THEORY AND PRACTICE IN ARCHAEOLOGY

This book aims to show through a series of examples that an interpretive archaeology dealing with past meanings can be applied in practice to archaeological data, and that it can also contribute effectively to social practice in the world of today.

Seven of the nineteen contributions included have been specifically written for this volume to act as an overview of the way archaeology has developed over the last ten years. Yet Ian Hodder goes beyond this: he aims to break down the separation of theory and practice and to reconcile the division between the intellectual and the 'dirt' archaeologist. Faced with public controversy over the ownership and interpretation of the past, archaeology needs a clear image of itself, be able to gain funding, win public confidence and manage the heritage professionally and sensitively. Hodder asserts that archaeologists cannot afford to ignore general theory in favour of practice any more than they can afford an ivory-tower approach. Theoretical debate is important to any discipline, particularly in archaeology, if it is not to become complacent, self-interested and uncritical

Theory and Practice in Archaeology captures and extends the lively debate of the 1980s over symbolic and structural approaches to archaeology. It will be essential reading for students of archaeology and for those involved in, and responsible for, heritage management.

Ian Hodder is a Reader in Archaeology at the University of Cambridge, a Fellow of Darwin College and a Director of the Cambridge Archaeological Unit.

MATERIAL CULTURES
Interdisciplinary studies in the material construction of social worlds

Series Editors:
Daniel Miller, Dept of Anthropology, University College London;
Michael Rowlands, Dept of Anthropology, University College London;
Christopher Tilley, Institute of Archaeology, University College London;
Annette Weiner, Dept of Anthropology, New York University

MATERIAL CULTURE AND TEXT
The Art of Ambiguity
Christopher Tilley

ARCHAEOLOGICAL THEORY IN EUROPE
The Last Three Decades
Edited by Ian Hodder

EXPERIENCING THE PAST
On the Character of Archaeology
Michael Shanks

THEORY AND PRACTICE IN ARCHAEOLOGY
Ian Hodder

TECHNOLOGICAL CHOICES
Transformation in Material Cultures since the Neolithic
Edited by Pierre Lemonnier

ARCHITECTURE AND ORDER
Approaches to Social Space
Edited by Michael Parker Pearson and Colin Richards

THE SWASTIKA
Constructing the Symbol
Malcolm Quinn

GIFTS AND COMMODITIES
Exchange and Western Capitalism Since 1700
James G. Carrier

ACKNOWLEDGING CONSUMPTION
A Review of New Studies
Edited by Daniel Miller

THEORY AND PRACTICE IN ARCHAEOLOGY

Ian Hodder

London and New York

First published in 1992
First published in paperback 1995
by Routledge
11 New Fetter Lane, London EC4P 4EE

Simultaneously published in the USA and Canada
by Routledge
29 West 35th Street, New York, NY 10001

Typeset in 10 on 12 point Palatino by
by Florencetype Ltd, Stoodleigh, Devon
Printed in Great Britain by
T J Press (Padstow) Ltd, Padstow, Cornwall

British Library Cataloguing in Publication Data
Hodder, Ian
Theory and practice in archaeology. –
(Material cultures)
I. Title II Series
930.1

Library of Congress Cataloguing in Publication Data
Hodder, Ian.
Theory and practice in archaeology/Ian Hodder.
p.   cm.   (Material cultures)
Includes bibliographical references and index.
1. Archaeology. I. Title. II. Series
CC173.H63 1992
930.1–dc20   91-38333

ISBN 0-415-127777

CONTENTS

CONTENTS

PART IV   Practising archaeology

ILLUSTRATIONS

SERIES PREFACE

The Material Cultures series crosses the traditional subject boundaries of archaeology, history and anthropology to consider human society in terms of its production, consumption and social structures. This approach breaks down the narrow compartmentalization which has until now obscured understanding of past and present societies and offers a more broadly-based (and coherent) set of explanations.

The series has developed from frustration with the conceptual limits imposed by a structure of separate disciplines. These divisions make little sense when so much of the most valuable work in many areas – in archaeology, consumption studies, architecture, museology, human geography, anthropology and communication science – grows from common roots and a shared intellectual framework.

The thrust of the series is to develop concepts necessary for understanding cultural and social form; but the editors' approach reverses the primacy often given to linguistic over material structures. This is deliberate after all, although structuralism borrowed from linguistics it took its most original shape through Lévi-Strauss's studies of kinship, myth and ritual. More recently a parallel process has taken place in architecture, which has been a crucial focus in the development of theories of post-modernism. This suggests that there are many advantages in attempting to construct approaches to the material world which consciously proclaim the distinctive nature of *objects* as against *language*.

This approach, central to all the books in the series, should be of particular benefit to those studies (like archaeology) which have artifacts as their main focus. But materiality provides new perceptions of cultural context over a much wider range of subject matter. It demands a conscious process of linking together the techniques and strategies of other disciplines. For example, a recognition of the issues of gender will infuse an historically based study with a deeper set of meanings; set the same work within an anthropological framework as well, and its value (and insights) are enhanced.

This broad sense of context allows us to publish work on the cultural politics of the body, on power systems of representation, on food and gender, and the experience of possession or alienation. All of them are rooted within a materialistic interpretation of culture.

The series will maintain a productive dialogue with developments in Marxist, as well as structuralist, post-structuralist and phenomenological thought, through focusing on the *specificity* of the material world and its particular forms and contents. Yet we recognize that it is the very materiality of that world which often presents a challenge to theory and promotes a critical approach to analysis.

Many of the disciplines which have a particular concern with material culture, such as museology and consumption studies, have tended to feel that their own developments in theory and analysis have been neglected over previous decades. They have become, relatively speaking, backwaters of the social science. This series is launched at a time when there are signs that this is about to be radically changed.

There are new advances in cultural theory which are not merely fetishistic and do not posit the object as distinct from social and cultural context. Advances in post-structuralism which have challenged the notion of the subject mean that we are now free to conceive of a new approach to material culture, which does not privilege or reify either objects or persons.

In planning and co-ordinating the series we wish to demonstrate above all the current intellectual excitement and potential for working within this field. Creating meaning from the material fragments of the past and the present now provides an arena for addressing some of the fundamental theoretical and philosophical issues of our time.

Daniel Miller, Michael Rowlands
and Christopher Tilley

PREFACE

In presenting a collection of some of my previously published papers there is perhaps an understandable desire to 'correct' all those commentators who argued that I whimsically shifted from one theory to another. Those who argued that my writings were confused and contradictory and that I just followed the latest trend, I now have the opportunity to show that they did not understand how all the pieces fit into a whole, an *oeuvre*. I can attempt to show how my work had a developmental coherence, if not predicted at the beginning, certainly guided by some big questions and dominant interests.

There is an impulse to 'put right' those 'mis'-readings of my writings. I can try to put the critics 'right' and show them what I had 'really' intended to say, explain what I 'really' meant. It is all to easy to argue that my critics, commentators, reviewers have not even read my work. Others sometimes seem wilfully to misunderstand what I have to say. It is tempting to take the chance now to argue that they read what they want into my writing, set me up as a straw man, and criticise me for what I have not written. Usually I have no opportunity to respond (see, however, Hodder 1986*). So at last, within the confines of these collected papers I could take the opportunity to 'set the record straight'.

I especially want to correct the impression that my work has only been about theory and has little relevance to what archaeologists actually do. People argue that I favour 'thinkers' over 'stinkers'. People say that the critique of processual archaeology was well established but that I have nothing to put in its place that 'lab' or 'dirt' archaeologists can use. They say that post-processual archaeology has led to an intellectualisation of debate so that few people want to be involved. Now I have the chance to show that the new theories can be linked to practice.

The problems raised by these impulses to 'put the record straight' will need fuller discussion from Chapter 10 onwards. For the moment, I wish to begin with the whole issue of theoretical debate and its relationship to archaeological practices.

* Hodder, I. (1986) 'Digging for symbols in science and history: a reply', *Proceedings of the Prehistoric Society* 52, 352–6.

ACKNOWLEDGEMENTS

I am grateful to Antiquity, Archaeological Review from Cambridge, Cambridge University Press, the Royal Anthropological Institute of Great Britain and Ireland, the Society for American Archaeology and the University of Calgary Archaeological Association for permission to reprint material here which was originally published by them.

The following papers were first published in the volumes listed below: Chapter 3: 'Conclusions and prospects', in I. Hodder *Symbols in Action*, Cambridge: Cambridge University Press, 1982, 212–29. Chapter 4: 'Burials, houses, women and men in the European Neolithic', in D. Miller and C. Tilley (eds) *Ideology, Power and Prehistory*, Cambridge: Cambridge University Press, 1984, 51–68. Chapter 6: 'Theoretical archaeology: a reactionary view', in I. Hodder (ed.) *Symbolic and Structural Archaeology*, Cambridge: Cambridge University Press, 1982, 1–16. Chapter 7: 'Archaeology in 1984', *Antiquity* 58, 1984, 25–32. Chapter 8: 'Politics and ideology in the World Archaeological Congress 1986', *Archaeological Review from Cambridge* 5:1, 1986, 113–19. Chapter 13: 'Interpretive archaeology and its role', *American Antiquity* 56 (1), 1991, 7–18. Chapter 14: 'Material practice, symbolism and ideology', *Proceedings of Theoretical Archaeology Conference, Bergen*, Bergen: Historical Museum, 1992. Chapter 17: 'Gender representation and social reality', *The Archaeology of Gender*, Calgary: University of Calgary, Archaeological Association, 1991, 11–16. Chapter 18: 'Writing archaeology: site reports in context', *Antiquity* 63, 1989, 268–74. Chapter 19: 'Archaeology and the postmodern', *Anthropology Today*, for the Royal Anthropological Institute of Great Britain and Ireland, 1990.

I would like to thank Sarah Tarlow for the preparation of the index.

1

THEORY, PRACTICE AND PRAXIS

This book deals with recent developments in archaeological theory which have come to be classified within the small world of archaeology as 'post-processual', but which in the wider world would be termed neo-Marxist, hermeneutic, critical and post-structuralist. The heavily theoretical nature of the post-processual debate is clear from even the briefest encounter with the literature (e.g. Shanks and Tilley 1987a; 1987b; Bapty and Yates 1990; Hodder 1991). Yet I have titled the book *Theory and Practice in Archaeology*. The emphasis on practice partly derives from a desire to show a wider relevance for post-processual ideas. If these new ideas are to have more than a superficial impact, they need to be related to the practice of archaeology. But I have also set myself a wider brief. Regardless of the overall impact of post-processual ideas, there is a need to break down the separation of theory and practice in archaeology.

In many countries with a large archaeological community, there is some form of division between, on the one hand, the intellectual, the interpreter, the academic, the theoretician and, on the other hand, dirt or white-coated archaeologists dealing with practical issues. Many people would feel that they fall somewhere between and temper these two extremes. But it is often the case that those most involved as practitioners are suspicious of and uninterested in abstract theory. It is probably true to say that most archaeologists are not specifically concerned with theoretical discussion, except perhaps when it creates the spectacle of a public oppositional debate. Archaeologists tend to be pragmatic and data-oriented, fascinated by specific technical and historical problems. In North America, for example, you only have to compare the Society for American Archaeology meetings (with their emphasis on middle-range theory, site formation processes, hunter-gatherer strategies and regional studies) with the meetings of the American Anthropological Association (where the emphasis is on power, gender, text, rhetoric etc.) to see the neurosis most archaeologists still feel towards saying anything which might have topical and general theoretical interest.

The lack of interest in general theory partly stems from the positivism which most archaeologists assume, however weakly. It has long been assumed that the source of theories and their internal coherence is of less concern than one's ability to test them against the archaeological data. The New Archaeology of the 1960s and early 1970s did lead initially to a refreshing concern with theory development as intuitive approaches were replaced by a 'loss of innocence' (Clarke 1973) and by a self-conscious concern with separating theory from data and providing rigorous methods for evaluating hypotheses. Through time, however, this approach has increasingly put all its eggs in the basket of neutral methods. Within positivist approaches in archaeology there is, on the whole, more emphasis on testability than there is on whether the theories being used are interesting, or valuable. So theoretical discussion in its own right is relatively unimportant, because we are supposed to be able to let method sort out the good and the bad theories.

Perhaps because of this positivism, perhaps because of the enormous difficulty of making sense of fragmentary data from long-gone societies, perhaps because of the difficulty of saying anything with any degree of certainty about the distant past, most archaeologists prefer to become absorbed in data and method. There are also institutional divisions between universities and heritage management which perhaps encourage the separation of theory and practice. This latter factor is especially severe in contexts of rapid site destruction. The past is being destroyed and we are wasting time if we gaze into our theoretical navels. We have to 'get our act together' rather than be involved in internal theoretical wrangles. What is needed is a discipline with a clear and certain image of itself, able to do the job of acting quickly and professionally to save the heritage, a discipline able to gain funding and win public confidence in conflicts over rights to the past.

A common view was expressed by Schiffer in a public debate at the Society for American Archaeology meeting at Atlanta, Georgia in 1989. 'High-level goals, I think, mostly generate conflict and ennui, whereas middle- and low-level goals generate productive research.' It is easy to sympathise with this 'let's get on with it' view (for a less absolute version see Flannery 1982). Theoretical discussion involves defining terms, stating positions, setting up categorical boundaries. It involves creating a coherent whole which is defined by its opposition to other wholes (for example, culture as text and as meaningfully constituted as opposed to culture as tool and as man's extrasomatic means of adaptation). General theories are heavily influenced by a priori judgements and taken-for-granteds. They are about ourselves. Even when describing the great thinkers and philosophers, it is possible to argue that they are expressing a certain way of looking at the world which is prefigured (White 1973).

But it is precisely this prefigured nature of theory which should entice us to look at theory more carefully rather than putting our blinkers on and getting our noses into middle- and low-level goals. The purer theory always asserts the interests of particular groups more obviously. This has been shown with great effect by Said (1978) in his analysis of the disciplines which have constructed the 'orient', which have reproduced over the long term certain stereotypical views of the orient, and which have thereby asserted the dominance of the 'occident'. In relation to Said's analysis it is interesting to note Rowlands' (1987) discussion about the study of European prehistory as a celebration of the peculiar dominance of the European occident against the stagnant and despotic orient. In more general terms, Fabian (1983) has shown how the anthropological creation of 'the other' as in another time asserts the dominance, dynamism and separation of the west. As a specific example of this tendency of theory to set up relations of domination, Trigger (1980) has shown how different phases of North American archaeologists have written the American Indian as unprogressive and lacking in dynamism.

archaeology

$$\left\{ \begin{array}{c} \text{theory} \\ | \\ \text{practice} \end{array} \right\} \underline{\quad\quad} \text{social practice}$$

Figure 1 The relationships between theory, practice and social practice (praxis)

One reason for a fuller consideration of practice is the need to evaluate the practical implication of our theories. Here I am talking about practice in the sense of social practice. Praxis is the Greek and German word for practice and in a long tradition of scholarship which includes Marx it has come to refer to social practice (Hoffman 1975). According to this view, theory and thinking are social and cannot be separated from the practices of social life. Theory and social practice are fused and the oppositions between fact and value, object and subject are demolished. The theory of praxis argues that theory is transformative and is potentially revolutionary. It asserts that we do not passively observe, contemplate the world, but that we create it. Science cannot, therefore, be separated from society.

Even by writing abstract theory in a proverbial ivory tower, apparently cut off from the world, the archaeologist is using and furthering a system of academic prestige, authority and privilege which has impacts on the conduct of education. Such theoretical labour, often supported by elitist institutions such as Cambridge University and its colleges, is part of a wider attempt to establish the independence and domination of intellectual endeavour. Recently the complacency of theoretical practices in archaeology has been under attack from several quarters. For

3

example, an awareness of gender issues has led to a rethinking not only of implicit androcentric assumptions in our theories but also to more general critiques of our understanding of power, domination and signification (Gero and Conkey 1991). A whole series of volumes following on from the 1986 World Archaeological Congress, itself a highly charged and politicised event (see Chapter 8), have expressed the claims made by minority groups against the theories about the past espoused by dominant traditions (e.g. Layton 1989a; 1989b; Shennan 1989; Gathercole and Lowenthal 1990 etc).

Intellectuals, including those on the 'left', have long spoken from the standpoint of the universal, as controllers of truth and justice. Foucault (1980, 126) argues that across the disciplines, the role of the intellectual has now changed from the universal to the specific. A new connection between theory and social practice has been established. As the example of archaeology shows well, 'intellectuals have got used to working, not in the modality of the "universal", the "exemplary", the "just-and-true-for-all", but within specific sectors, at the precise points where their own conditions of life or work situate them. . . . This has undoubtedly given them a much more immediate and concrete awareness of struggles. And they have met here with problems which are specific, non-universal' (ibid.). As archaeologists are embroiled in reburial issues, land claims, feminism, heritage management and the planning process, as they stand up in court as 'expert witnesses' in the management of cultural resources, they fit better the picture of the specific intellectual than the universal scholar of the nineteenth and early twentieth centuries.

As well as considering archaeological praxis, it is necessary to bring to the fore archaeological practice in a more conventional sense. By practice here I mean the application of theory in specific contexts. There is a potential link between praxis and practice which can be exploited in order to limit the closure, self-sufficiency and self-interest of abstract theoretical schemes. Almost by definition, theory describes abstractions and generalities which go beyond the specific instances with which it may be concerned. Even theories which purport to explain only particular events involve translating those events into terms which we can understand and which therefore have some generality. In more general theory, concerned with defining rules and principles, the specific instances are examples which illustrate the general point. In neither the particular nor the general types of theory is the theory reducible to the practices being explained. Even in the case of an exhaustive catalogue there are theoretical underpinnings which go beyond the cataloguing practice. There is, therefore, a gap between theory and data. I realise that this notion of a separation of theory and practice might be seen as a hangover from positivism and from the separation of science from value judgement. This is a problem to which I will return (Chapter 12). But for

4

the moment I wish to assert that in relating theory to data there is always a tension, a need for adjustment and interpretation of the general in relation to the particular. While the human ability to twist and turn until theory and data are made to fit is remarkable, there is at least the potential that in accommodating theory to unexpected data we will be confronted by problems that force reconsideration of general theory. This may be a pious hope when the theories are strongly grounded in ideologies as I demonstrate in Chapter 8, but in other cases I will argue that we do adjust our taken-for-granteds (Chapters 15 and 16). Relating theories to practice potentially opens them up to reflection and to the evaluation of archaeological praxis (Chapter 16). For example, it might be argued that the hard archaeological and geological evidence for the 'antiquity of man' contributed to a shaking of beliefs in Biblical accounts of origins. Equally, the discovery of indigenous traditions of cultural development in South Africa and North America ultimately provided a basis for the critiques of white supremacy and legitimacy.

But it is not enough to focus on practice alone. I have so far been providing grist for the mill of those like Schiffer and Flannery who say we should 'get on with' practice. But if theory is inadequate on its own, so is practice. Schiffer (1976; 1987) does of course use theories but would claim that middle- and low-level theories can to some extent be separated from abstract general theoretical argument. Otherwise his statement quoted earlier (p. 2) would make no sense. In fact, however, all middle- and low-level theory must involve higher level generalities in order for us to understand them, know their relevance and place them within a disciplinary framework. For example, in Schiffer's account of site formation processes, his a priori assumptions (high-level theory) lead him largely to ignore the issue of whether discard is meaningfully constituted. We cannot hide in empiricism, description, field archaeology, applied science and middle-range questions, hoping to avoid general theoretical issues. Our practices always necessarily employ generalities in order to make sense of what we find and do. What we measure and how we measure it are theoretical. The assumption that artifacts are the result of human action is theory. The concepts of a site, a pot, an axe are theoretical and dependent on the historical development of disciplinary knowledge. After all, we used to think axes were thunderbolts. Archaeology, perhaps more than any other discipline, is forced to use theory to construct statements on the basis of highly fragmented and partial evidence.

So if archaeologists just want to 'get on with it' and ignore general theory, they are simply being uncritical and doing bad science. But the need for theory as well as practice takes me back to praxis. In fact many of the social implications of archaeological assumptions have come about through theoretical critique – for example, of the 'man the hunter'

5

hypothesis (Gero and Conkey 1991) or 'optimal foragers'. However much archaeological data and contemporary social practices confront archaeological theories and taken-for-granteds, there is still a need for theoretical reflection of the implications raised. Theory allows the possibility of critique.

But theory is also needed for archaeology if as a discipline it is to make an impact in current society and in competition with other disciplines. It is through theory, which systematises and forms a body of knowledge according to specified principles, that the discipline takes its form. The discipline so defined adjudicates the appropriate data and methods. It is through apprenticeship in the theoretically formed body of knowledge that professionals are defined. Such a disciplinary discourse, formed through theoretical praxis, has to be the subject of critique in order to expose its exercise of power as repressive. But power is also enabling and productive (Foucault 1980). If archaeology as a discipline is to act effectively in relation to a quickly diminishing heritage, and if it is to achieve a wider public participation in the past, it must claim a certain coherence (Chapter 12). While it might be argued that such coherence can be given by common methods and techniques, the decision about which methods are allowable (such as systematic sampling or open as opposed to 'box' excavation or the collection of botanical remains) can only be based on theoretical considerations.

The difficulty is that any such coherence, while it may have the advantage of empowering the discipline as a whole to play an effective role in society, threatens to stifle diversity, critique and change. Such coherence and self-confidence may disempower alternative and subordinate voices. This is a central problem which I will explore later in this book. For the moment, I have argued that archaeologists use theory whether they like it or not. The 1980s, at least in some parts of Europe and America, have seen an enormous expansion of theoretical debate. Such theoretical debate is a necessary part of a self-conscious discipline. But it has to be related both to practice and to praxis if it is not to become self-interested, complacent, inward-looking and uncritical.

Perhaps a simpler way of making the same point would be to say that both theory and practice (including praxis) are necessary to each other. On its own, either can become blind to its follies, dangerous in its implications. It is in the movement across the gap between theory and practice, between the general and the particular, that change is safeguarded.

REFERENCES

Bapty, I. and Yates, T. (1990) *Archaeology after Structuralism*, London: Routledge.
Clarke, D. L. (1973) 'Archaeology: the loss of innocence', *Antiquity* 47, 6–18.
Fabian, J. (1983) *Time and the Other*, New York: Columbia University Press.

Flannery, K. V. (1982) 'The Golden Marshalltown: a parable for the archaeology of the 1980s', *American Anthropologist* 84, 265–78.

Foucault, M. (1980) *Power/Knowledge. Selected Interviews and Other Writings*, ed. C. Gordon, New York: Pantheon Books.

Gathercole, P. and Lowenthal, D. (1990) *The Politics of the Past*, London: Unwin Hyman.

Gero, J. and Conkey, M. (eds) (1991) *Engendering archaeology*, Oxford: Basil Blackwell.

Hodder, I. (1991) *Reading the Past*, 2nd edn, Cambridge: Cambridge University Press.

Hoffman, J. (1975) *Marxism and the Theory of Praxis*, New York: International Publishers.

Layton, R. (1989a) *Conflict in the Archaeology of Living Traditions*, London: Unwin Hyman.

——— (1989b) *Who needs the Past? Indigenous Values and Archaeology*, London: Unwin Hyman.

Rowlands, M. (1987) 'Europe in prehistory', *Culture and History* 1, 63–78.

Said, E. (1978) *Orientalism*, Harmondsworth: Penguin.

Schiffer, M. (1976) *Behavioural Archaeology*, New York: Academic Press.

——— (1987) *Formation Processes of the Archaeological Record*, Albuquerque: University of New Mexico Press.

Shanks, M. and Tilley, C. (1987a) *Re-constructing Archaeology*, Cambridge: Cambridge University Press.

——— (1987b) *Social Theory and Archaeology*, Cambridge: Polity Press.

Shennan, S. (1989) *Archaeological Approaches to Cultural Identity*, London: Unwin Hyman.

Trigger, B. (1980) 'Archaeology and the image of the American Indian', *American Antiquity* 45, 662–76.

White, H. (1973) *Metahistory: the Historical Imagination in Nineteenth Century Europe*, Baltimore (MD): Johns Hopkins University Press.

Part I

SYMBOLIC AND STRUCTURAL ARCHAEOLOGY

2

SYMBOLISM, MEANING AND CONTEXT

For many people, one of the most fascinating aspects of archaeology is that it straddles the gulf which separates the arts from the sciences. More specifically, it brings together the 'softer' humanities and social sciences with the 'harder' physical and natural sciences. The underlying reason for this link is the dual character of material culture. The artifacts studied by archaeologists tell us about history but not in the language of the historian. The archaeologist deals in things and not words. Material culture is both the product of human purpose and yet it is material following the laws of the non-human world. The term itself captures the duality of 'material' and 'culture'.

Archaeologists increasingly use a battery of scientific techniques to deal with the material side of this duality. In the 1960s and 1970s, however, so-called New Archaeologists tried to extend a natural science approach into all areas of the discipline. Even cultural issues were thought to be accessible using a philosophy derived from the natural sciences, emphasising general laws, hypothesis testing and independence of theory and data. This approach was most successful in areas of cultural life such as subsistence which were more closely integrated with the natural environment. It paid little attention to the social world and even less to symbolic and ideological issues. Using the metaphor of the natural sciences, archaeology was seen to be dealing with only one hermeneutic. By this I mean that archaeologists and the data they studied were thought to be within one framework of meaning, one hermeneutic, called western science.

But it is also possible to view material culture as part of cultural expression and conceptual meaning. It is possible to go beyond the immediate physical uses and constraints of objects to the more abstract symbolic meanings. In this case, understanding material culture is more like interpreting a language because it is dealing with meanings which are only loosely, if at all, connected to the physical properties of objects. These symbolic meanings are organised by rules and codes which seem to be very different from culture to culture and which do not seem to be strongly determined by economic, biological and physical matters. Faced with this historical indeterminacy, the natural science model for archaeology breaks down. Using the metaphor of the humanities and social sciences, archaeology can be seen to be dealing with a double hermeneutic. As well as the framework of meaning of western science within which archaeologists work, there is also the framework of meaning, perhaps constructed very differently and according to different rules and principles, of the culture being studied. The problem then becomes one of how to translate from one hermeneutic to the other.

In the two chapters which follow, the point is made that material culture has to be interpreted within its own hermeneutic. However, at the time they were written I had not recognised the problem of translating from one culture to another. Indeed, I had not even recognised the world of western science within which I worked *as cultural*. My aim was simply to show the inadequacy of a universalising natural science approach which treated objects as if they were only products of the physical world. As a result of detailed ethnoarchaeological work undertaken in Africa and published in *Symbols in Action* (1982), of which the concluding chapter is reprinted here as Chapter 3, I wanted to make three points (see also Hodder 1986).

First, material culture is meaningfully constituted. As is clear from Chapter 3, I understand this to mean that there are ideas and concepts embedded in social life which influence the way material culture is used, embellished and discarded. All human action is meaningful not simply because it communicates messages to other people. Information-processing approaches have the danger of reducing the meanings of objects to 'bits' of information which are studied simply in terms of their effectiveness in conveying messages. But whether material culture is functioning as a tool or as information, it is organised by concepts and ideas which give it meaning. While I would now doubt that these concepts are necessarily rigidly organised into 'codes' and 'sets' and 'structures', I take the line in Chapter 3 that some form of structuralist analysis is appropriate. In Chapter 4, on the other hand, the organising scheme that 'tombs mean houses' derives from, although it cannot be reduced to, a specific social and economic context and is not seen as being organised by abstract structures. Whether one thinks that our concepts are deeply structured by binary oppositions and the like (the approach taken in Chapter 3) or whether the meanings are closely tied to a specific social context (as is attempted in Chapter 4), the claim is made that material culture is constituted within frameworks of conceptual meaning.

Although material culture is always meaningfully constituted, it can be given conceptual meanings in different ways. For example, it is important to distinguish meaning from intention. At one level, it is possible for an archaeologist to ask questions about intentions such as 'What was the purpose of the shape of that ditch?', 'Why is this wall made of turf and that of stone?', 'Why does this tomb look like that house?' Merriman (1987) has shown that prehistoric archaeologists can answer questions about even the most abstract intentions. He shows that a wall built in Iron Age central Europe was built like examples in the Mediterranean in order to gain prestige by association with the exotic Mediterranean civilisations. Indeed, archaeologists routinely argue that certain items have high value, indicate high status or give prestige. In all such cases, the archaeologist must be assuming that to some degree the participants in the culture being studied purposively gave prestige connotations to the objects concerned. After all, it would be difficult to see how an object could give prestige if nobody at the time recognised it as such. Even if the initial producer of an artifact did not intend it to have prestige, a prestigious object would normally be used intentionally.

But the intentions do not exhaust the meanings of the objects. This is because there may be conceptual meanings which are not recognised by the makers and users of objects. Unrecognised and unintended meanings can perhaps be distinguished. *Unrecognised meanings*: on the one hand, there are the realms of meaning of which actors are unconscious or only dimly and infrequently conscious. We are able to act effectively without calling up into our conscious minds all the cultural meanings of the things we do. For example, I might show a visitor to my house the living room and dining room but not the bedroom and kitchen without realising that I am using a code common in England which separates public from private in a particular way. *Unintended meanings*: on the other hand, different people will read different things into actions. The producer or user of an object is always to some degree uncertain about how the object will be given meaning by others. Different people might link the same object to different conceptual schemes. With speech, it is possible to some degree to monitor the effects of what one is saying and then emphasise, recapitulate, rephrase a sentence so that the intended meaning is got over. But with writing, and with much material culture, the text and the object become separated from the author and producer. Over space and time, distant from their production, texts and objects can be given numerous meanings in different contexts. One has only to look at the different meanings which have been given to Stonehenge (Chippindale 1983) to appreciate the way in which archaeological objects, enduring for millennia, can be given new interpretations.

Because of these unrecognised and unintended areas of meaning, and because different groups in society can give their own, often contrasting, meanings to the same objects, the emphasis placed in Chapter 3 on structured 'wholes' needs to be tempered with a fuller understanding of socially embedded, conflicting meanings. In other words, conceptual schemes and symbolic meanings need to be related to practice. In the practices of daily life, whether they be primarily economic, social or ideological, actors draw upon conceptual schemes and resources, but they do so differently depending on their economic, social and ideological position and intentions. In the Nuba case discussed in Chapter 3, it is quite possible that deeper study would have shown that men and women viewed the pure/impure = cattle/pig = male/female oppositions differently (see Hodder 1986). Barrett (1987b) has pointed out in relation to the study presented in Chapter 4 that no account is given of whether tombs meant houses to all or just some people. It may of course be the case that the different meanings given by groups within society are in some sense subsets of a larger 'whole', but such integration needs to be demonstrated rather than assumed.

The second general point that resulted from writing *Symbols in Action* followed on from the first. If material culture was meaningfully constituted, and if the conceptual meanings were at least partly arbitrary, then material culture had to be studied contextually. The notion of arbitrariness needs some clarification. I have argued above that the abstract and symbolic meanings of material culture objects cannot be reduced to their biological and physical properties nor to the uses to which they are put. For example, there is no intrinsic religious significance in two pieces of wood nailed together in the form of a cross. To say that the meanings of material culture objects are partly arbitrary is to say that those meanings cannot be determined from cross-cultural scientific study of the material properties and functions of objects. While material culture meanings may be historically arbitrary in this sense, they are not arbitrary in another sense. Any use of an artifact depends on the previous uses and meanings of that artifact or of similar artifacts within a particular historical context. However fast that context is changing the meanings of artifacts at time t are not arbitrary because they are partly dependent on the meanings of artifacts at time $t-1$.

The symbolic meanings of artifacts are thus not entirely arbitrary because they are bounded within contexts. For the archaeologist wishing to understand past meanings of objects it is thus essential to define the context within which an object has associations which contribute to its meaning. I will discuss the definition of context more fully in Chapter 11. For the moment, I would define context as the totality of the relevant environment (Hodder 1991, 143). The context of an archaeological 'object' (including a trait, a site, a culture) is all those associations which are relevant to its meaning. This totality is of course not fixed in any way since the meaning of an object depends on what it is being compared with, by whom, with what purpose and so on. There is thus a relationship between the totality and the question of relevance. The definition of

14

the totality depends on perspective and interest and knowledge. In addition, there is a dynamic relationship between an object and its context. By placing an object in a context, the context is itself changed. There is thus a dialectical relationship between object and context, between text and context. The context both gives meaning to and gains meaning from an object.

Contextual archaeology thus involves 'thick description' (Geertz 1973) in the sense that it emphasises the need to understand the meanings of an object by placing it more and more fully into its various contexts. But on the other hand, as is made clear in Chapter 3, any such contextualisation depends on generalities. As noted in Chapter 1, any account of the past involves translating the 'other' into 'our' terms. We cannot even begin to make sense of the archaeological data without making general assumptions. But the danger has been in archaeology that these generalisations have been applied without sensitivity, without recognition of that aspect of human culture which is historically non-arbitrary. It is necessary to interpret generalisations in relation to specific contexts. As such, a contextual archaeology is not relativist. By this I mean that it accepts the ability to move between cultural contexts, using generalisations, in order to understand the 'other'. But it does argue that these generalisations have to be accommodated to the 'other' context in sensitive and 'thick' ways. The generalisations are, in the process, themselves transformed. The movement between generalisation and context, like that between context and object, is continual and unstable.

The third main point that resulted from *Symbols in Action* was that material culture is active, not passive. This essential point underlies the first two. It argues that material culture is not a passive by-product of human behaviour. In essence an argument is being made here against a mechanistic view of society. With the attempt to see societies and human culture through approaches championed in the natural sciences, archaeologists had come in the 1960s and 1970s to emphasise predictable relationships between behaviour, material culture and environment. Thus we were told with statistical precision that settlements with a certain floor area would contain a certain number of people, or that burial complexity related to social complexity in some direct manner. In fact, of course, societies are not made up of people doggedly following ahistorical rules. Groups in society have different goals and strategies for attaining them and they give different meanings to the world around them. As a result, individuals face some degree of uncertainty in applying historical rules in social action. Because of the unrecognised and unintended meanings and consequences of action, monitoring and interpretation of action are continually needed. All human action is thus creative and interpretive. General rules have to be interpreted in relation to context in the same way that archaeologists have to interpret generali-

15

sations in relation to the contexts they are studying. In both cases the meanings are not self-evident. They cannot be passively absorbed. They have to be actively constructed.

VERIFICATION

The three points discussed above raise a host of difficult questions. For example, if material culture is meaningfully constituted, how can archaeologists reconstruct the different meanings given to objects by long-dead people? If meanings are contextual, how do we know what the relevant context in the past was? If material culture is active and the meanings constructed, how can we use generalisations? Is not the whole attempt to get at 'their' meanings doomed? How can we hope to get into 'their' minds?

Some archaeologists find these questions so difficult that they prefer to throw up their hands and argue that we should not try to get to 'their' meanings. Clearly there is a view, which I will discuss in Chapter 11, that we should simply accept that archaeologists cannot reconstruct the past. All they can do is construct it, impose our meanings on the data and leave it at that. In Chapter 11 I will reject this view as too extreme. I will argue that we can to some extent accommodate our constructions to an understanding of 'their' meanings. But for those who do aim to reconstruct rather than just construct the past, what I do find totally incomprehensible is the view that we can do this without getting at 'their' meanings. Many people seem to accept that human culture is meaningful and purposive and yet at the same time they seem to convince themselves that human culture can be studied without recourse to meaning.

Originally, the idea that it was difficult for archaeologists to gain access to past symbolic meanings was encouraged by an empiricism and scepticism expressed in Hawkes' (1954) ladder of inference. According to this ladder it was possible for archaeologists to reconstruct past technologies and economies with relative ease in comparison with past social organisation and ideas. This separation of the material and the cultural has often been associated with a materialism, from Childe to Binford, according to which it is possible to infer the social and ideational from the material. Many archaeologists would today reject such approaches and would accept that material culture is both materially and meaningfully constituted. But because of the hangover from empiricism, positivism and materialism, such archaeologists, in the same breath, deny the possibility of getting at past minds. For example, Earle and Preucel (1987) accept the importance of symbolism but say we cannot get at the minds of prehistoric people. The same is true of Bintliff (1990, 13). But what would be the point of interpreting past symbols (as symbolising prestige, status, inside or outside) if we did not think they had those meanings to 'them'?

Binford has often argued that it is necessary to avoid making interpretations of the role of mind and symbolic meanings in understanding both archaeological and 'actualistic' data. But then he suggests the following generalisation that 'if one plans to occupy the site for some time and *does not care to* have the debris from one activity inhibit the performance of another, one develops special use areas peripheral to the domestic area' (1989, 256, my italics). At the heart of this generalisation is a belief or perception which 'they' held: 'one does not care to'. At the core of all generalisations about discard are such assumptions about 'their' minds.

As another example, Barrett (1987b) argues that it is dubious and unnecessary to claim that we can understand 'their' world. He says we can study discourse without discovering ideas in people's heads, and that we can reject a 'text' model for material culture even though he sees social action as meaningful, as constructed, as active. 'I do not believe that such texts are capable of adequate translation' (Barrett 1987a, 6). Yet his whole approach to discourse accepts that material culture does not have single objective meanings (ibid., 9), that the material world is used to give signification, and that it is invested with meaning. He asserts that authoritative codes are signified by symbols through which 'the participants know' (ibid., 10) and accept the validity of the conditions under which they act. Since Barrett seems to reject a naive materialism, he must, in order to apply his approach, interpret meanings in 'their' heads, despite his rhetoric to the contrary. And this is indeed abundantly clear in his own applied work. For example, he has stated the need to get at the 'subjective geography' of how people 'perceived' their landscape (Barrett 1989, 122–3). He has interpreted the location of a cemetery on the edge of agricultural fields as being determined 'by the acts of growth and fertility' (ibid., 124). For this interpretation of how the burials gave authority to people in the past to make any sense at all, it must be assumed that, at some level, the ideas of growth and fertility were in 'their' heads.

Willy-nilly, Barrett has, like the rest of us, found himself interpreting conceptual meanings in 'their' heads. I have never read an archaeological text in which some interpretation of what 'they' were thinking has not been a necessary part of the argument, however much it might be denied by the author. When I call some remains on a site a house or dwelling I must mean that 'they' used it and recognised it in a house-like way. Otherwise, presumably I would call it a storage facility or something else. Of course, I can claim that the term 'house' is a neutral label, but I suspect that the analysis would proceed rather differently, with different conclusions if I were to give the remains other supposedly neutral labels such as shrine, cattle byre, or even dance floor or gambling den! Similarly, interpretations of what things meant to 'them' underlie 'neutral' labels such as settlement, wall, pit. If 'they' did not see the settlement as settlement-like and therefore did not use it in a settlement-like way, it would be meaningless to talk of it as a settlement. Even when I reconstruct an economy from animal bones on a site I must at least be assuming that 'they' thought of the animals from which the bones derive as useful for food, clothing, etc. When Renfrew (1982) reconstructs an ancient system of weights and measures, we must assume that 'they' understood the system themselves. Otherwise, how could it have worked? I have already given the example of artifacts which archaeologists designate as prestigious or of high or low status. How could an object have had prestige or have given status if 'they' did not perceive it as prestigious or of a particular status?

In my view, the idea that archaeologists can get away without reconstructing ideas in the heads of prehistoric peoples is pure false consciousness and self-delusion. It derives from an earlier commitment to empiricism, positivism and materialism and from a narrow view of what scientists do. It should be clear, however, that the ideas that archaeologists reconstruct are not necessarily the conscious thoughts that would have been expressed if we could travel backwards through time and talk to people in prehistory. As I made clear above, there is a difference between meaning and intention. No social actor can be aware of all the extent and levels of meanings within a particular context. For the ethnographer as for the time-travelling prehistorian, what is said can never exhaust all the levels of meaning. On the whole, archaeologists will often concentrate on larger and longer-term scales of context, which help to frame meanings of which 'they' may rarely have been consciously aware.

If it can be accepted that archaeologists do indeed attempt to reconstruct past conceptual meanings which are in some sense in 'their' heads, the onus is on us to try and get as close as possible to those past meanings. But how are we to know how close we have come to getting it right? And if another archaeologist comes up with a competing theory, how can we verify our different claims? An important initial step in answering such questions is to return to the dual nature of material culture. As much as artifacts are organised by conceptual schemes, they are also made to do something in the world. They are real objects which people made, held, used, exchanged, buried, discarded, etc. We need also to return to the idea that conceptual meanings exist in relation to social, political and economic contexts. They are not purely abstract. They are embedded in real world contexts. The emphasis on symbols *in action* is that conceptual meanings both give meaning to and derive meaning from action. Theory and practice are in a relation of dependence and tension.

18

Conceptual schemes thus have effects on the material visible world. They contribute to the patterning of the material world and they are themselves constrained by that world. Although heavily transformed by survival and recovery factors, the patterning of material remains is recovered by archaeologists. The associations of artifacts of different types in layers and pits, in sites and regions, in cemeteries and land-scapes, retain a trace of an original patterning which was itself produced by actions informed by conceptual schemes.

It would be wrong to claim that the surviving archaeological patterning can be interpreted in a simple and objective way. We cannot hope to avoid dealing with the problems raised by the double hermeneutic. Rather, we have to accept that, in order to make sense of the patterned remains, we have to approach them with questions and a relevant general anthropological and historical understanding. As noted above, archaeologists sometimes approach the search for and interpretation of patterning by placing too much emphasis on the universality of their ideas and measuring devices. Indeed, in the study presented in Chapter 4 (Hodder 1984), I made a number of invalid cross-cultural assumptions about women, labour and land. These ideas were simply imposed on the data in ways that were typical of much processual archaeology (cf. Barrett 1987b). I made no attempt to understand the tomb–house link in terms of particular strategies as I was later to do by using the concept of the domus (Hodder 1990; see Chapter 16). In other cases, too, I had too much hope in universal 'objective' links between material culture and its meanings. For example, I assumed that material culture was organised by a universal 'language' (Hodder 1986). While it clearly is the case that we need to use generalisations and that we need to work on refining them and understanding how they work in different contexts, they can never be claimed to be neutral or objective. The more universal a relationship, the more likely we are to have confidence in it, but in the end we always have to accept that the past may have been different. If they did things differently there, we always have to interpret our generalisations in relation to those differences.

While now embarrassed by the processual aspects of Chapter 4, it is useful in demonstrating another aspect of the verification procedure that archaeologists routinely use. As well as referring to generalities to support their arguments, they also try to find as much of the evidence that they can account for in their theories. The more data that can be accommodated by a particular theory, the more likely we are to find it preferable. In Chapter 4 the claim that tombs meant houses is a claim about prehistoric meanings which at some point and at some time were in some people's heads. This claim about an historically non-arbitrary and contextual meaning is supported by the fact that this 'thought' was translated into physical evidence by making the tombs look like houses. The claim also uses generalities which allow us to label evidence 'houses' and 'tombs'. But no claim is made in this work that tombs mean houses cross-culturally. Neither is it argued that in certain social and economic conditions tombs are universally built like houses. Rather an attempt is made to support the theory that tombs meant houses by looking for internal links and associations. This interpretation is plausible because a good number of specific formal links can be made between the houses and the tombs and because of temporal and spatial overlaps between the occurrences of the two types. Similarly, the interpretation of the Orkney evidence in Chapter 3 is supported by the repetition of the same schemes within different categories of material.

I do not think that it would be possible to 'verify' these interpretations in any absolute or final sense. Indeed I doubt whether one can reach this type of certainty with any but the most banal of archaeological statements. But I do think it is clear that further evidence could be collected which would either strengthen or weaken the interpretations made. For example, in the cases of the European tombs and houses, further evidence might show a considerable gap in time between the houses and tombs, thus weakening the hypothesis that the tombs copied the earlier houses. Or else, further evidence might show that the internal ordering of space in the two types of monument is clearly different.

One of the reasons for including Chapters 3 and 4 in this book is that since they were written new material has been excavated which confirms rather than weakens the suggested meanings. In my undoubtedly partisan view the hypotheses have been positively 'tested' by new evidence. Take for example the hypothesis that tombs meant houses in Chapter 4, and take the eight points of similarity. Some of these now seem ruled out (Hodder 1990). For example, it is now clear that the pits along the sides of the houses are an early feature and thus cannot be compared with the ditches along the sides of the later tombs. And there seems to be little evidence for the use of decoration in the houses. But in other ways the points of similarity have been increased. Both Midgley (1985) and Bogucki (1987) have argued that the Polish tombs are like houses in that they tend to form clustered patterns similar in form to the Kujavian 'villages' of houses. Perhaps the strongest evidence, however, is that in many areas in northern Europe the tombs seem to be located directly over earlier settlements (Midgley 1985) and over dumps of domestic rubbish. There does seem to be a close association between the tombs and houses.

Other supporting evidence has come from excavations which have shown links between the Danubian cultures which built the long houses and the construction of the tombs (Hodder 1990). For example, the trapezoidal tomb of Les Fouaillages in the Channel Islands has pottery from a late Danubian tradition (Kinnes 1982). In Burgundy, at Passy, a series of linear funerary monuments associated with Danubian material culture shows the appearance of the idea of linear tomb burial even within cultures associated with long houses (Thevenot 1985). Indeed, the evidence for a link between houses and tombs was recently seen to be strong enough for Sherratt (1990) to suggest a general interpretation for the processes of transformation in north and west Europe.

It is not necessary to assume that builders of burial monuments throughout northwest Europe 'remembered' their derivation in central European houses. But it is possible to argue that the tradition that tombs represented houses was a long one, as is suggested by the frequent siting of tombs over settlements or houses. Further evidence to support a local link between tombs, other ritual monuments and houses in Orkney, as argued in Chapter 3, has come from recent excavations at Barnhouse (Richards 1992). Here Structure 2 (Figure 2) has close similarities to the tombs, with six recessed chambers (as at Quanterness) or rooms placed around a central area with hearth. Structure 8 allows parallels to be drawn between houses, tombs and the henge at the nearby Stones of Stenness. Richards (1991; 1992) emphasises the common use of similar types of central hearth. Despite the chronological difficulties with the arguments presented in Chapter 3 (see Sharples 1985), new evidence, which could easily have undermined the interpretation of meaning, has in fact supported it.

I do not conclude from these examples that I have in some ultimate way been proved right in my interpretations of these meanings in the heads of prehistoric peoples. I fully expect other interpretations to be suggested which overthrow or transform my own. This must always be the case with any historical or anthropological reconstruction. But I do conclude from these examples that it is possible to make statements about past meanings which can be strengthened or weakened by consideration of the evidence. On this basis it is possible to prefer one hypothesis, which fits the data better, over another. Of course, as I will argue later in this book, archaeologists also have other grounds for preferring particular hypotheses. And it is undoubtedly the case that the data themselves can be redefined to favour preferred hypotheses. Much as they may seem to be, the data are not 'set in stone'. And yet, however subjective it may be, the patterning in the data is real and there is only so much that can plausibly be distorted. There is a very real sense in which my hypothesis that tombs meant houses in Neolithic Europe will have to stand the test of time, both as perspectives and theories change and as more data are collected and old data re-examined.

A final aspect of the strengthening of the interpretation of meaning is to provide a plausible social and economic context within which the meaning can be situated as discourse (Barrett 1987b). After all it is only by showing how the meaning worked in practice that we can say that we have properly provided it with a context. The attempts to provide such a context in the following chapters are relatively unsuccessful, especially in Chapter 4 where, as already mentioned, there was too much depen-

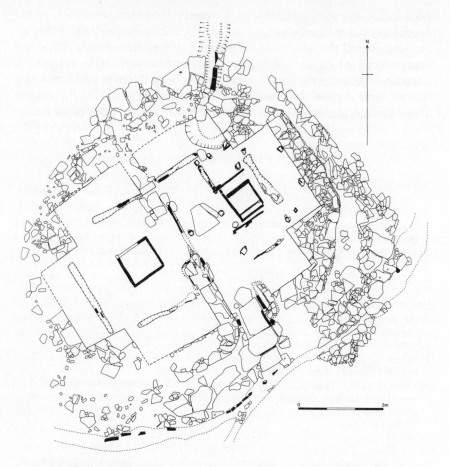

Figure 2 Barnhouse, Orkney, Structure 2 (with permission of C. Richards).
Compare with Figure 5.

dence on cross-cultural hypotheses based on inadequate social theories. A fuller account (see Hodder 1990) would interpret the tombs as often providing a stable 'home' in a dispersed and relatively mobile settlement pattern. In a northwest European context without long-term stable houses or villages, the tombs provided the only focus for stable long-term social structures which were needed in an agricultural system increasingly based on delayed returns for the input of labour.

The following chapters, then, present a contextual approach to past symbolic meanings. They demonstrate the potential for interpreting specific, not general meanings. Unlike most other approaches in archaeology, the contextual approach, close to thick description, seeks to ask questions such as 'Why was this particular shape or decoration of pot used rather than any other?', 'Why were the tombs this shape?', 'What specifically did the tombs mean?' It is only by asking such questions that we can understand the way in which material culture was socially active and was involved in long-term change. What the chapters do not do, however, is adequately consider the social context, incorporate different and competing 'voices', and explore the relationship between 'their' and 'our' contexts. These failings, and others, will be dealt with in the later parts of the book.

REFERENCES

Barrett, J. (1987a) 'Fields of discourse', *Critique of Anthropology*, 7, 5–16.
—— (1987b) 'Contextual archaeology', *Antiquity* 61, 468–73.
—— (1989) 'Time and tradition: the rituals of everyday life', in H.-A. Nordstrom and A. Knape (eds) *Bronze Age Studies*, Stockholm: Statens Historiska Museum.
Binford, L. R. (1989) *Debating Archaeology*, New York: Academic Press.
Bintliff, J. (ed.) (1990) *Extracting Meaning from the Past*, Oxford: Oxbow Books.
Bogucki, P. (1987) 'The establishment of agrarian communities on the north European plain', *Current Anthropology* 28, 1–24.
Chippindale, C. (1983) *Stonehenge Complete*, London: Thames and Hudson.
Earle, T. and Preucel, R. (1987) 'Processual archaeology and the radical critique', *Current Anthropology* 28, 501–38.
Geertz, C. (1973) *The Interpretation of Cultures*, New York: Basic Books.
Hawkes, C. (1954) 'Archaeological theory and method: some suggestions from the Old World', *American Anthropologist* 56, 155–68.
Hodder, I. (1982) *Symbols in Action*, Cambridge: Cambridge University Press.
—— (1984) 'Burials, houses, women and men in the European Neolithic', in D. Miller and C. Tilley (eds) *Ideology, Power and Prehistory*, Cambridge: Cambridge University Press.
—— (1986) *Reading the Past*, Cambridge: Cambridge University Press.
—— (1990) *The Domestication of Europe*, Oxford: Basil Blackwell.
—— (1991) *Reading the Past*, 2nd edn, Cambridge: Cambridge University Press.
Kinnes, I. (1982) 'Les Fouaillages and megalithic origins', *Antiquity*, 61, 24–30.
Merriman, N. (1987) 'Value and motivation in prehistory: the evidence for "Celtic spirit" ', in I. Hodder (ed.) *The Archaeology of Contextual meanings*, Cambridge: Cambridge University Press.
Midgley, M. (1985) *The Origin and Function of the Earthen Long Barrows of Northern Europe*, Oxford: British Archaeological Reports International Series 259.
Renfrew, C. (1982) *Towards an Archaeology of Mind*, Cambridge: Cambridge University Press.
Richards, C. (1991) 'The late Neolithic house in Orkney', in R. Samson (ed.) *The Social Archaeology of Houses*, Edinburgh: Edinburgh University Press.
—— (1992) 'Monumental choreography: architecture and spatial representation in late Neolithic Orkney', in M. Shanks and C. Tilley (eds) *Interpretative Archaeology*, London: Routledge.
Sharples, N. (1985) 'Individual and community: the changing role of megaliths in the Orcadian Neolithic', *Proceedings of the Prehistoric Society* 51, 59–74.
Sherratt, A. (1990) 'The genesis of megaliths', *World Archaeology* 22, 147–67.
Thevenot, J.-P. (1985) 'Informations archeologiques: circonscription de Bourgogne', *Gallia Prehistoire* 28, 171–210.

3

SYMBOLS IN ACTION

Environments to which societies are adjusted are worlds of ideas, collective representations that differ not only in extent and content, but also in structure.

(Childe 1949, 22)

In the preceding chapters it was suggested that there are few areas in prehistoric archaeology in which there has been sufficient emphasis on symbolism and conceptual schemes. Such an emphasis is of importance in reconstructing the past since material culture transforms, rather than reflects, social organisation according to the strategies of groups, their beliefs, concepts and ideologies. In this chapter I wish to consider briefly some broader aspects of a less behaviourally and less ecologically oriented archaeology.

'WHOLENESS'

It is suggested that interpretation of the past might make use of a concept of structure as demonstrated in the Nuba study (Hodder 1982). Each aspect of the material culture data, whether burial, settlement pattern, wall design or refuse distribution, can be interpreted in terms of common underlying schemes. These structures of meaning permeate all aspects of archaeological evidence. Each material item has significance in terms of its place in the whole. This is not to say that the patterns in the different types of data are always direct mirror images of each other. Rather, the identifiable patterns are transformations, often contrasting, disrupting or commenting on basic dichotomies and tensions within the social system and within the distribution of power. Yet the emphasis on 'wholeness' remains. The structures behind the patterning in one type of data must be interpreted by reference to other structures in other categories of information.

An emphasis on wholeness is also the hallmark of the application of systems theory in processual archaeology. But it is possible to identify differences in the concept of wholeness or totality as used by systems theorists and as described here. All applications of systems theory in archaeology have begun with a definition of a subsystem, or with a list of all subsystems (e.g. Clarke 1968; Renfrew 1972). The aim of the analysis is then to examine the interrelationships between the different subsystems, and to explain one in terms of its connections to others. Indeed, it is the very essence of systems theory that the behaviour of one subsystem can be understood and predicted from its functional links to others. As one part of the system changes, the others regulate and adapt to regain homeostasis (Hill 1971, 407; Binford 1972, 20; Flannery 1972, 409; Plog 1975, 208). One subsystem which has recently been seen as important is the 'ideational' (Drennan 1976; Flannery and Marcus 1976; Fritz 1978). Flannery (1972, 409) accepts that the human population's 'cognised model' of the way the world is put together is not merely epiphenomenal but plays an essential part in controlling and regulating societies. Everything ideational is put in a separate subsystem and then the functional links between this and the other subsystems are examined in terms of regulation and management.

The concept of wholeness in archaeological systems theory thus concerns the functional relationships between separate subsystems. In assessing this viewpoint it should first be recognised that the subsystems are of the analyst's own making. She decides on separating out, for example, everything ideational, and then examines the links between categories which have been arbitrarily defined (Sahlins 1976). Second, the structure of the whole derives from the functional links between the parts, and there is no real concept of wholeness itself except as a by-product of the relationships between parts. Few archaeologists have claimed that there are absolute one-to-one behavioural links between environments and human societies. So if one asks 'Why does the system have the form it does?', 'What structures the whole?', the functional view inherent in systems theory can only provide partial answers.

On the other hand, it may be easier to answer such questions satisfactorily if archaeologists consider the symbolic principles which link the parts together. These principles permeate the functional relationships, and they form the whole. The whole does not come from the parts but from the underlying structures. It is not adequate to separate everything ideational into a separate subsystem. Rather, idea and belief are present and are reproduced in all action, however economic or mundane. Structures of meaning are present in all the daily trivia of life and in the major adaptive decisions of human groups. Material culture patterning is formed as part of these meaningful actions and it helps to constitute changing frameworks of action and belief. The concept of wholeness from this structural point of view is more absolute and more far-reaching than in systems theory as used by archaeologists.

In practical terms the need for systems theorists to locate separate subsystems has been associated with a concern for identifying variability (e.g. Binford 1978, 3). In its annual adaptive cycle, a community is seen as going through different tasks at different positions on the landscape. In different environmental and strategic contexts, different assemblages will be left as a result of variation in adaptive behaviour. So the search of the archaeologist is for adaptively linked variation in cultural assemblages. This approach pays little attention to schemes common to the varying assemblages. Binford (ibid., 3) accepts that adaptive responses 'draw upon a repertoire of cultural background', but this cultural component is considered peripheral and unimportant. Under this behavioural view, there is little emphasis on methodologies for examining how variability can be studied and interpreted as transformations following underlying rules. That which articulates and gives meaning to the variability is given less attention than the variability itself and its functional relationships.

On the other hand, the traditional 'normative' emphasis (see Binford 1978) concerned with cultural norms and mental templates has contrasting limitations. Here the examination is of the cultural codes held in common by members of society regardless of the setting in which they find themselves. This approach is less able to cope with variability and with expedient adaptive responses.

It is necessary then to bridge the gap between the emphasis on variability and the emphasis on static, shared norms and templates. There is a need to move away both from studying variability without examining the structures which bind that variability together, and from studying cultural codes which do not allow for adaptive intelligence. In ethnoarchaeological studies (Hodder 1982) I have tried to examine symbols in action, and I have shown how structures of meaning relate to practice – how symbol sets are negotiated and manipulated in social action. Cultural patterning is not produced by a set of static fixed norms but is both the framework within which action and adaptation have meaning, and it is also reproduced in those actions and in the adaptive responses that are made. There is no dichotomy between an interest in culture and meaning and a concern with adaptive variability. Indeed, interpretation of the past must integrate both research aims. The examination of variability on its own is insufficient.

Processual, behavioural and systems theory archaeology have accompanied a massive fragmentation and compartmentalisation of archaeological research. The discussion above suggests one of the reasons why this should be so. The emphasis in recent archaeology has been on defining subsystems and their law-like behavioural links with an 'environment'. The initial need to define subsystems in analytical research has provided a framework for the specialisation of methods, theories and generalisations relevant to each subsystem. There are those who work on settlement studies or spatial analysis, while others write books or conduct cross-cultural research on burial, exchange, subsistence economies, art and so on. Despite attempts to break down these barriers (e.g. Flannery 1976), each subsystem realm is developing its own vocabulary which is fast becoming incomprehensible to specialists in other fields. Much of the literature, teaching and research in archaeology is divided along these lines. There is a need for integration, which would be the logical result of a symbolic and 'contextual' archaeology.

THE PARTICULAR HISTORICAL CONTEXT

The type of prehistory that is implied by a concern with the meaningful constitution of material culture patterning is likely to be more particularistic and less concerned with cross-cultural behavioural laws. Material culture patterning cannot be derived directly from the 'environmental' conditions of behaviour. But this is not to say that some form of generalisation will not be used in interpreting the past. If the Nuba data and some of the ethnoarchaeological information (Hodder 1982) are considered as if prehistoric and archaeological, it can be seen that, in giving 'meaning' to the finds and in placing them in a structured 'whole', two broad types of generalisation might be used.

1   Symbolic or structural principles occur widely although they are used and emphasised in different ways in each society. In the Nuba case, the structural oppositions clean/dirty, male/female and life/death would be seen to be marked. These symbolic principles are found in most societies, and knowledge of them aids the analysis in the particular case. The identification and analysis of symmetry in the Nuba art and decoration might make reference to general studies of types of symmetry (e.g. Washburn 1978). We might also include generalisations concerning the relationships between structural principles. For example, in the Nuba case, Douglas' (1966) model for the link between pure/impure and an emphasis on categorisation is applicable.

2   As well as generalisations concerning structures and symbolic principles themselves, there are also models and analogies concerning the way man gives meaning to actions. Such generalisations give indications about the way beliefs and concepts can be integrated into social and ecological strategies, and about the way the structures of the first type of generalisation are used in day-to-day life. In chapter 8 (Hodder 1982), Douglas' model for the relationship between the principle pure/ impure and sex dichotomies was described, while it has also been suggested (ibid.) in the accounts of the Njemps, Nuba and British Gypsies that dependent subgroups within larger dominant societies often have a strong sense of purity and boundedness, and place an emphasis on classification and categorisation.

Despite the use of these two types of generalisation, the interpretation of each set of material culture data is unique. The general principles are rearranged into unique patterns in each 'whole'. The particular nature of each set of cultural data occurs for two reasons.

i   The general symbolic principles of the first type are assembled in particular ways. In the archaeological study of the Nuba, it would first be necessary to identify the particular use of general structural oppositions such as clean/dirty, life/death, male/female and the degree of emphasis on classification and categorisation. In comparing the Moro and Mesakin areas (ibid.) it would be noted that decoration surrounds zones with more refuse, suggesting the marking of boundaries between clean and unclean, while the decoration around the flour in the grinding huts and in the toilet areas might also be identified. Many of the rituals marking the life/death boundary could be recovered archaeologically, and if the grave fills were sieved some idea of the association of grain with death might be found. Within the compounds, the division into two halves, male and female, could be identified in the distribution of male and female artifacts and in the overall arrangement of the different types of buildings. An emphasis on symbolic categorisation and separation would be recovered from the distributions of cattle and pig bones, and body and skull bones, while in the art of the Nuba a series of simple but distinct rules would be found.

It would also be necessary to examine the relationships between these different symbolic oppositions. It would be found that cattle/pig could be associated with male/female because of the association of male items with cattle remains in cattle camps and in burials, and because of the association of female items with pigs. So male/female = cattle/pig rather than pig/cattle. This is a particular relationship. In the art, general principles (rotational symmetry etc.) are assembled by the idea of a particular cross or star design. The particular way the elements are arranged into a whole is aided by general hypotheses concerning the relationships between types of symbolic principle. The Nuba dichotomy clean/dirty could be linked to the emphasis on categorisation and boundedness by posing Douglas' (1966) model concerned with purity. By suggesting an additional dichotomy such as pure/impure, it may be easier to tie different components into the 'whole'. But the arrangement pure/impure = cattle/pig = male/female = clean/dirty = life/death is particular and specific to the Nuba context.

ii Really inseparable from (i), except in the stages of analysis, is the articulation of the symbolism and beliefs in social and ecological action. In the archaeological study of the Nuba, reference could be made to models and analogies in the second type of generalisation. Economic evidence and the regional distributions of cultural material would indicate the overt separation of a distinct Nuba group with economic and resource interchange with their more widely spread neighbours (the Arabs). The minority, dependent but symbolically separate position of the hill communities in relation to the Arabs is consistent with the overall concern with the marking of conceptual boundaries and with the principle of purity. Although in this case the Nuba fit one of the models in (2), we cannot predict that the same integration of structure and practice will occur in all similar social and ecological environments, nor that material culture will always be involved in the same way. Other groups in similar situations may manipulate concepts and material symbols differently. As the Nuba communities undergo radical changes, with outmigration, closer contacts with Arabs, and the break-up of family groupings, interest groups have chosen to emphasise certain traditional values and certain concepts have come to the fore. The ideological manipulation of symbolism to justify, disrupt, mask or comment on aspects of social reality was examined especially in the studies in Baringo and Zambia (Hodder 1982). In each particular context, beliefs and material symbols are negotiated and manipulated in different ways as part of individual and group strategies.

Because of the transformations in (i) and (ii), we cannot *predict* what material culture patterning will result in any human and physical environment, but we can *interpret* the past by using our contemporary knowledge of symbolism and ideologies (1 and 2). There can never be any direct predictive relationships between material culture and social behaviour because in each particular context general symbolic principles, and general tendencies for the integration of belief and action, are rearranged in particular ways as part of the strategies and intents of individuals and groups. The 'whole' is particular, dependent on context.

An archaeology in which an emphasis is placed on the particular way that general symbolic and structural principles are assembled into coherent sets and integrated into social and ecological strategies can be called a 'contextual' archaeology. The advantage of the term 'context' is that it can be used to refer both to the framework of concepts and to the articulation of that framework in social and ecological adaptation. As in the Nuba example, a cultural item or a social or ecological action can be interpreted in terms of its place within a structured set or whole. But the notion of context must be extended to include historical context. The framework within which actions and strategies are given meaning is built up over time and at each new development this framework is itself altered and transformed from within. The structures at phase B cannot be understood without reference to the structures in phase A. In the Nuba study, the ideology which accompanies the present changes and flux derives from a traditional framework with a long history. In the example of the Merina of Madagascar (Hodder 1982, Chapter 9), the ideal of stable descent groups which contrasts with the day-to-day links and social relations derives from an older structure of beliefs. Equally, reference to the history of a particular cultural trait is fundamentally important in the interpretation of its position and use within a new phase. Amongst the Dorobo (ibid., Chapter 6), the Maasai quality of the cultural items is critical, while spear and weapon types may be borrowed from successful groups within the Baringo area (ibid., Chapter 4) precisely because the types have a history of association with highly esteemed warrior groups.

APPLYING THE CONTEXTUAL APPROACH IN ARCHAEOLOGY

It has been suggested as a result of the ethnoarchaeological studies that material culture is meaningfully constituted. Material culture patterning transforms structurally rather than reflects behaviourally social relations. Interpretation must integrate the different categories of evidence from the different subsystems into the 'whole'. It has also been suggested that each particular historical context must be studied as a unique combination of general principles of meaning and symbolism, negotiated and manipulated in specific ways. I have already indicated briefly how these points might be followed up in the practice of archaeology by imagining what the Nuba would look like if dug up. This is, of course, a slight of hand. It is now necessary briefly to describe a truly archaeological analysis which illustrates the points made so far in this chapter. The case study cannot be exhaustively described here. It is introduced simply as an illustration, to demonstrate the feasibility and potential of the approach and to provide some flavour of its nature.

Late Neolithic Orkney

The archaeological study concerns the late Neolithic on the Islands of Orkney in northern Britain (Figure 3). In Orkney, settlements have been excavated at Skara Brae (Childe 1931; D. V. Clarke 1976), Rinyo (Childe and Grant 1939; 1947) and at the Knap of Howar, Papa Westray (Traill and Kirkness 1937; A. Ritchie 1973; 1975). Excavations of communal burial tombs have provided general information on ritual and form (Henshall 1963), while the recent excavations at Quanterness (Renfrew 1979) provide an important account of the detail and dating of an Orkney tomb. The 'henges' of Stenness (J. N. G. Ritchie 1976) and Brogar represent a third type of site on Orkney connected with 'ritual' but not demonstrably primarily concerned with burial. The settlements, burials and ritual sites all occur within a relatively small area, the

30

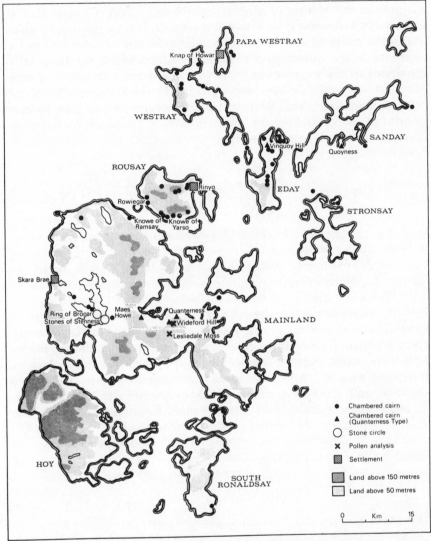

Figure 3 The distribution of Neolithic sites on Orkney. *Source*: Renfrew 1979

Orkney Islands, and a relatively short period of time, the second half of the third millennium bc. It is possible, then, to compare the information excavated from the different types of site.

Within the terms of the 'processual' approach in archaeology such comparison of information from different types of site would, as has been shown, be of interest. Indeed, in the site report of Quanterness, it is stated (Renfrew 1979, 160) that the comparison of Quanterness and Skara Brae should allow the special factors governing the selection of the

31

fauna used in funerary practices to be assessed. Yet such a comparison is never carried out in the report, and there is no comparison of the information from the different types of site. As was indicated above, this lack of integration is paradoxically symptomatic of much of recent archaeology. The systems approach involves the separation of spheres, subsystems, and then the analysis of the links between them. But the initial separation hinders the further integration. All that can be achieved is a demonstration of the possible functional links between subsystems, and there is no method for examining the structure which runs through the whole. A systems framework has not provided methods or theories which would focus attention on the comparison of faunal material from a burial (such as Quanterness) and a settlement (Skara Brae). These two types of site are in separate subsystems and the functional links are obscure. It is perhaps partly for this reason that a comparison between the different types of site is never carried out in the Quanterness report.

On the other hand, the focus of interest in the contextual approach is precisely on the comparison of information from different spheres within the same cultural frame and on the identification of common structural schemes. So what similarities and differences do occur between the settlement, burial and ritual sites? In general, there are many similarities in the artifacts found. On the Orkney mainland, Grooved Ware is found at all three types of site, as are particular artifacts such as a highly distinctive decorated three-spiked macehead which occurs at both Skara Brae and in the Quoyness chambered cairn.

Yet there are also major differences in the artifacts found in the different types of site. Although the mainland Orkney pottery is all of the same Grooved Ware tradition, there are distinctions. At the Skara Brae and Rinyo settlements, decoration is more elaborate and more common than at the Quanterness tomb and Stenness henge (although such differences could be due to variation in recovery methods, with more attention paid to decorated pottery in the earlier excavations of the settlements). Applied decoration is common at the settlements but rare at Quanterness and absent from the small sample at Stenness. Some particular decorative motifs occur at Quanterness but not at Skara Brae (ibid., 79). While many of these pottery differences could be due to chronological variation which is too slight to be identified by radiocarbon dating, the distinctions are supported in other spheres. For example, beads, extremely common at Skara Brae where they often occur in large concentrations in 'stores', are extremely rare in the burial and ritual sites.

The faunal assemblages also vary between the different site types, although the discussion here is hampered by only approximate recording of the faunal material and by the fact that some of the recent excavations have yet to result in fully published bone reports. Yet there are certainly differences in the percentages of animal bones (cattle, sheep, pig) present in the different types of site. There are also differences in the ages of the animals. The bones which occur in both the Skara Brae and Knap of Howar settlements indicate large proportions of very young cattle with sheep being of all ages, while this situation is reversed at the Quanterness tomb. Here there are very many young sheep but relatively few young cattle. Different parts of the animal carcasses are also predominant in the different types of site. Childe's Skara Brae report gives indications of the presence of all parts of the animal carcass including skull, jaw, ribs and vertebrae. Although the account of the Skara Brae animal bones is inadequate for the purposes of detailed comparison with the tombs and henge, the latter sites are distinctive in showing a lack of particular parts of the animal carcass. At Quanterness the sheep bones include many limbs and feet, but few skull fragments. At Stenness both cattle and sheep are represented by very few ribs, vertebrae, scapulae and skulls. The magnitude of these variations is considered in both bone reports to be too great to be due to differential survival and some cultural selection is assumed.

So the artifactual evidence, including animal bones, from Orkney suggests major differences between the settlement, burial and ritual sites, and in particular between the settlements and the other two types of site. Although slight chronological variation may account for some of these differences, the substantial series of radiocarbon dates from Orkney demonstrate contemporaneity in the late third millennium bc. It would also be possible to argue that the coastal settlement sites, partly dependent on fish (D. V. Clarke 1976) and shells, are different from other, as yet unexamined, inland sites whose assemblages may prove to be more similar to the inland henges and tombs. This would seem to be a difficult hypothesis to support in view of the short distances from interior to coast, and in view of the artifactual evidence of the social and economic integration of the different sites (similar pottery styles and other artifact types) but it must remain a competing hypothesis to be examined by future fieldwork.

In any case there is other evidence of the special conceptual importance of the boundary between life and death, settlement and tomb, in Orkney. This evidence resides in the long sequence of complex ritual that can be associated with death as a result of the detailed analyses by Chesterman (in Renfrew 1979) of the human bones from Quanterness. Analysis of the bleached condition of the bones, their fragmentation and placing in the tomb, suggested excarnation of the bodies outside the communal tombs, selection of certain parts of the body, and the placing of these parts in the tombs. There is a large preponderence of feet over hand bones. In the tomb the bones were burnt in a central fire. All this,

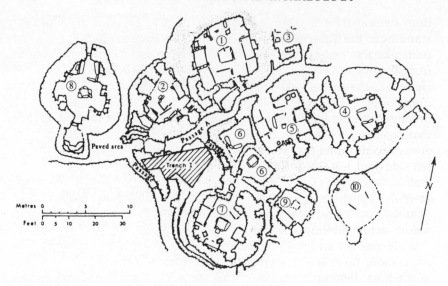

Figure 4 Plan of the Skara Brae settlement on Orkney. *Source*: Clarke 1976.
Reproduced by permission of the Controller, HMSO

and the very existence of these large burial structures, suggest the special importance attached to the life/death boundary in the particular context of late Neolithic Orkney.

While such evidence of the special distinctiveness of the boundaries between life (settlement) and death (burial) and ritual (henge) is unlikely to be of any surprise to archaeologists, it is important for my purposes to document the importance of the boundaries before moving on to a further characteristic of the Orkney data. This further aspect is that what is reconstituted on each side of the boundaries has many structural equivalencies.

Structural similarities across conceptual boundaries

The overall plans of the Skara Brae and Rinyo settlements are markedly *cellular* with huts leading off long corridors and, within the huts, small 'cupboards' leading off the central area (Figure 4). The entrances to both the hut 'cells' and the cupboard 'cells' are small and low.

In the centres of the Skara Brae huts there is always a hearth surrounded by stones placed on edge. Adjacent to the hearth are frequently found artifacts such as flint and stone tools, bone adzes and piercing tools. Although the hearth is usually seen as central, many of the huts have the entrance door slightly to the right of the hearth on entering (e.g. huts 2, 4, 5 in Figure 4).

Despite the slightly off-centre position of the hearth and door, the huts demonstrate a clear left/right symmetry (as seen by a person standing in the hut entrance). The overall plan shows similar features, in particular the 'beds', in the left and right of the approximate central axis from the door to the hearth to the 'dresser' at the back of the hut. Yet closer examination shows that this apparent symmetry hides repeated differences, left from right. The right hand bed is always larger (1.5 to 2 m long) than the left hand bed (1.1 to 1.7 m). Childe records (1931, 15) that receptacles (for example of whalebone) containing traces of paint always occur under the left bed, while beads are also distinctively on the left side (ibid.). It would be tempting to relate this right/left difference to male/female. However, such an interpretation is not part of my argument and other interpretations are possible – for example, an adult/child distinction or some difference in function which is not involved in sex, age or status differentiation.

While the left and right halves of the huts show both symmetry and opposition, there is also a cross-cutting distinction between the interior of the huts, behind the hearths, and the front of the huts between the hearths and the entrances. The back half of the hut contains a major 'dresser' set in the back wall, and frequently contains 'limpet boxes' set in the floor. The precise interpretation of the functions of these features is unclear although some type of storage is usually supposed (D. V. Clarke 1976). At the Rinyo settlement (Childe and Grant 1939) a large pot was found in a recess in the wall facing the door in hut D. Near the hearth and the front of the hut are the main activity areas at Skara Brae (as seen in the distributions of tools) and the right-hand near corner is interpreted by Childe, especially in hut 7, as a kitchen or dining area.

A final characteristic of the arrangement of information in the huts to be mentioned here is the positioning of some engraved decoration around the walls within the settlement and huts.

The main structural components of the Skara Brae settlement, apparently duplicated in the less extensively excavated Rinyo site, are the cellular arrangement with cells linked by small, low and often long entrances, the hearth approximately on the central axis of the hut with the entrance slightly to the right, the left/right symmetry and opposition, and the decoration of the inside of the settlement boundary. Many of these structural characteristics also occur in the chambered tombs. Most obviously, the overall plan of the tombs is cellular, with six chambers leading off the central chamber at Quanterness (Figure 5) and Quoyness, and with three side chambers at Maes Howe. At Quanterness, as at Skara Brae, the entrances are low, narrow and long.

This parallel between the cellular structure of the settlements and chambered tombs is so obvious that it has rarely been remarked or thought to be of importance. But the particular similarity between the settlements and burials on Orkney mainland is given special significance

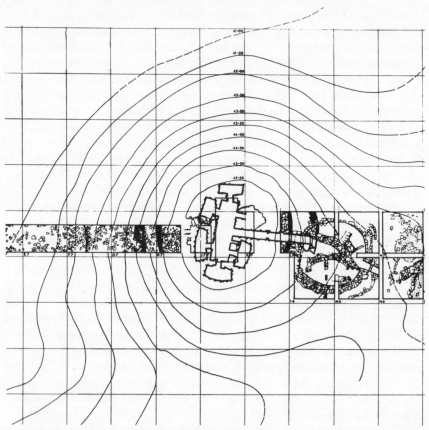

Figure 5 Plan of the Quanterness tomb on Orkney (compare with Figure 2, p. 22).
Source: Renfrew 1979

by a contrast with the settlements and tombs on the more northerly islands. On Rousay and the northern isles a few chambered tombs do occur, but the great majority of the tombs are 'stalled cairns'. The tombs here are made up of single galleries divided at intervals by stones partially inserted into the long sides. The 'stalled' aspect is also found at the Knap of Howar settlement on Papa Westray (Figure 13, p. 61). The two huts excavated (Traill and Kirkness 1937) are divided into two or three sections by stones projecting out of the side walls. Although aspects of the Skara Brae structure occur at the Knap of Howar, such as the positioning of cupboards mainly at the end of the hut opposite the entrance, and the location of beds to the sides, the linear partitioning into segments is clearly different and comparable with the stalled cairns.

A further distinctive aspect of the Orkney settlements is the central location of the hearth. In the Quanterness tomb, evidence of burning is confined to the central chamber and does not occur in the side chambers. There may also be some indication of more burning in the central part of the central chamber. To the sides, left and right, of the main central chamber are higher concentrations of human bones and higher densities are also found in the side chambers. Pottery, animal bones and other artifacts are more common in the central area of the main chamber. The overall arrangement of burning and artifacts at the centre, with lower artifact densities and higher human bone densities at the edges, is a parallel to the central hearth and artifacts in the huts with the beds, dressers and storage facilities around the sides.

The offset entrances in the huts are paralleled in the placing of the side chambers in many of the tombs. For example, at Quoyness the entrances are offset to the right as they are in the huts.

The plans of all the tombs show a left/right symmetry as has already been identified in the concentrations of human bones at Quanterness. The decoration around the sides of the chambers in the tombs is similar to the huts both in its rectilinear zig-zag content and in its placing often round entrances to side chambers (in the huts the decoration often occurs around entrances to different types of side cubicle).

The settlements and tombs thus demonstrate many structural parallels which must be examined against the extensive ritual surrounding the life/death boundary. Some of the same structures can be identified in the henge at Stenness (Figure 6). At the centre of the stone circle is a rectangular setting of stones on edge and there is evidence of burning, particularly in the form of burnt sheep bones, within this feature. The shape, position, construction and contents of this feature are parallel to the hearths in the huts.

The axis from the henge entrance to the central square of stones divides the henge into two symmetrical halves, but the bones from the ditches surrounding the two halves indicate an opposition within the symmetry. While sheep bones are found in the ditch to the left of the entrance, no sheep bones are found to the right.

Behind the central stone setting at Stenness are pits, one of which contains a concentration of pure barley while another contains the lower part of a pot. These pits behind the central stone setting are analogous to the storage tanks and facilities behind the hearths in the huts. There is an additional structural parallel between the Maes Howe tomb and the Stenness henge: both have banks *outside* the ditches.

The structural similarities between the settlements, tombs and 'ritual' henges have been described. The parallels concern the cellular arrangement with complex entrances (not found in the henges – see below), the hearth position as part of a centre/periphery pattern, a left/right symmetry and opposition, and a front/back division. The existence of these structural equivalencies on each side of marked boundaries (e.g. between settlement (life) and tomb (death) suggests that the activities

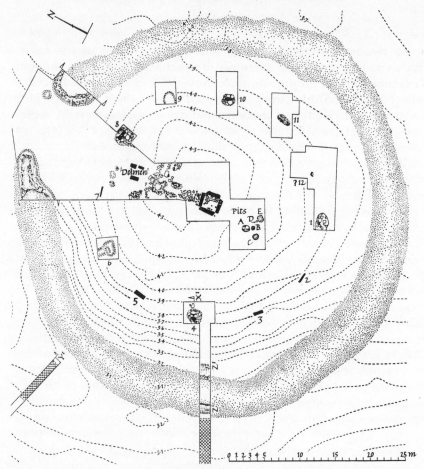

Figure 6 Site plan of the Stones of Stenness, Orkney, showing the ring of stones (numbers 1 to 12), the outer bank and inner ditch, and the central setting of stones. *Source*: J. N. G. Ritchie 1976

carried out in each context reconstituted and reinforced particular dimensions of order. In ritual and in death the structure is first broken down at the boundaries and then reconstituted on the other side, reinforcing and naturalising the day-to-day order of life in the settlements.

Yet in discussing the henge at Stenness one major aspect of the structure was not examined. Neither the Ring of Brogar nor the Stones of Stenness are in any sense cellular in plan. The henges have centres and encircling rings; they have no cubicles nor cells nor long narrow entrances. Everything is organised around one centre, and in this the plan of the henge denies or leaves out the multi-centred form which is so distinctive of both the burial and settlement plans.

Henges and change

In one respect the Orkney henges reverse the settlement and burial structures. To examine this difference in structure it is necessary to begin to examine changes through time. Renfrew (1979) has suggested that the earlier Neolithic on Orkney is characterised by an egalitarian society. This conclusion is derived from the form and distribution of burials, settlements and artifacts in Orkney which show no indication of ranking. But in the later part of the Neolithic (late second millennium bc) a few monuments of larger scale were constructed such as Maes Howe and the henges themselves. The major monuments occur in close proximity in the central part of mainland Orkney and for the first time suggest some form of centralised organisation. It should be emphasised that the settlements and many of the tombs continue in use during both periods.

The suggested change from local and equivalent communities to some degree of centralisation is supported by evidence from other parts of Britain. The change in burial may indicate a real change in Orkney social organisation. But carbon 14 for the Orkney sequence is of particular interest in that the dates place the Stenness henge earlier than the Maes Howe tomb. A bridge between the decentralised and the centralised phases of the Orkney Neolithic occurs in the 'ritual' of the henges.

The denial in the ritual sites of an aspect of the structure found in the other classes of site marks a contrast. This ritual contrast in structure is similar to what Turner (1969) has termed 'antistructure'. Turner suggests that it is often in the sacred or 'holy' undermining of structure that the structural order is in fact revitalised. The reconstitution of structure out of contrast is often associated with a feeling of community he calls 'communitas'. The central location of the henges in the Orkney Islands suggests a general community focus in ritual even prior to the development of an elite and it indicates that significance may reasonably be given to the lack of cellular structure in the henges. The later association of the especially large tomb of Maes Howe with these central henges is taken here as indicating that the 'communitas' and subversion in ritual were manipulated so that they became associated with the emerging status group. The elite could develop out of the pre-existing system only through the ritual reversal of structure, from cellular to centred, within an otherwise familiar setting in which the settlement and burial activities were repeated and supported. The one part of the structure which was changed concerned the new centred arrangement, the lack of equivalent cells. A henge expressed in one unit the images in numerous individual components in settlements and burials. It provided a ritual symbol of unity which could in turn be used to support an elite. In addition, the reconstitution of the settlement structure in a ritual setting associated with a dominant group may indicate that knowledge

39

about ritual and the symbolic significance of daily activities was controlled by high-status individuals and contributed to their legitimation.

Returning to the earlier Neolithic in Orkney, related arguments may be used to account for the similarity between burial and settlement forms. Although Renfrew has described society at this earlier stage as egalitarian, senior males or lineage heads would have been socially dominant within local groups (Bloch 1975) and the burial ritual may have legitimated their authority through ties with the ancestors (Friedman and Rowlands 1977). The burial form, as an image of the settlement form, would relate the ancestors, the past and the ritual to the daily activities within the settlements. The links made in this way between seniors, ancestors, burial and settlement would act to legitimate the dominance of seniors and their central focus in daily activities within settlements and in the social relations there symbolised. The increased dominance of the social group buried at Maes Howe was also based on the manipulation of a familiar organisation of space within the tomb and on symbolic references in the burial ritual to the mundane activities of the individuals inhabiting settlements such as Skara Brae.

Review of the Orkney study

Since the archaeological analysis of the Orkney material was introduced here as an illustration, it may be helpful to examine the procedure of analysis in order to refer back to the more general conclusions at the beginning of this chapter.

(a) 'Wholeness'. In the initial stage of the Orkney analysis a set of structural relationships was identified and then 'tested' across different spheres (settlement, burial and ritual) and in different regions (mainland and northern Orkney). It was not assumed that the structure in each sphere should reflect that in others, but rather transformations and contrasts were identified. This stage of analysis, demonstrating and identifying pattern, took up the major part of the account.

In the second stage an idea was taken from Turner that structure and antistructure reinforce each other, that structure exists in reference to antistructure in ritual. This hypothesis expresses a principle concerning the way in which humans construct meaning. It is not a behavioural law since it does not say 'if there are certain conditions, then there will be an interplay between structure and antistructure'. Rather, it suggests that structure and antistructure are logically linked.

(b) The particular context. The hypothesis was then made that the structural transformations could have been manipulated as part of social action (the development of an elite), so influencing the particular way in which hierarchisation occurred. It was suggested (again from Turner) that the organisation of ritual may provide 'communitas', and the further hypothesis was then made that this sense of community in an earlier phase could be appropriated by an emerging elite to form a new system in the following phase. Here a general functional model has been used, but understanding of the particular way in which hierarchisation had developed by the end of the period is contributed to by the structural analysis. The structure in the later phase is transformed out of the structure in the earlier phase, manipulated as part of the strategies of groups within societies.

SUMMARY AND SOME FURTHER PROSPECTS

The ethnoarchaeological studies in Kenya and Zambia (Hodder 1982) led to a realisation that symbols are actively involved in social strategies. Because of the active involvement, the symbols may be used to mask, exaggerate or contradict certain types of information flow and social relationships. The Sudan example (ibid.) showed that the form of these transformations depends on general conceptual principles. An archaeology which accepts and develops these points would probably be relatively particularistic in the sense that the conceptual framework within which humans acted and constructed meaning would be seen as being unique to one spatial and historical context. The conceptual framework itself would be seen as having been built up strategically from general and widely found principles. The various principles are combined to provide a structure which runs through the whole of the material culture patterning, through all the types of archaeological evidence. The different subsystems and the behavioural variability from site to site are interpreted in terms of the principles and concepts which play a part in all social and ecological actions.

But it is insufficient merely to describe what might be done in archaeology in reaction to the ethnoarchaeological studies, so in this chapter I have provided a brief archaeological illustration. The particular interpretations provided, like most explanations, will ultimately be proved to be wrong. But the very possibility of proof and disproof is important in demonstrating the feasibility of following up the general implications of the ethnoarchaeological work. The archaeological example in this chapter suggests that studies and interpretations of the past may be able to incorporate symbolic principles and the framework within which humans give meaning to their actions.

As the quote at the beginning of this chapter indicates, the conclusions reached in this book (Hodder 1982) are hardly new. Many of the suggestions made here in relation to prehistory are accepted within historical archaeology (Deetz 1967; Glassie 1975; Ferguson 1977; Leone 1977; Schmidt 1978). Yet I think the conclusions have been worth

41

describing in view of the functional, behavioural and ecological emphases in many recent prehistoric studies. Recent approaches in many fields of archaeological research were described and contrasted with the ideas resulting from the ethnoarchaeology in (Hodder 1982, Chapter 9).

The prospects for the further development of a non-behavioural, contextual archaeology, depend to a large extent on the further expansion of ethnoarchaeological investigations. We need to know much more about the role of material culture patterning in reproducing conceptual frameworks, and about the ideological manipulation of material items in social and ecological strategies. On a broader front there is a need for archaeologists to integrate theories and ideas from a wide range of studies concerned with structure, meaning and social action. The prospect is for a debate in archaeology concerning structuralism (Lévi-Strauss 1963; Piaget 1971) and its various critiques (Sperber 1974; Pettit 1975; Bourdieu 1977), post-structuralism (Ardener 1978; Harstrup 1978), structural-Marxism (Friedman and Rowlands 1977; Godelier 1977) and contemporary social theory (Marsh, Rosser and Harré 1978; Giddens 1979). What is meant by concepts such as ideology, legitimation, power, symbol and social structure must be argued within the archaeological literature and the concepts must be incorporated into interpretations of the past. The ethnoarchaeological studies presented in this book (Hodder 1982) have resulted in the asking of many more questions than have been answered. But they have at least suggested the urgency of developing a broader archaeology, more fully integrated into the social sciences.

REFERENCES

Ardener, E. (1978) 'Some outstanding problems in the analysis of events', in E. Schwimmer (ed.) *The Yearbook of Symbolic Anthropology*, London: Hurst.

Binford, L. R. (1972) *An Archaeological Perspective*, New York: Academic Press.

—— (1978) *Nunamiut Ethnoarchaeology*, New York: Academic Press.

Bloch, M. (1975) 'Property and the end of affinity', in M. Bloch (ed.) *Marxist Analyses in Social Anthropology*, London: ASA.

Bourdieu, P. (1977) *Outline of a Theory of Practice*, Cambridge: Cambridge University Press.

Childe, V. G. (1931) *Skara Brae. A Pictish Village in Orkney*, London: Kegan Paul.

—— (1949) *Social Worlds of Knowledge*, Oxford: Oxford University Press.

Childe, V. G. and Grant, W. G. (1939) 'A Stone-age settlement at the Braes of Rinyo, Rousay, Orkney', *Proceedings of the Society of Antiquaries of Scotland* 73, 6–31.

—— (1947) 'A Stone-age settlement at the Braes of Rinyo, Rousay, Orkney', *Proceedings of the Society of Antiquaries of Scotland* 81, 16–42.

Clarke, D. L. (1968) *Analytical Archaeology*, London: Methuen.

Clarke, D.V. (1976) *The Neolithic Village at Skara Brae, Orkney: 1972–73 Excavations: an Interim Report*, Edinburgh: HMSO.

Deetz, J. (1967) *Invitation to Archaeology*, New York: Natural History Press.

Douglas, M. (1966) *Purity and Danger*, London: Routledge and Kegan Paul.

Drennan, R. D. (1976) 'Religion and social evolution in Formative Mesoamerica', in K. Flannery (ed.) *The Early Mesoamerican Village*, New York: Academic Press.

Ferguson, L. (ed.) (1977) *Historical Archaeology and the Importance of Material Things*, Society for Historical Archaeology, Special Series Publication 2.

Flannery, K. V. (1972) 'The cultural evolution of civilisations', *Annual Review of Ecology and Systematics* 3, 399–426.

——— (1976) *The Early Mesoamerican Village*, New York: Academic Press.

Flannery, K. V. and Marcus, J. (1976) 'Formative Oaxaca and the Zapotec cosmos', *American Scientist* 64, 374–83.

Friedman, J. and Rowlands, M. (eds) (1977) *The Evolution of Social Systems*, London: Duckworth.

Fritz, J. M. (1978) 'Paleopsychology today; ideational systems and human adaptation in prehistory', in C. Redman (ed.) *Social Archaeology*, New York: Academic Press.

Giddens, A. (1979) *Central Problems in Social Theory*, London: Macmillan Press.

Glassie, H. (1975) *Folk Housing in Middle Virginia: a Structural Analysis of Historical Artifacts*, Knoxville: University of Tennessee Press.

Godelier, M. (1977) *Perspectives in Marxist Anthropology*, Cambridge: Cambridge University Press.

Harstrup, K. (1978) 'The post-structuralist position of social anthropology', in E. Schwimmer (ed.) *The Yearbook of Symbolic Anthropology*, London: Hurst.

Henshall, A. S. (1963) *The Chambered Tombs of Scotland*, Edinburgh: Edinburgh University Press.

Hill, J. N. (1971) 'Report on a seminar on the explanation of prehistoric organisational change', *Current Anthropology* 12, 406–8.

Hodder, I. (1982) *Symbols in Action*, Cambridge: Cambridge University Press.

Leone, M. (1977) 'The new Mormon temple in Washington DC', in L. Ferguson (ed.) *Historical Archaeology and the Importance of Material Things*, Society for Historical Archaeology, Special Series Publication 2.

Lévi-Strauss, C. (1963) *Structural Anthropology*, New York: Basic Books.

Marsh, P., Rosser, E. and Harré, R. (1978) *The Rules of Disorder*, London: Routledge.

Pettit, P. (1975) *The Concept of Structuralism: a Critical Analysis*, Dublin: Gill and MacMillan.

Piaget, J. (1971) *Structuralism*, London: Routledge and Kegan Paul.

Plog, F. T. (1975) 'Systems theory in archaeological research', *Annual Review of Anthropology* 4, 207–24.

Renfrew, C. (1972) *The Emergence of Civilisation*, London: Methuen.

——— (1979) *Investigations in Orkney*, London: Society of Antiquaries.

Ritchie, A. (1973) 'Knap of Howar, Papa Westray', *Discovery and Excavation in Scotland* 1973, 68–9.

——— (1975) 'Knap of Howar, Papa Westray', *Discovery and Excavation in Scotland* 1975, 35–7.

Ritchie, J. N. G. (1976) 'The stones of Stenness, Orkney', *Proceedings of the Society of Antiquaries of Scotland* 107, 1–60.

Sahlins, M. (1976) *Culture and Practical Reason*, Chicago: University of Chicago Press.

Schmidt, P. R. (1978) *Historical Archaeology. A Structural Approach in an African Culture*, Westport, Connecticut: Greenwood Press.

Sperber, D. (1974) *Rethinking Symbolism*, Cambridge: Cambridge University Press.

Traill, W. and Kirkness, W. (1937) 'Howar, a prehistoric structure on Papa Westray, Orkney', *Proceedings of the Society of Antiquaries of Scotland* 71, 309–21.

Turner, V. W. (1969) *The Ritual Process*, London: Routledge and Kegan Paul.

Washburn, D. K. (1978) 'A symmetry classification of Pueblo ceramic designs', in P. Grebinger (ed.) *Discovering Past Behaviour*, New York: Academic Press.

4

BURIALS, HOUSES, WOMEN AND MEN IN THE EUROPEAN NEOLITHIC

The history of research on the megalithic monuments of western Europe provides a clear illustration of the deleterious effects of the split between historical and processual approaches in archaeology. In this paper, some of these effects will be illustrated, but then, using essentially the same material, an alternative approach will be examined. A perspective that treats the evidence as ideologically informed representations can resolve the previous dichotomies and indicate the potential in the study of prehistoric social relations. Initially the Neolithic tombs and monuments were seen as caused by a spread of megalith builders or of the megalithic idea (Montelius 1899; Childe 1925; 1957; Crawford 1957; Daniel 1958). For example, Piggott (1965, 60) saw the adoption or propagation of the collective chambered tombs linked to a spread of new religious ideas, and the link between megaliths, frameworks of ideas and world pictures continues to be stressed by, for example, Kinnes (1981, 83). Recently, however, some archaeologists have criticised this use of historical and distributional arguments and have suggested that the occurrence of megaliths cannot simply be explained in cultural terms (for example, Chapman 1981, 72). In some of these more recent works there has been a tendency to be concerned mainly with generalisations, such as the use of megaliths as markers of territory, or of social and economic tensions. This has had the effect of removing megaliths and Neolithic burials from their historical context in western Europe, and from the domain of the ideological, by which I refer to meaningful social action and negotiation within specific historical contexts.

Several writers have emphasised the role of Neolithic megalithic monuments in western Europe as social centres (Case 1969; Fleming 1972; 1973; Reed 1974; Kinnes 1975; Whittle 1977; Jarman, Bailey and Jarman 1982). Specifically reacting against diffusionist arguments, Renfrew (1976) has suggested a social role for the tombs as territorial markers in segmentary societies. A central question posed concerned the restricted occurrence of megaliths on the 'Atlantic facade' – western Europe (France, Britain, Spain, Portugal, Netherlands), northwest

Europe (Scandinavia and north Germany), and the western Mediterranean (south France, Italy and the west Mediterranean islands). Renfrew suggested that territorial markers were needed in this area because of greater population stress which itself had two sources. First, the westward spread of the Neolithic was halted by the Atlantic coast such that birth rates had to be cut back as population reached its saturation point. Excess population could no longer split off and expand westwards. The resulting social stress was further aggravated by a second factor, the existing high levels of hunter-gatherer-fisher populations in the rich coastal and estuarine regions. These two conditions led to the building of tombs for the ancestors to act as foci for equivalent segmentary units.

Chapman's (1981) anti-diffusionist arguments are based on an hypothesis suggested by Saxe (1970) and Goldstein (1980) and it is claimed that interment in cemeteries or monuments will emerge in periods of imbalance between society and critical resources. Late Mesolithic cemeteries, Neolithic central European cemeteries, and the megaliths of western Europe are seen as related to increasing territorial behaviour and the use and/or control of crucial but restricted resources.

The first problem with such arguments is that it appears difficult, if not impossible, to identify social stress or restricted resources in the general terms used by Renfrew and Chapman. In reference to Renfrew's argument there is no evidence that demographic stress was greater in Atlantic Europe than in central Europe. There is good evidence of concentrated Mesolithic occupation in areas which do not have megaliths (for example Geupel 1981, and in southeast Europe, Srejovic 1972). The adoption of agriculture in western Europe was often different from that in central Europe (there is evidence for slow and gradual adoption in Britain, and in south France where cereals were not cultivated until well after the first animal domesticates) and the rate of population growth (if any proves to have occurred) is unknown. Certainly there is no evidence for higher population densities in western than in central Europe. Indeed, during the period of megalithic monument construction (approximately fourth to second millennia BC), much of the clearest evidence we have of 'filling up' of the environment and dense occupation comes from central Europe (Meier-Arendt 1965; Sielman 1972; Kruk 1980). Chapman recognises this fact and suggests that both the megaliths of western Europe and the inhumation cemeteries of central Europe are like responses to an imbalance between society and critical resources. But how is one to recognise territorial behaviour and the use and control of restricted resources? Almost by definition, all societies and all animal species have such characteristics. Certainly, following Meillassoux (1972 – adequately criticised by Woodburn 1980), one of Chapman's own sources, one would expect all agricultural societies to have a need to control restricted resources.

But it is not so much the lack of evidence of social and economic stress, territoriality and restricted resources that is my concern here, and I will be using the same sources of evidence in the interpretation to be offered in this paper. Rather, the second and more important criticism concerns the weak link between burial, megalithic monuments and the processes described. In Renfrew's model, it is not at all clear how megalithic monuments helped to control the birth rate. Any marker or inhumation cemetery could have functioned as a focus or as a symbol of the ancestors. Chapman's arguments are very general and his hypothesis is described as being as relevant to Lepenski Vir, where burial under houses is referred to as indicating formal disposal areas (1981, 75), as to inhumation cemeteries and megalithic monuments. It is even implied that a role similar to formal burial is played by enclosed habitation sites (ibid., 78). As Kinnes (1981, 86) remarks, 'a central place for any social group might be a mortuary site: equally it could be any other structure, boulder or tree'. In both Renfrew's and Chapman's and in other work of this type, the megalithic monuments lose most of their specificity. Megaliths are seen as indicating more social stress and acting as better foci than other types of burial, and in the Saxe and Goldstein model, the formal burial is seen as legitimating control of resources by reference to the ancestors. But large enclosed settlements, significant points in the physical landscape, distinctive portable artifacts or enclosed urned cremation cemeteries might have done equally well. The megalithic monuments have not really been explained at all.

Closely linked to this second point is a third, that no attempt is made in recent, 'processual' studies, to account for the form of the megalithic monuments themselves (see, however, Fleming 1973). While there is great variation in type of monument, most authors cite general similarities in passage and gallery graves and associated art and ritual which occur in many, if not all, the various areas where Neolithic megalithic monuments are found. There are round mounds, rectangular and trapezoidal mounds. There are earthen and stone barrows, timber and stone chambers. There is often, but not always, evidence of multiple interments, excarnation of the bodies prior to burial in the tombs and of careful arrangement of the bones. The facades of the tombs are often elaborate, and are associated with high artifact densities while in many cases, few artifacts are found within the tombs. The tombs are often orientated in specific directions. Widespread similarities are not just a late phenomenon but occur at an early stage, for example at Hoedic and Teviec. All this detail, and much more, is lost in the cross-cultural, processual approach that has been applied recently. The explanations provided have been inadequate because there is a disproportionate amount of information that has to be left aside.

The processual studies of Renfrew and Chapman and the others cited above have been widely accepted and discussed, but in view of the criticisms above it is argued here that alternative explanations must be sought. The inability of recent interpretations to account for the mega-lithic monuments of western Europe derives, in this author's view, from the artificial split made in archaeology between history and process. It will become clear in this article that a previous generation of archaeol-ogists attracted by the megalithic problem (such as Childe, Clark, Daniel, Piggott), but dubbed diffusionist, historical or even culturalist by processual archaeologists, were concerned with megaliths as megaliths. They did consider the monuments in their own right within a specific historical context. They attempted to explain the shape, orientation and content of the tombs and the tomb ritual. However inadequate their results, the meaning of the tombs and monuments themselves was considered. More recently archaeologists moved to an opposite and more extreme position in which the meaning of the tombs, what they signified in a particular historical context, was entirely disregarded.

This reaction against a consideration of specific cultural meaning necessarily led to a failure of the attempts at a processual and functional explanation. The processual explanations could not cope with the rich-ness of information relating to the things to be explained. Since one had no idea what, for example, the shape of the tomb meant in its particular historical context, one could have absolutely no idea of how it might have functioned. Even if one was content only to explain the fact that megaliths existed, there could again be no successful outcome. It can *never* be possible to 'test' the hypothesis, or support the analogy, that the tombs functioned as territorial markers or legitimated rights to resources without also having some hypothesis concerning the meaning of the tombs in the society and time period concerned. The tombs and monuments of the Neolithic in western Europe had symbolic associ-ations and meanings and this meaningful context must be considered if we are to understand how they worked within social processes. But equally, archaeologists working within an historical and cultural frame-work had limited success because symbolic meaning was discussed with limited reference to social process, function and legitimation. It is the divide between the consideration of history and particular symbolic meanings on the one hand and the consideration of process and func-tion on the other, a divide set up and encouraged by the 'New Archaeology' of the sixties and seventies (Hodder 1982a), which has held back explanation in archaeology. The problem of the megaliths of western Europe is just one example of the difficulties that have arisen. Any rigorous and adequate explanation must allow that symbolic mean-ing and social process are actively and recursively related and must apply integrated social models.

In particular, the dichotomy set up between meaning and function had the effect that ideology became a problematic area of enquiry which could have no successful issue. There has, of course, been a recent increase in attempts made within a processual framework to discuss ideology and legitimation, and the hypothesis of Saxe concerning the use of burial to legitimate access to resources, and applied by Chapman to European Neolithic burials, is an example of such developments. But, as already indicated, such a framework tends to relegate ideology to an epiphenomenon of the assumed primacy of functional contingencies and does not adequately consider the particular symbolic meanings of the monuments and rituals. The Saxe hypothesis not only presents a relatively passive view of society, but also, and more clearly, it disregards the cultural context so central to ideology and ideological functions. When individuals act socially, and represent their actions to others, they necessarily do so within a framework of meaning, and this framework is relative and historically constructed. Without consideration of the cultural context one cannot hope to understand the effects of past social actions.

While a number of recent articles have examined megalithic monuments as symbolic and as socially active, legitimating internal social strategies (Gilman 1976; Tilley 1981; Hodder 1982b; Shanks and Tilley 1982; Shennan 1982), they have again failed adequately to consider the particularity of the historical context in which megaliths are found. It is the aim of this article, however, first to demonstrate that there is considerable evidence that many of the earthen and chambered tombs of western Europe referred symbolically to earlier and contemporary houses in central Europe and, to a lesser extent, in western Europe (Figure 7). The tombs signified houses. To examine the significance of this symbolic association it will then be necessary to assess the symbolic and social context of long houses in central Europe. It will be shown that there is evidence for elaboration of domestic space and that this elaboration of houses and domestic pottery increases and then decreases through time into the later Neolithic. It will be argued that the type of house and pottery symbolism identified in the central European early and middle Neolithic is appropriate in a social context where primary social strategies revolve around male–female relationships, which are themselves linked to competition between lineages for control of labour. It will be argued that long barrow burial and long houses are two ways of coping with and involving material culture in similar social strategies and that the existence of the long mound tradition can only be partially explained in terms of adaptive behaviour. Rather, the way megaliths were involved actively in social strategies in western Europe depended on an existing historical context. The existence of the tombs, their form and function can only be adequately considered by assessing their value-laden meanings within European Neolithic society.

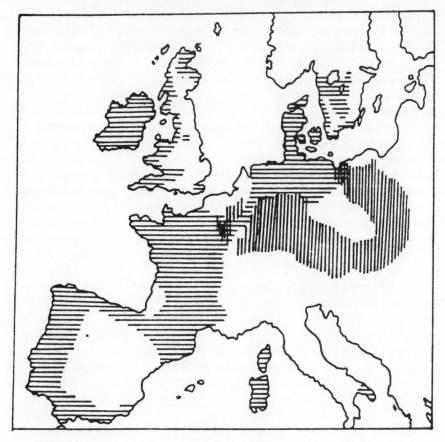

Figure 7. The distribution of Neolithic chambered tombs in Atlantic Europe (horizontal shading), and of Bandkeramik settlements and finds with long houses (vertical shading)

TOMBS AND HOUSES

Many timber and stone chambered tombs in Atlantic Europe are enclosed within a rectangular or trapezoidal mound (Figure 8). The apparent similarity between these shapes and the plans of Linearbandkeramik (LBK), Stichbandkeramik (SBK), Lengyel and Rössen houses in central and east-central Europe in the fifth and fourth millennia bc (Figure 9) has been noted by many scholars, although significantly not by those explicitly espousing a processual view (Renfrew 1976; Chapman 1981) or an ecological approach (Jarman, Bailey and Jarman 1982). Daniel (1965, 86) speculated that Oscar Montelius may not have been so wrong in thinking that the European passage graves may have been lithic funerary versions of wooden dwelling houses. Childe

50

(1949a), Sprockhoff (1938) and Glob (1949) compared the long cairns and barrows of northern and north-central Europe with long houses. The use of LBK houses as a model for the long mound tradition has been suggested by Case (1969), Ashbee (1970), Whittle (1977, 221), Kinnes (1981, 85), Powell *et al.* (1969) and a detailed case has been made by Reed (1974) and Marshall (1981). Grahame Clark (1980, 96) noted that the trapezoidal burial mounds of Brittany and Kujavia recall domestic house structures associated with the Lengyel culture of north-central Europe and the trapezoidal houses of the Iron Gates on the lower Danube.

The long houses of central Europe cover the late fifth and fourth millennia bc. The earth and stone long barrows on the other hand cover the later part of the fourth millennium and continue in use in different areas into the late third and early second millennia bc. Reference to formal similarities between the houses and tombs thus implies transformation from the houses to the tombs. In the anti-diffusionist framework within which some archaeologists have recently worked the stylistic similarities between houses and tombs have either been disregarded, as we have seen, or various alternative and more functional explanations of 'coincidental' similarities have been sought (Fleming 1973). It is necessary, therefore, to go beyond the numerous general statements of affinity and to show that there are sufficient numbers of similarities between houses and tombs to make the 'null hypothesis' of

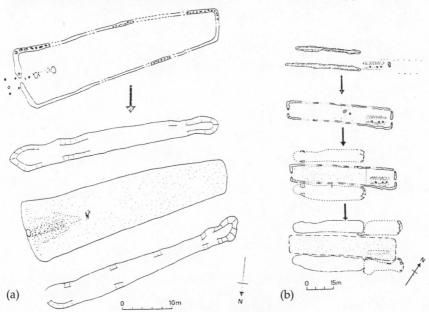

Figure 8 Long mound burial. The structural sequence at (a) Fussell's Lodge, (b) Kilham. *Source*: Kinnes 1981

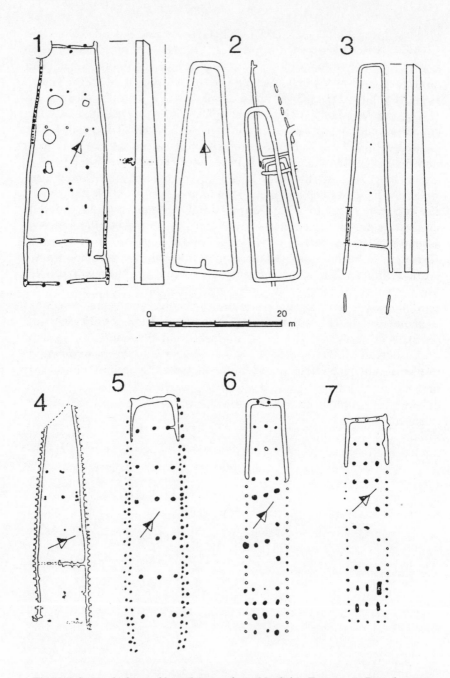

Figure 9 Ground plans of long houses from Neolithic Europe. 1: Postoloprty, Czechoslovakia; 2: Brzesc Kujawski, Poland; 3: Biskupin, Poland; 4: Aldenhoven, Germany; 5: Zwenkau, Germany; 6–7: Geleen, Netherlands. *Source*: Marshall 1981

no diffusion appear unreasonable. But it is of interest to note at the outset that the similarities between long houses and long tombs are such that Barkaer, long thought to be a site containing long houses, has recently been convincingly reinterpreted as a site with long burial mounds (Glob 1975; Madsen 1979).

Since long houses and long burial mounds overlap chronologically in the second half of the fourth millennium bc, it is in the cultures of that period in central and east-central Europe that we should search for the closest parallels for the burial monuments of Atlantic Europe. Both the Rössen and Lengyel cultures of central and east-central Europe respectively continue into this period and both have rectangular and trapezoidal long houses. It is the construction and shape of these houses that provide the first two specific parallels for the Atlantic long burial mounds (see Figures 8 and 9). First, timber long barrows either have continuous bedding trenches for the walls or lines of posts, or some mixture of the two, and the same variety is found for the houses. Second, Soudsky (1969) suggests that the distinctive trapezoidal house form develops only after the early Neolithic in central Europe, and it is clearly associated with the SBK, Rössen and Lengyel contexts. However, some LBK houses at Elsloo, Netherlands, already begin to show a trapezoidal form. For the tombs, the Fussell's Lodge long barrow, dated to the second half of the fourth millennium bc, has traces of vertical timbers in its trapezoidal enclosure and must have looked from the outside very similar to the trapezoidal timbered houses of central Europe. Earthen long barrows are generally trapezoidal in shape in Britain and more triangular in Poland. Trapezoidal barrows are also known from Denmark and north Germany but in these areas rectangular barrows are more common (Madsen 1979, 318) and can be compared with the rectangular long houses which continue in use alongside the trapezoidal forms. Trapezoidal cairns, limited by a wall or by boulders, are found in Britain in the Severn-Cotswold group, Clyde, Irish Court cairns and in the Orkney-Cromarty long cairns. There are also examples to parallel the rectangular earth barrows (Ashbee 1970, 90). Rectangular and trapezoidal chambered cairns also occur in Brittany and the Paris Basin.

While the rectangular and trapezoidal shapes of the houses and barrows can be compared, it should be emphasised that the formal similarities do not imply equivalence of size. Reed (1974, 46) notes that while the lengths of a good many south English long barrows fall comfortably within the range of LBK and Rössen long houses, most long barrows are about twice the width and length of most long houses. Marshall (1981) in a detailed quantitative study has shown that the earthen long barrows, the gallery graves of the Severn-Cotswold group and of the Scottish-Irish group are generally larger and wider than the trapezoidal long houses but that the ratio between length and maximum width is similar, especially when comparing the trapezoidal houses and the gallery graves. Thus the tombs studied are normally larger than the houses but they retain the same shape.

A further point of comparison between houses and tombs concerns orientation, since both generally have their long axis aligned E–W or NW–SE. However, it is first necessary to consider the position of the entrance of the houses and tombs. This is normally at the broader end of the trapezoidal houses, and the main burial chamber and entrance facade in the long barrows are also at the broader end although, in certain cases, other burial chambers in the barrow can be entered from the side. It is at the broad end of the trapezoidal houses that breaks occur in the wall foundations, and an entrance is clearly visible in this position at Postoloprty (Figure 9:1). The highest concentrations of arti-facts occur outside the presumed entrance at the wider end of the trapezoidal long houses at Brzesc Kujawski (Bogucki and Grygiel 1981). While it is possible that the tombs are broader and higher at one end in order to accommodate the stone or wooden chamber, rather than be-cause of any formal similarity with trapezoidal long houses, such an argument ignores the orientation of the buildings: that the broader end of the trapezoidal tombs and houses is generally towards the east or southeast.

Madsen (1979, 318) notes that in Britain, Poland, north Germany and Denmark the broader end of the trapezoidal earthen long barrows is to the east. In Britain Colt Hoare noted in 1812 that the earthen long barrows had the broad end pointing to the east. In Brittany the entrances of the passage graves are generally to the southeast especially in the case of the long passaged dolmens (L'Helgouach 1965, 76–9). The entrances of the gallery graves in the same area are to the east. The Cotswold-Severn tombs mainly face towards the east and in Shetland the entrances face east or southeast, as do the stalled Orkney cairns. Burl (1981) provides other examples of the overall tendency for the broader ends of trapezoidal mounds or the entrances of rectangular or circular passage grave mounds to face east. This is not to say that exceptions do not exist. The Clava passage graves and ring cairns of northeast Scotland generally face southwest and the chambered tombs on Arran show no preferred orientation. However, the overall tendency, particularly of long barrows, is for the entrance and the broader end to face east and southeast (Figure 10). Soudsky (1969) has demonstrated that the broader end of trapezoidal long houses faces southeast, in the quadrant betwen 90° and 180° from north. The rectangular long houses are, like the tombs and trapezoidal houses, orientated NW–SE (see Marshall 1981 for quantitative data). But the location of the entrance(s) in these houses has not been determined with any certainty. In view of the similarity with trapezoidal houses it would seem likely that the entrance is at the southeast end. Certainly, it is the northwestern end which often has a continuous bedding trench, while the sides are often flanked by continuous ditches from which it is presumed that earth was taken to form the daub walls. Thus it seems likely that the southeastern portion of the rectangular long houses contained the entrance, and fourth millennium bc models of houses have the entrance at one shorter end (Piggott 1965, 46). However, a side entrance has at times been claimed for LBK long houses with the 'Y' posts in the central section of the house being used to frame a door (Meyer-Christian 1976). Startin (1978) suggests that the 'Y' posts functioned as a brace against lateral winds and there is no evidence of an entrance in the central side area.

Thus, the third point of similarity between long houses and long barrows is that the entrance in the trapezoidal forms is at the broader end, while the fourth similarity is that the entrances of the trapezoidal and rectangular forms generally face the east or southeast. The fifth point is that there is considerable elaboration of the entrance itself. The long barrows and passage graves frequently have large facades, with 'horns' pointing forwards from the entrance, forecourts and ante-chambers. There is often evidence for rituals and offerings in the fore-

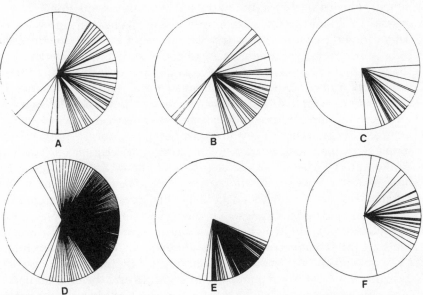

Figure 10 The orientation of tombs and long houses in Europe. A: Armorican gallery graves (L'Helgouach 1965); B: Armorican tombs with short and medium passages (L'Helgouach 1965); C: Armorican tombs with long passages (L'Helgouach 1965); D: Earthen long barrows from the southern and northern regions of Britain (Ashbee 1970); E: Rectangular and trapezoidal Neolithic long houses (Marshall 1981); F: Megalithic tombs in Holland (Bakker 1979)

court area, leading to a distinction between the outer, entrance area with many artifacts, and the inner tomb frequently with few artifacts to accompany the skeletal remains. The entrance is often blocked by massive boulders, but may equally be a 'false' entrance, the real entrance being to the side of the mound. Many of these characteristics are found in both stone and earthen barrows. Wooden porches which have been effectively blocked by posts, as at Fussell's Lodge, recall the so-called 'false portals' of the Severn-Cotswold laterally chambered stone long barrows (Ashbee 1970, 92). There is a similar emphasis on facades and most of the Scandinavian earthen barrows have a substantial transverse bedding trench in the eastern end holding a timber facade. In Britain and Scandinavia the facade sometimes has projections at the sides forming 'horns' (e.g. Lindebjerg (Madsen 1979), East Heslerton, Skendleby and Willerby Wold (Ashbee 1970)). These various characteristics are also found in the long houses of central Europe. Side projections or 'horns' at the broader, eastern end of trapezoidal long houses are found at, for example, Inden-Lamersdorf, Zwenkau and Brzesc Kujawski (Soudsky 1969) and a distinct entrance area has been identified at Postoloprty and Biskupin (ibid.). Occupation horizons have almost everywhere been removed by later land use but, as already noted, the late Lengyel sites of Brzesc Kujawski and Biskupin in the Polish lowlands have the highest concentrations of refuse pits near the entrance.

There is good evidence of a tripartite division of the long houses which can to some extent be paralleled in the tombs. It has long been recognised that LBK houses are divided into three sections although the central section may occur on its own or with only one of the two end sections. In line with the fifth point made above, the clearest division of the trapezoidal long houses is that which separates the room at the entrance or the entrance area from the inner portion of the house. For example, in the Rössen trapezoidal house at Deiringsen-Ruploh (Günther 1973) a clear division occurs one-third of the way into the house. At Postoloprty the interior area with four hearths is partitioned off from the entrance room (Soudsky 1969). In his review of the trapezoidal long house Soudsky notes that many show no evidence of any internal divisions, but where there is one it is tripartite, with antechamber, central main room and store at the back. At Bochum-Hiltrop, for example, there is a partition separating off the back third of the house. The smaller Rössen and later houses which are divided into two rooms will be discussed below, but once again the division of space often occurs one-third of the way into the house, near the entrance, in the classic 'megaron' plan. The earthen tombs frequently show a similar division, with the main burial chamber occurring in the third of the mound nearest the entrance in Britain and/or in the central portion in Scandinavia. At Bygholm Norremark, a house beneath the barrow has clear traces of a threefold division, while at Skibshoj and Troelstrup the eastern third is partitioned from the western two-thirds (Madsen 1979). A similar division in Britain can be seen at Kilham (Figure 8:b). Multiple partitioning of long barrows is a general characteristic in both Britain and Scandinavia, but it is the gallery graves of the Paris Basin that again show the specific principle at work. The 'allées couvertes' are divided one-third of the way in (Figure 11) and in Brittany the gallery graves normally have an antechamber and sometimes a back room. The rock-cut tombs (hypogées) of the Paris Basin are often divided into three distinct rooms, the inner room being the largest and containing the majority of the skeletal remains. It should be recognised that, in comparing long houses and French gallery graves parallels are being sought across at least a millennium, from the late fourth millennium to the late third millennium bc. It is not the contention here that the houses acted as direct and immediate analogies for the late third- and early second-millennia gallery graves, and there are intermediary forms in various parts of Atlantic Europe. A general and continuous underlying tradition is claimed, lasting millennia, finding surviving expression in different ways at different times in different places.

The seventh point of comparison between long tombs and long houses concerns the use of decoration. The stone-built houses at Skara Brae, Orkney, contained stones incised with geometric decoration similar to that found in contemporary chambered tombs on Orkney, often in similar positions above and near entrances and within rooms (Hodder 1982c). The rich decoration of tombs in western Europe has long been of interest, the decoration occurring on the sides of galleries and transepts, on capstones, and in the Paris Basin for example, particularly in the entrance area (Figure 11). The decoration of long houses in central Europe may be less widely recognised because of the non-surviving timber and daub structures and removal of the occupation horizon. However, models of houses frequently have decoration similar to that on Danubian pottery. Decorated walls occur at Karanovo in southeast Europe and designs resembling pottery decoration are found on fourth-millennium bc houses in Hungary (Piggott 1965, 90). Neolithic huts at Grossgartach have wall plaster with red and white zig-zags on a yellow background. Specific links between decoration in tombs and the domestic context are also suggested by the frequent similarities between the designs used in the tombs and on domestic pottery. While it will be shown below that special funerary or ritual decorated pottery does exist (for example in Chassey and north European contexts), the decorated pottery of the earlier Breton Neolithic, for example, has concentric arc designs recalling those found in the tombs in the same area. The use of features such as an eye motif on 'pots, bones and stones' in Spain and elsewhere in Atlantic Europe has been described by Crawford (1957, 60).

Eighth, both long houses and burial mounds are frequently associated with ditches flanking the long sides (see Figures 8 and 12) although in some cases the tombs (for example Giants' Hill, Skendleby earthen long barrow) also have ditches at the rear and/or front. Quarry ditches along the barrows are a normal feature in Britain and Poland but are less common in Scandinavia and north Germany (Madsen 1979, 318). While it can of course be claimed that such ditches are simply functional consequences of the need to provide material for the house walls or barrow mounds, there is no necessary relationship: the material could

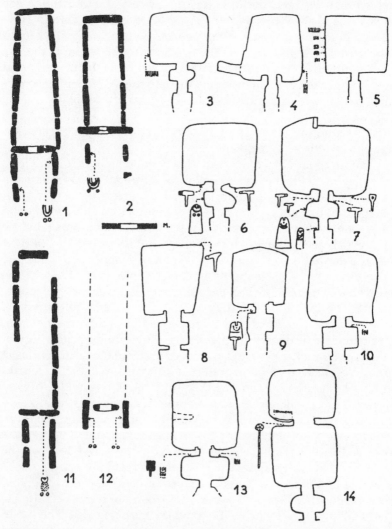

Figure 11 Gallery graves (allées couvertes) and rock-cut tombs (hypogées) from the SOM culture in the Paris Basin. *Source*: Bailloud 1964

have been obtained from elsewhere, or from differently shaped hollows. Whatever the reason for the construction of the side ditches, they do exhibit a close formal similarity between the houses and the mounds which suggests one type of monument evoked the other. In fact there are often precise similarities between the ditches in the two cases. Both are frequently irregular in outline (for example, see Willerby Wold (Ashbee 1970, 39)) and are sometimes dug as a series of interconnecting pits. In view of the other similarities between the houses and tombs noted above, it is argued here that the similarity in the form and placing of the quarry ditches is significant.

Eight points of similarity between Neolithic houses in central Europe and long burial mounds in Atlantic Europe have been identified, although each comparison involves a number of more detailed attributes. The main points can be summarised as follows.

1 Construction of houses and earthen long barrows includes use of continuous bedding trenches, lines of simple posts and some combination of the two techniques.
2 Trapezoidal and rectangular shapes with similar length/maximum breadth ratios for trapezoidal forms.
3 The entrance of the trapezoidal mounds and houses are at the broader end.
4 The entrances of the rectangular and trapezoidal houses and barrows frequently face towards the southeast.

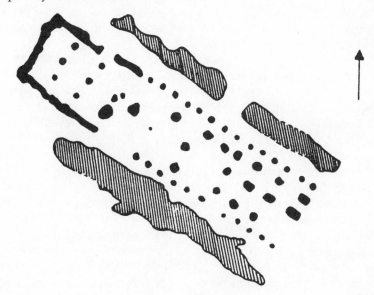

Figure 12 An example of a LBK house with site ditches: Building 32 at Elsloo, Netherlands

5 The entrances are elaborated, specifically with facades, antechambers, 'horns', or activity concentrations.
6 There is a tripartite division of the long house or mound, although frequently only one division is found one-third of the way along the length from the entrance.
7 Tombs and houses frequently have internal decoration.
8 Ditches flank the long sides of houses and barrows.

This list of similarities concerns specifically the long barrows, gallery graves, rectangular and trapezoidal long houses. But other traditions are known such as the circular house and the passage grave with circular or polygonal inner chamber. It has already been noted that some scholars have drawn parallels between houses and tombs for these types also (Daniel 1965, 86). Clark (1980, 96) has drawn specific attention to the domestic connotations of the stone-built ritual hearths in Hoëdic and Teviec (see below) and in the trapezoidal tombs of Kujavia, and the burning found at the front of many tombs may recall the elaborate stone hearths in houses at Lepenski Vir on the lower Danube. In comparing the houses, tombs and ritual monuments in the Neolithic of the Orkney Islands, similarities were noted in the central position of a stone-lined hearth or area with burning and occupation debris, in the left/right symmetry, and in the use of the back area for storage. Similarities between the houses and tombs of Skara Brae and Quanterness were observed in the use of decoration, in the cellular plan, and in the long narrow entrances (Hodder 1982c). In addition, in the Orkney Islands, the protruding side stones at intervals along the interior walls of the 'stalled cairns' are constructionally and formally similar to the divisions in the Knap of Howar houses (Figure 13).

As in any analogical argument, any one point of comparison, on its own, could be seen as coincidental. But as the numbers of similarities increase it becomes unreasonable to argue for a lack of any significant relationship. It is claimed here that specific parallels exist in the fourth millennium bc between houses in central Europe and contemporary tombs in Atlantic Europe. But there is also a longer European tradition from the late fifth to the early second millennia bc which can be followed at different times in different areas. For example, the early Neolithic LBK houses in the late fifth and early fourth millennia show most of the eight characteristics, while the gallery graves which continue in use into the early second millennium in Brittany and the Paris Basin contain aspects of the same style. There is continuity in the tradition in Europe throughout the whole period although particular areas, such as the Paris Basin, may only have surviving evidence intermittently. In some local areas, such as the Orkneys, the idea of tombs representing houses (and vice versa) takes on a particular local form. In the Channel Islands a link between tombs and the domestic context is suggested by the finding of querns at La Hougue Mauger and La Hougue Bie.

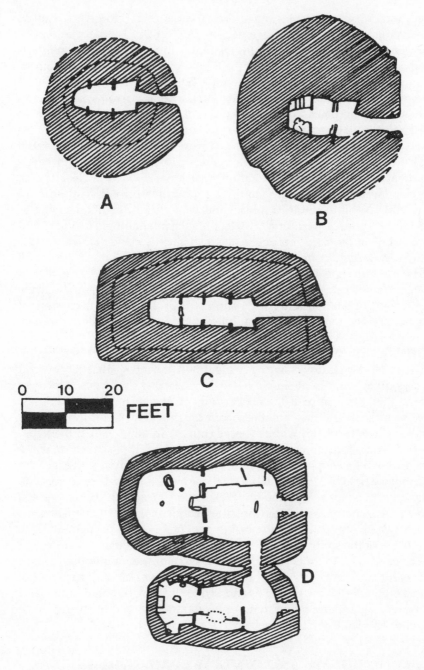

Figure 13 Comparison of tombs (stalled cairns – A, B, C) and houses (D) in the Orkney Neolithic. A: Kierfea Hill; B: Knowe of Craie; C: Knowe of Yarso; D: Knap of Howar

Although local examples, as in the Orkneys, serve to give weight to the overall relationship between houses and tombs, it is the relationship between long houses and long tombs that is the primary concern in this study. It has been suggested that the long burial mounds evoke symbolically the earlier and contemporary long houses of central Europe. The complementarity in time and space of the long barrows and houses needs to be emphasised. Not only are the relevant types of houses earlier than and overlapping in time with the long barrows, but they also have a different spatial distribution (Figure 7), being found in central and east-central Europe where they are mainly associated with single inhumation graves and inhumation cemeteries. There is clear spatial overlap between long houses and long mounds in the Paris Basin, but here early Neolithic and Danubian houses with inhumation cemeteries are followed, after an interval, by late Neolithic chambered tombs, and some similar overlaps occur in northwestern Europe. However, the tombs are largely confined to Atlantic Europe where houses are small and varied in appearance. Put crudely, the long houses occur earlier in the centre of Europe, while the long burial mounds in Atlantic Europe begin later, overlap in time, and continue later. It is a question, then, of the transmission and transformation of an idea, a way of doing things, from east to west, and from settlement to burial.

While certain aspects of the symbolic meaning of the megalithic monuments of western Europe have been suggested (essentially that they evoked houses), it is insufficient simply to catalogue formal similarities. However many points of comparison can be found between tombs and houses, further support for the hypothesis can be provided if the forms being discussed can be placed within a social context. In other words, the hypothetical symbolic meaning carries greater conviction if it can be seen to play a part within a developing world of practice. It is necessary to consider why tombs were built like houses. If the symbolic evocation can be recognised to play an active part within the societies being considered, it becomes still more unreasonable to reject the formal similarities as coincidental. The close link between form and function, history and process is here apparent. Any restriction of the study to one side of the unity is inadequate.

The next task, then, is to examine the place of the long houses within the early and middle Neolithic societies of central and east-central Europe. It will then be possible to return to the long burial mounds, and consider what they might have evoked and how they might have functioned ideologically in their own social context.

LONG HOUSES AND CENTRAL EUROPEAN SOCIETY

Because occupation and habitation horizons have rarely survived in central European settlements it is difficult to assess the functions carried out in the different sections of the Neolithic long houses. In the trapezoidal house at Postoloprty, Bohemia, four hearths have been identified in the inner room (Figure 9:1 and Soudsky 1969), but there is little other direct and reliable evidence. Inference concerning the function of three- and two-roomed long houses in central Europe has therefore been based on smaller houses of the fourth and third millennia bc in central Europe and adjacent areas. For example, in the two-roomed houses at Aichbühl and Riedsachsen on the Federseemoor (Schmidt 1930–6) a clay oven generally occurred in the outer room in the inner right-hand corner with an open hearth immediately in front of it. In the inner room there was also an oven or an open hearth, generally against the partition to the right of the door. A hearth or oven occurs in both rooms at the Tripolye settlement at Ariuşd in Transylvania. At Niederwil in the Pfyn culture in Switzerland in the early third millennium, thirty one- or two-roomed houses have hearths inside one or both rooms (Waterbolk and Van Zeist 1978). At Karanovo in Bulgaria, by the third millennium bc a tripartite division of the houses occurs. Soudsky (1969) suggests that the antechamber has a religious function because of the occurrence of figurines, the large central room is for the main habitation, and the inner room has cooking functions as indicated by the finds of grinding stones, storage jars and hearths. As Childe was already able to remark in his 1949 review of house types in temperate Europe, the timber buildings north of the Balkans have been compared with the megara of late Neolithic Thessally 'ad nauseam'. Soudsky (1969) has re-emphasised the similarities in the bipartite with small front room and tripartite plans, particularly in the presence of a 'forecourt' entrance area. Overall, Soudsky suggests that the LBK, SBK, Rössen and Lengyel rectangular and trapezoidal long houses had a front antechamber, a main central room, and a back store. In the very different settlement of Skara Brae on the Orkney Islands, the entrance leads into single-roomed houses, with the main occupation area in the centre around the hearth, and the main storage area at the rear (Childe 1931; Hodder 1982c).

The functions to which particular rooms were put will have varied through time and space, but the main point to be emphasised here is that a linear organisation of space and of activities occurred, from the front to the back. The entrance of fourth and third millennia houses in central Europe was, as far as we can observe, universally in one of the shorter sides. From there, a series of rooms and differences in activity led to the back enclosed end of the house. At Ariuşd the inner room is rather higher than the outer room (Childe 1949b). It is of interest that in the LBK houses it is often only the back end (the northwest end) that has a continuous bedding trench. Space is graded from front to back in that the back cannot be reached except by going through the front rooms or activity areas. The long rectangular and trapezoidal shapes reinforce the graded sequence. Elaboration of the entrance area noted in the houses, further emphasises the distinction between a front or public area and the inner recesses of the houses. The trapezoidal shape itself, with the entrance at the broader of the two short ends, brings the front into prominence in relation to the back.

A number of trapezoidal long houses, for example at Postoloprty, Bylany and Bochum-Hiltrop, have an alcove on the right after entering, between the antechamber and central room. At Postoloprty the alcove occurs at the point where a ritual foundation deposit was found. In the foundation trench were recovered a stone box made of grinding stones containing pottery, a bone pin, and bones including a pig's skull. Soudsky (1969) has suggested that the small alcove thus had a ritual function and has drawn parallels with the ritual animal deposits in the Tripolye culture.

Through time, the size and elaboration of houses increase and then gradually decrease. It has already been noted that by the end of the fourth millennium small rectangular houses, still with the tripartite or bipartite division and entrance at a short end, occur in central Europe. In the late fourth and early third millennia small two-roomed houses occur in the Michelsberg culture, but for much of the third millennium, small unicellular houses are more common in Horgen and Baden contexts and in Britain and in the TRB culture in Atlantic Europe. The latter houses show little elaboration and complexity of the domestic context, and there is less of the earlier separation of activities.

Another aspect of the domestic context to which the archaeologist has ready access in the central European Neolithic is pottery. However produced, the majority of the pottery seems to have had a domestic use and it occurs richly in association with houses. Models of pots in use within houses are known from southeast Europe (Childe 1949b; Clark 1952), and the similarity between designs found on pots and on houses has already been described. Throughout Europe there is a clear trend for the gradual disappearance of elaborate, decorated pottery in the period under consideration, in line with the gradual disappearance of large and complex house structures. In the Danubian areas in the early Neolithic there is much fine, decorated and, in the southeast, painted pottery. The complexity and richness of the LBK pottery at first increases through time (Hodder 1982b) and decorated pottery continues in, for example, the Rössen culture. But by the time of the Michelsberg culture in the late fourth and early third millennia bc, decorated pottery is rare. A similar sequence has been noted in Hungary (Sherratt 1982). The early Körös phase has dispersed settlement and non-complex pottery, but the pottery of the following Tisza phase is elaborate, associated with long houses and defended aggregated settlement. In the ensuing Tiszapolgar phase pottery is little decorated and houses are small and dispersed. In the Paris Basin, decorated pottery occurs in association with long houses but is rare in the following Chassey and SOM phases when the substantial long houses are no longer found. In Brittany pottery decoration is more elaborate in the early phases (L'Helgouach 1965). The increase and then gradual disappearance of decoration and formal complexity in the TRB sequence has been documented in detail for the Netherlands (Hodder 1982b). In Jutland, Denmark, Gebauer (1978) has noted that ritual vessel forms like clay ladles and pedestalled bowls are only present in the early part of the middle Neolithic TRB and the amount of fine ornamented pottery gradually reduces. Conversely the storage vessels increase markedly through time. Going farther afield, the early Neolithic pottery in south France is largely restricted to fine, decorated wares. Similarly, in Calabria in south Italy, the early Stentinello pottery is fine and richly decorated, but through time the amount of coarse pottery gradually increases and by the Diana phase in the third millennium, pottery is plain.

In general, then, the Neolithic of the late fifth and fourth millennia in central Europe, in contrast to the third millennium, is characterised by gradually increasing elaboration of the domestic context through the organisation of space and activities, ritual and decoration. It is now possible to consider this domestic symbolic elaboration, and thus the significance of the long houses, in the context of central European Neolithic society. It is widely accepted that social groups were at this time small-scale, largely acephalous, although with some degree of differentiation between lineages gradually emerging. Settlement pattern evidence shows the gradual increase in size of small, dispersed population units. By the late fourth and third millennia villages, often defended, occur but the degree of internal social differentiation in settlement and burial remains slight.

As a result of ethnoarchaeological studies on small-scale, dispersed, acephalous lineage groups in east Africa, and as a result of more general comparative studies, it has been possible to suggest the hypothesis that 'in small-scale lineage-based societies in which the major concern is to increase labour power, the control of women by men and the negotiation of position by women will become the dominant feature of social relations and will often involve cultural elaboration of the domestic sphere' (Hodder 1985, 157). This hypothesis involves two relationships which need to be explained. The first concerns the link between domestic symbolic complexity and male–female negotiation of social position, and the second concerns the link between male–female relationships and the control of reproduction.

In the Baringo district in Kenya, it was noted that containers were decorated, house compounds were large and the internal arrangement of houses was complex in areas and in societies in which lineage groups were trying to expand and to compete with other groups through increased reproduction. The restricting resource was labour rather than land, and women as reproducers could negotiate social position but men were concerned to control women and their reproduction. Put more generally, the maternal and paternal lines competed for the control of offspring and labour power. Women occupied a focal point in this tension, as the reproducers of labour, and it was in terms of the control of women and the domestic context and in terms of the negotiation of power by women that social conflict and much material patterning developed. The domestic context was the scene for the playing out of competition between lineages based on the control of women, and women used such strategies as the decoration of food containers in order to draw attention to and increase their focal role. A related argument, with direct relevance to the type of use of space identified in this study, is made by Donley (1982). The Swahili houses on the east African coast (and similar to Islamic houses in several parts of the world) are internally divided into a linear sequence of rooms. One enters at one of the shorter ends of the house and proceeds through the rooms to the back. The rooms are higher as one moves inwards, and they become more private and secluded. Decoration is used to protect areas of defilement. Donley demonstrates that the elaboration of the Swahili domestic context is concerned with control over women and of the purity of descent groups. While the wider social and political context of the recent east African coast differs markedly from the central European Neolithic, a link between domestic symbolic elaboration and the position of women has been recognised in a wide range of societies from Braithwaite's (1982) study in south Sudan, to Okely's (1975) interpretation of Gypsy society, and to the South American groups examined by Hugh-Jones (1979).

Although it would be difficult to place much reliance on these ethnographic analogies without a careful consideration of the contexts involved, the widespread relationship between varying elaboration of the domestic context and the varying position of women is suggestive. This suggests that the type of organisation of space found in the long houses of central Europe is likely to be linked to social strategies of control and seclusion. We are not dealing here with houses or rooms with multiple access, with courtyard plans or agglomerations of single rooms. Inner rooms can only be reached through outer rooms, in a linear sequence. The inner rooms are secluded and access is controlled. Also, house and pottery decoration draws attention to the domestic space and to food and drink which must at least partly have been prepared by women. The preparation and provision of food in the domestic context, for adults and offspring, has great symbolic potential in any society concerned with the reproduction and expansion of its labour power and with the control over its reproductive and productive potential.

The elaboration of the domestic world as part of male-female relationships occurs cross-culturally in a variety of different social contexts. But in the early Neolithic of central Europe a relevant context is immediately apparent. Settlement initially spread into relatively empty but rich and easily worked areas of loess soil. It is clear that labour, not land would have been the limiting resource. Competition between groups would have been in terms of control over reproduction. Productive success would have depended on women as reproducers, and descent groups would compete for the control of the labour power of offspring. In all this, women and the domestic world would have played a central role, the foci of social tensions. The elaboration of the material culture was part of the strategies of men and women, through maternal and paternal lines, to obtain access to labour.

As the social process of lineage competition built up through time, control of women in the house and settlement, and thus of descent and labour, would have assumed an increased importance, with women as the focal points of reproduction and exchange. Through time, houses became more substantial (Sherratt 1982), pottery more decorated, figurines more elaborate (ibid.). The agglomeration of settlements, a process seen in the fourth millennium in many parts of central Europe, not only allowed greater control over women and descent, but also allowed co-operation between women leading to a greater need to seclude and control them through the organisation of house space. Through the late fifth and early fourth millennia all aspects of material culture from pottery and houses to figurines and settlement organisation demonstrate attempts to use materials to naturalise and mark out the position of women in the domestic context. In this way the central importance and power of women as reproducers and as the nodes of links to other lineages was emphasised but they were also secluded and controlled. The multivalent, ambiguous nature of material culture was played to the full.

By the late fourth and third millennia, however, there is increased evidence for 'filling up' of the environment, further expansion of settlement onto less productive soils, the use of the plough and increased use of secondary animal products (Sherratt 1981). Gradually, through time, land became the major limiting resource, not labour. As Goody (1976) and Ingold (1980) have noted, in societies (such as hoe agriculturalists and milch pastoralists) where the amount of resources in the possession of a productive unit is a direct function of labour supply, there will be little attempt to restrict inheritance to particular descent lines and, as we have seen, competition between descent lines for the control over offspring will lead to multiple descent claims and affiliations of individuals. But where (as amongst plough agriculturalists) there is a scarcity of productive resources rather than labour, there will be a pressure to restrict the number of dependants in a household and to confine the range of potential heirs to direct descendants. Thus as land became the critical resource as a result of the competition between descent groups, women would have less ability to negotiate their social position since they would no longer be at the focus of the competing claims between descent lines for the control of offspring. The domestic context would no longer be relevant as a forum for symbolic elaboration. Houses decrease in size and become simple in construction and content, pottery is plain, the role of women in the domestic context (but not necessarily in other spheres) is devalued. From another point of view, the decrease in house size and the removal of decoration from the domestic context can be seen as an active process. The 'closing' of lineage groups and the restriction of descent must involve strategies of legitimation in order to exclude certain individuals from inheritance and access to resources. The removal of elaboration from the domestic context devalues the woman as reproducer and the claims to inheritance made through women. The removal of complexity from domestic space and from pottery decoration helps to establish absolute control of descent lines by lineage heads. The woman is less able to use her position as reproducer to promote competing claims from other groups.

It would be of interest, in view of the above hypothesis, to examine changes in pottery production in the late fourth and third millennia bc. For example, the uniformity of the plain Chassey, Michelsberg, Diana and other pottery may prove to indicate specialist and centralised production, and Peacock (1969) has demonstrated petrologically the centralised manufacture of plain Hembury ware in southwest England. Since such increases in the scale and organisation of production are often linked to shifts to male potters (Balfet 1966), it would be possible to see the changes in the third millennium as involving removal of pottery and its associated symbolism from the domestic sphere of production in order to increase male dominance and control. However, much work remains to be done on the organisation of Neolithic pottery-production before such an hypothesis can be entertained.

It has been suggested that the long houses of central Europe were large and elaborate and were internally organised so that they played a part in the competition between descent groups for the control over reproduction and labour. The major division in the houses between entrance and interior, between outside and inside is part of the strategy of seclusion by men of women and control of maternal ties. The trapezoidal form has been explained as part of the same contrasts, front against back. Soudsky (1969) suggests that the trapezoidal shape gives a better aerodynamic quality against increased winds. There is little evidence for changes in Neolithic wind speed and such an hypothesis carries little conviction in relation to the trapezoidal shape of the long barrows.

Climatic arguments have also been suggested for the orientation of long houses. Marshall (1981) shows that modern wind directions are considerably more varied than are the long house orientations, but reconstructions of central and eastern European Neolithic wind patterns have suggested a predominance of northwesterlies. However, even if wind direction is part of the explanation of the long house orientations, the relationship between house, wind and orientation could have been invested with further significance. Certainly the equivalent orientation of many long mounds, the constructions of which are less likely to have been harmed by weather and wind, argues that the placing of the houses and mounds was significant. Relationships to the winds, sun, moon or stars could have produced a higher authority, a naturalisation of the social processes centred on the house itself.

LONG MOUNDS

It is now possible to return to Atlantic Europe and to consider the social context of the long burial mounds. The spread of farming into western Europe from central Europe and the Mediterranean occurred mainly in the later fourth and third millennia as part of the process of infill and intensification noted above (Whittle 1977). There is evidence of ploughing under barrows and it seems likely that a range of secondary animal products was in use, allowing occupation of a wider variety of environments. In line with the hypothesis already presented, houses are small and there is little elaboration of domestic space. A number of individual huts are known in Britain, and at Knardrup, Denmark, an early Neolithic TRB settlement consisted of three small single-celled houses (Larsen 1957). Initially, however, there is likely to have been a concern to increase reproduction and labour power. In the first stages of agricultural development aspects of the domestic context such as pottery may have been marked out and emphasised as part of the processes already outlined and the early appearance of decorated pottery in Scandinavia and Brittany has been mentioned. Generally, however, the Atlantic facade is characterised by poor and crudely decorated or undecorated pottery in relation to the wares of central and southeast Europe, and those areas with decorated pottery change to plainer pottery during the third millennium.

According to the models used in this study, the Atlantic Neolithic should include societies in which the limiting resource is productive and in which attempts are made to restrict and control descent. It is in the same terms that the long mounds are described by Chapman. But it is now possible to reconsider these burial monuments in the light of the symbolic associations with central European long houses. The transference of the Neolithic house form to western European burial involved a large number of specific and complex symbolic meanings which must affect the way the functions of the tombs are interpreted.

69

The association between the house form and male-female relationships is strengthened by a consideration of the tombs. Here the surviving art, whether from stone monuments in Malta or France, shows clear depictions of women and female breasts. In the tombs of the Paris Basin shown in Figure 11, these depictions are often set beside drawings of axes, although the male connotations of the latter cannot be demonstrated with any certainty. Other aspects of the tombs emphasise the principles already identified. In particular the elaboration of the entrance area, the facades and forecourts, the closing of the tombs and the difference in ritual and artifacts inside and outside the tombs all indicate the same concerns with an inner/outer dichotomy, with control and seclusion. No more eloquent testimony of the latter principles could be provided than the false portals. In nearly all types of chambered tomb the organisation of space is largely sequential and controlled, and several of the temples at Tarxien in Malta have the same structure as has been identified for central European houses – there is an overall trapezoidal form as one moves from the large front chambers to the small rear chambers.

But the long mounds are not houses, they are tombs. They bring the above signification to the context of the ancestors, death and the past. Also the context is not one of everyday experience. The long mounds form a separate ritual context. Links can be made, then, between the control of reproduction, ancestors and ritual. But there are other aspects of the tombs and the burial ritual which need to be included in any explanation. The first involves communality and participation. The labour involved in the construiction of stone and earth tombs itself involves participation by the group and it is for this reason, and because of their monumentality, that they have been seen as social and territorial foci. Participation is also seen in other aspects of the tombs. In particular the partitioning of the mounds at South Street and Barkaer, for example, has suggested the division of the construction task between different work groups. Similarly, the discontinuous nature of the long barrow ditches at Wor Barrow and elsewhere (Ashbee 1970, 47) recalls the discontinuous construction of causewayed enclosures in Britain and the suggestion made by Startin and Bradley (1981) that different task groups were involved. As has long been recognised, the tombs are usually communal in nature and provide a special focus for the group as a whole. The rearrangement of skeletal remains and the 'mixing' of bones can again be seen as denying and resolving within-group differences. It can even be suggested, following Lévi-Strauss (1969), that the removal of flesh from bones may be associated with relationships between the maternal and paternal sides, with continuity and order (Rowlands 1980, 51).

A second aspect of the symbolism of the tombs concerns their orientation. As already described, many of the long tombs are aligned axially so that the entrances face to the southeast. The Clava passage graves are aligned to certain positions of the moon and sun (Burl 1981). There is no need to evoke Neolithic astronomer-priests and mathematicians for general relationships to, for example, the rising sun. The concern with time and with the movements of the sun and moon in relation to burial and the mundane world provide a higher authority for the social strategies symbolised and mediated in the tombs. The orientation to the sun and moon provided a naturalisation of the social order.

Having outlined various components of the symbolism of the long burial mounds it is now possible to see how they may have been used in social strategies. It has been suggested that an initial concern of social units in Atlantic Europe in the late fourth and early third millennia may have been to control women as reproducers. In the early stages of the Atlantic Neolithic, strategies similar to those outlined for central Europe may have been followed. But through time, again as in central Europe, extra-lineage ties established through women would have been restricted and controlled, and it has been shown that areas which do have decorated pottery in the early phases of the Neolithic (TRB in Scandinavia and Holland for example) gradually lose elaborate decoration. But in Atlantic Europe in both early and later phases, the position of women is emphasised in the context of communal ritual, outside the domestic sphere. Here women are depicted and the domestic 'house' context is elaborated. Women as reproducers, as the source and focus of the lineage, are here celebrated. But only in the house of the ancestors does this occur, in a context in which communal participation is stressed, and in which differences are denied. Domestic houses themselves, and in some areas pottery, are rarely elaborate. Women as reproducers and their position in the domestic context are, in the context of ritual, appropriated for the lineage as a whole. Their services are for the lineage alone and this control is legitimated by the ancestors and by higher authorities.

The above hypothesis is seen as plausible because it accounts for the richness and complexity of megalithic burial ritual and for other aspects of the data from the Neolithic of Europe. There is a potential for the collection and consideration of further data to support or throw doubt on the hypothesis. In particular, more information is needed on economic subsistence strategies, on the organisation of craft production, on the internal organisation of houses, on pottery design, on the symbolism of axes and so on. I have not considered the evidence from the southeast of Europe, or the significance of figurines. But the steps so far taken indicate at least the potential of an approach which integrates the study of meaning and function. Other explanations are not so much wrong as limited. I have tried, in this section, to incorporate reference to existing theories concerning western Neolithic burial and society. It is possible to see now why and how collective monumental burials acted as territorial markers and legitimated access to restricted resources and such arguments have been developed and extended by the consideration of meaning and an active social context.

Other hypotheses which can be incorporated concern the development of social hierarchy in relation to megaliths in Atlantic Europe (Renfrew 1979; Shennan 1982). In reference to the Orkney Neolithic, it has been suggested that a centralised hierarchy developed through the control of rituals which were represented as being for the society as a whole (Hodder 1982c). By repeating in one ritual centre the patterns of activity found within dispersed groups, the major henges and those controlling the rituals in the henges could rise to dominance. It was through the appropriation of rituals for the larger society that individual lineages could come to dominate others (cf. Friedman 1975). Similarly, in western Europe generally, each burial mound formed the focus for members of a descent group. Because the burial house was the house of the whole descent group, those sections of a lineage most closely linked to the burial ritual could rise to dominance through the ideology of communal care. The elders or sub-groups most closely connected with the tombs could control the reproduction and continuation of the lineage itself and would be legitimated not only by the symbolism of reproduction, communality and denial of differences, but also by appeal to higher, 'natural' authorities. In the larger-scale competition between tomb-centred lineage groups, those groups which performed and acted more competently in relation to the symbolism and meaning of the tombs could also control and increase productive resources more successfully and would be able to rise to a superior position. As Shennan (1982) has noted, communal burial is in many areas associated with, but also masks, increasing social differentiation.

ATLANTIC AND CENTRAL EUROPE COMPARED

As described in this article and in the work of, for example, Chapman (1981), Sherratt (1981) and Whittle (1977), similar social and economic developments occurred in west and central Europe during the Neolithic. In both areas competition for productive rather than reproductive resources became the major concern in the late fourth and third millennia BC. There is widespread evidence for settlement infill, expansion of settlement into less productive areas, and intensification as seen in the use of the plough and secondary animal products. In both areas, as described by the model of Ingold (1980) and Goody (1976) and utilised in this study, attempts were made in conjunction with these developments to restrict inheritance and to 'close' lineage groups. Why then are long mounds part of these processes in Atlantic Europe, but not in central Europe?

One type of explanation for the occurrence of long mound burial in

Atlantic but not central Europe concerns ecological conditions. The greater variety of subsistence resources available in the Atlantic zone (Clarke 1976) may have led to different adaptations and the megalithic monuments could be seen as part of a 'technocomplex' (Madsen 1979). It has been shown above that arguments for higher population density in Atlantic Europe, leading to greater stress and competition and hence to megaliths, have little sound basis. There is, however, some ground for viewing monumental mound burial as being linked to greater mobility of settlement in Atlantic Europe. Jarman, Bailey and Jarman (1982) have documented the frequent occurrence of communal burial mounds in areas of low arable potential, including the limestone plateaux of southern France and it has been suggested that the tombs in the Netherlands provided a focus for dispersed and relatively mobile groups. Within such an hypothesis, the tombs as houses would be appropriate symbols of continuity, stability and the lineage itself.

On the other hand, there is little evidence that any significant difference existed between degrees of dispersal in central and western Europe by the third millennium bc. As already noted, by the late fourth and third millennia bc, settlement had expanded, a more varied suite of environments was in use, and evidence for long-term stable occupation is infrequent. It is difficult to argue for any major difference in economic adaptation in central and Atlantic Europe at this time. Equally, monumental burial occurs in a great variety of ecological contexts in Atlantic Europe. For example, in southern Sweden Clark (1977) notes megalithic tombs on both high-quality and on very poor soil associated with the use of coastal resources. Tombs connected with a largely fishing economy are known from the Scilly Isles (Clark 1980, 98) and from Carrowmore, Ireland (Burenhult 1980a; 1980b; 1981). Frequently, however, they occur in predominantly agricultural contexts. It is not possible to see megaliths as linked to any one subsistence strategy, in any one environment. Even if such a relationship were to be substantiated, it is not possible to derive a burial ritual directly from a type of subsistence. The types of adaptation that occurred in Atlantic Europe were enabled by the same framework of meaning that produced the tombs, and a two-way interaction between culture and ecology must be assumed.

Atlantic Europe is characterised by a series of burial and other traits which go to make up a tradition which needs to be explained in its own terms, in its own historical context. This is not to say that a static set of ideas determined the production of long barrows, since we have seen how the symbolism of the tombs and of pottery was actively involved in social change, as a medium for action. It may be helpful to consider the historical tradition as a 'coping system' which enabled, but was also changed by, practical decisions and their effects.

It is possible to argue in Iberia, Brittany, England, Ireland and

Scandinavia for some local contribution to the emergence of megalithic burial. The important evidence from Hoëdic and Teviec in Brittany for a Mesolithic origin for aspects of the megalithic and communal burial tradition is underlined by the uncalibrated C^{14} date of 4625 ± 300 bc from Hoëdic. At Teviec inhumations in graves with up to six individuals are found in clear mausolea with piles of stones on the bodies, while at Hoëdic small slabs of stones were placed over the graves (Pequart and Pequart 1954). There is evidence in both places for the addition of bodies and removing earlier bones into a pile with a skull on top, in the style of many Neolithic megalithic rituals. Although evidence for Mesolithic burial is limited, it would be possible to argue for an earlier tradition of various aspects of the megalithic burial ritual in Atlantic Europe.

But the difference between Atlantic and central Europe does not only concern the use of megaliths. Monumental burial involves an emphasis on ritual outside the domestic context which is also seen in other spheres and in other times in Atlantic Europe. The precise nature of the ritual activities at English causewayed camps is yet to be determined but was frequently on an impressive scale (Mercer 1980). In Scandinavia, settlements are not known inside causewayed camps (Madsen 1977). The general tradition of major ritual monuments continues into the late third millennium and the second millennium in Britain where henges act as distinctive ritual centres with varying degrees of occupational activity. From Carnac to Stonehenge and to the 'temples' of Malta, Atlantic Europe is characterised by an investment in separate, non-domestic ritual which is wholly alien to the central European tradition. In the latter area and in southeast Europe, 'ritual' in the form of figurines, foundation deposits and shrines does occur, but within houses and settlements, closely linked to the domestic context. In Atlantic Europe the ritual is outside the domestic context, or at least it extends into a separate sphere on which most of the art and cultural elaboration often centre.

I have shown how these differences in the traditions of the two areas were related to generally similar social strategies. In other words, two rather different coping systems were described, and these involved similar successful adaptations in the two regions. There also seems to be evidence for continuity in the tradition from earlier into later times and a major concern must be to examine the longer-term historical continuities. Shennan (1982) has noted differences in the development of hierarchy and in the adoption of metallurgy in the two areas. In addition, I find it provocative and potentially exciting to note that in the Upper Palaeolithic in Europe painted caves are found in western Europe but not in central Europe despite careful research in the latter area, despite the existence of appropriate caves, and despite the occurrence of portable art in domestic contexts in central Europe. Upper Palaeolithic cave art is largely confined to Atlantic Europe and often occurs in clearly non-domestic contexts, in caves and parts of caves which are not used for habitation. Other similarities in the tradition which can be examined are that the Palaeolithic art uses methods which demonstrate participation (Marshak 1977) and the resolving of differences (Conkey 1982). Clearly the identification of these continuities requires further research and further papers, but the possibility exists of identifying long-term cultural traditions which are actively implicated in social change.

CONCLUSION

In the above account the megaliths have been placed within a social context. This article thus continues in the directions taken by Renfrew, Chapman, Fleming and Reed. However, there are two differences from such work. First, I have not been concerned simply with the general appearance of societies – territorial behaviour and the use of restricted resources. All societies have such characteristics, but competition and access to resources vary structurally in different societies. In this article, following Goody and Ingold, I have used a model that, in the European Neolithic, competition was initially based on control of reproduction but later productive rather than reproductive resources became the limiting factor. It has been suggested that these organisational differences are associated in the Neolithic with changes in patterns of inheritance, in the relations between maternal and paternal claims on offspring and resources, and in the relations between men and women. The model allows the mundane and ubiquitous archaeological evidence of houses and pots to be incorporated directly in models of social change. These artifacts act ideologically in the sense that they are involved in objectifying and giving meaning to social strategies. In the first phase the domestic context is the central focus of competing claims to reproductive resources. Material culture is used to form a world in which women are to be emphasised, celebrated but controlled as reproducers of the lineage, and in which women and extra-lineage ties have a central importance. In the second phase the domestic context is withdrawn from its central focus by changes in material culture, and these changes are part of the developing social control of productive resources. Competing claims to the inheritance of those resources, whether land or livestock, are restricted by de-emphasising and devaluing the domestic context, the role of women as reproducers and the extra-lineage ties.

In reaching such a conclusion, and in relating the hypothesis to megalithic burial, it has been necessary, in contrast to published 'processual' studies, to consider the particular historical significance of houses, mound shapes, decoration and orientation, and this is the second difference from the 'processual' studies of megaliths. Individuals can only act socially within ideologies which are historically contingent. The particular symbolism of artifacts can be examined by considering associations of form and use, and by showing that the symbolic significances inferred 'make sense' within active social strategies. It has been possible to see the diffusion of an idea, of a style of construction, as a socially active process. The house form which diffused from central Europe to Atlantic European burial had the significance of a domestic context in which reproductive potential and the control of that potential were marked out. In Atlantic Europe, however, this significance, further elaborated by the use of art depicting women, was transformed. In a ritual and ancestral burial context, female reproduction was appropriated by the lineage and competition between maternal and paternal claims to reproductive and productive resources was resolved in a non-domestic context. All aspects of burial and other rituals can be linked to the same concern with legitimating control of reproductive and productive resources through an ideology of communal work and participation for the lineage.

Ultimately the ideology, the way of coping, associated with the megaliths of western Europe cannot be explained only in terms of social strategies and adaptive potential. While ideas and practices diffuse from central to Atlantic Europe, the latter area transforms the meanings and uses the symbolism in rather different ways. While environmental differences between Atlantic and central Europe can be identified, the successful adaptations to those environments cannot be explained solely in terms of those adaptations. There is much scope for examining the varied appearances in different times and in different areas of the 'style' of the Neolithic of the Atlantic facade. While only brief reference has been made to possibilities of remarkable continuities in 'ways of doing things' in Atlantic Europe, it is now necessary to examine further the historical tradition which gives the appearance of monumental burial its specificity. The playing out of the historical tradition of Atlantic Europe must be understood partly in its own terms and the task is scarcely begun.

REFERENCES

Ashbee, P. (1970) *The Earthen Long Barrow in Britain*, London: Dent.
Bailloud, G. (1964) *Le Neolithique dans le Bassin Parisien*, supplement to *Gallia Prehistoire* 2.
Bakker, J. A. (1979) 'July 1878: Lukis and Dryden in Drente', *Antiquaries Journal* 59, 9–18.
Balfet, H. (1966) 'Ethnographic observations in North Africa and archaeological interpretation of the pottery of the Maghreb', in F. R. Matson (ed.) *Ceramics and Man*, Viking Fund Publication in Anthropology 4.
Bogucki, P. and Grygiel, R. (1981) 'The household cluster at Brzesc Kujawski 3:

small-site methodology in the Polish lowlands', *World Archaeology* 13, 59–72.

Braithwaite, M. (1982) 'Decoration as ritual symbol: a theoretical proposal and an ethnographic study in southern Sudan', in I. Hodder (ed.) *Symbolic and Structural Archaeology*, Cambridge: Cambridge University Press.

Burenhult, G. (1980a) *The Archaeological Excavation at Carrowmore*, G. Burenhults Förlag, Stockholm.

—— (1980b) *The Carrowmore Excavations: Excavation Season 1980*, Stockholm Archaeological Reports 7, Institute of Archaeology, University of Stockholm.

—— (1981) *The Carrowmore Excavations: Excavation Season 1981*, Stockholm Archaeological Reports 8, Institute of Archaeology, University of Stockholm.

Burl, A. (1981) ' "By the light of the cinerary moon": chambered tombs and the astronomy of death', in C. L. N. Ruggles and A. W. R. Whittle (eds) *Astronomy and Society in Britain During the Period 4000–1500 BC*, British Archaeological Reports British Series 88.

Case, H. (1969) 'Settlement patterns in the North Irish Neolithic', *Ulster Journal of Archaeology* 32, 3–27.

Chapman, R. (1981) 'The emergence of formal disposal areas and the "problem" of megalithic tombs in prehistoric Europe', in R. Chapman, I. Kinnes and J. Randsborg (eds) *The Archaeology of Death*, Cambridge: Cambridge University Press.

Childe, V. G. (1925) *The Dawn of European Civilisation*, 1st edn, London: Kegan Paul.

—— (1931) *Skara Brae*, London: Kegan Paul.

—— (1949a) 'The origin of Neolithic culture in northern Europe', Antiquity 23, 129–35.

—— (1949b) 'Neolithic house-types in temperate Europe', *Proceedings of the Prehistoric Society* 15, 77–85.

—— (1957) *The Dawn of European Civilisation*, 6th edn, London: Routledge.

Clark, J. G. D. (1952) *Prehistoric Europe: the Economic Basis*, London: Methuen.

—— (1977) 'The economic context of dolmens and passage graves in Sweden', in V. Markotic (ed.) *Ancient Europe and the Mediterranean*, Warminster: Aris and Phillips.

—— (1980) *Mesolithic Prelude*, Edinburgh: Edinburgh University Press.

Clarke, D. L. (1976) 'Mesolithic Europe: the economic basis', in G. Sieveking, I. H. Longworth and K. Wilson (eds) *Problems in Economic and Social Archaeology*, London: Duckworth.

Colt Hoare, R. (1812) *The Ancient History of South Wiltshire*, London.

Conkey, M. (1982) 'Boundedness in art and society', in I. Hodder (ed.) *Symbolic and Structural Archaeology*, Cambridge: Cambridge University Press.

Crawford, O. G. S. (1957) *The Eye Goddess*, London: Phoenix House.

Daniel, G. E. (1958) *The Megalith Builders of Western Europe*, London.

—— (1965) 'Editorial', *Antiquity* 39.

Donley, L. (1982) 'House power: Swahili space and symbolic markers', in I. Hodder (ed.) *Symbolic and Structural Archaeology*, Cambridge: Cambridge University Press.

Fleming, A. (1972) 'Vision and design: approaches to ceremonial monument typology', *Man* 7, 57–72.

—— (1973) 'Tombs for the living', *Man* 8, 177–93.

Friedman, J. (1975) 'Tribes, states and trasformations', in M. Bloch (ed.) *Marxist Analyses and Social Anthropology*, London: Malaby Press.

Gebauer, A. B. (1978) 'The Middle Neolithic Funnel Beaker culture in south-west Jutland. An analysis of the pottery', *Kuml* 1978, 117–57.

Geupel, V. (1981) 'Zum Verhältnis Spätmesolithikum–Frühneolithikum in mettleren Elbe-Saale-Gebiet', *Mesolithikum in Europa. Veröffentlichungen des Museums für Ur- und Frühgeschichte Potsdam* 14/15, 102–12.

Gilman, A. (1976) 'Bronze Age dynamics in southeast Spain', *Dialectical Anthropology* 1, 307–19.

Glob, P. V. (1949) 'Barkaer, Danmarks aeldste landsby', *Fra Nationalmuseets Arbejdsmark* 1949, 5–16.

—— (1975) 'De dødes lange huse', *Skalk* 1975, 6.

Goldstein, L. G. (1980) *Mississippian Mortuary Practices: a Case Study of Two Cemeteries in the Lower Illinois Valley*, Northwestern University Archaeological Program, Scientific Papers 4, Illinois: Evanston.

Goody, J. (1976) *Production and Reproduction*, Cambridge: Cambridge University Press.

Günther, K. (1973) 'Eine neue Variante des mittelneolithischen Trapezhauses', *Germania* 51, 41–53.

Hodder, I. (1982a) 'Theoretical archaeology: a reactionary view', in I. Hodder (ed.) *Symbolic and Structural Archaeology*, Cambridge: Cambridge University Press.

—— (1982b) 'Sequences of structural change in the Dutch Neolithic', in I. Hodder (ed.) *Symbolic and Structural Archaeology*, Cambridge: Cambridge University Press.

—— (1982c) *Symbols in Action*, Cambridge: Cambridge University Press.

—— (1985) 'Boundaries as strategies: an ethnoarchaeological study', in S. Green and S. Perlman (eds) *Frontiers and Boundaries in Prehistory*, New York: Academic Press.

Hugh-Jones, C. (1979) *From the Milk River*, Cambridge: Cambridge University Press.

Ingold, T. (1980) *Hunters, Pastoralists and Ranchers*, Cambridge: Cambridge University Press.

Jarman, M. R., Bailey, G. N. and Jarman, H. N. (1982) *Early European Agriculture*, Cambridge: Cambridge University Press.

Kinnes, I. (1975) 'Monumental function in British Neolithic burial practices', *World Archaeology* 7, 16–29.

—— (1981) 'Dialogues with death', in R. Chapman, I. Kinnes and K. Randsborg (eds) *The Archaeology of Death*, Cambridge: Cambridge University Press.

Kruk, J. (1980) *The Neolithic Settlement of Southern Poland*, Oxford: British Archaeological Reports International Series 93.

Larsen, K. A. (1957) 'Stenalderhuse på Knardrup Galgebakkez, *Kuml* 1957, 24–43.

Lévi-Strauss, C. (1969) *The Elementary Structures of Kinship*, 2nd edn, Boston: Beacon Press.

L'Helgouach, J. (1965) *Les sepultures megalithiques en Armorique*, Rennes.

Madsen, T. (1977) 'Toftum near Horsens. A causewayed camp from the transition between Early and Middle Neolithic', *Kuml* 1977, 180–4.

—— (1979) 'Earthen long barrows and timber structures: aspects of the early Neolithic mortuary practice in Denmark', *Proceedings of the Prehistoric Society* 45, 301–20.

Marshak, A. (1977) 'The meander as a system: the analysis and recognition of iconographic units in Upper Palaeolithic compositions', in P. J. Ucko (ed.) *Form in Indigenous Art*, London: Duckworth.

Marshall, A. (1981) 'Environmental adaptation and structural design in axially-pitched longhouses from Neolithic Europe', *World Archaeology* 13, 101–21.

Meier-Arendt, W. (1965) *Die bandkeramische Kultur im Untermaingebiet*, Bonn.
Meillassoux, C. (1972) 'From reproduction to production', *Economy and Society* 1, 93–105.
Mercer, R. J. (1980) *Hambledon Hill: a Neolithic Landscape*, Edinburgh: Edinburgh University Press.
Meyer-Christian, W. (1976) 'Die Y-Pfostenstellung in Häusen der älteren Linear-Bandkeramik', *Bonner Jahrbücher* 176, 1–25.
Montelius, O. (1899) *Der Orient und Europa*.
Okely, J. (1975) 'Gypsy women: models in conflict', in S. Ardener (ed.) *Perceiving Women*, London: Malaby Press.
Peacock, D. (1969) 'Neolithic pottery production in Cornwall', *Antiquity* 43, 145–9.
Pequart, M. and Pequart, S.-J. (1954) *Hoëdic*, Anvers: De Sikkel.
Piggott, S. (1965) *Ancient Europe*, Edinburgh: Edinburgh University Press.
Powell, T. G. E., Corcoran, J. X. W. P., Lynch, F. and Scott, J. G. (1969) *Megalithic Enquiries in the West of Britain*, Liverpool: Liverpool University Press.
Reed, R. C. (1974) 'Earthen long barrows: a new perspective', *Archaeological Journal* 131, 33–57.
Renfrew, C. (1976) 'Megaliths, territories and populations', in S. J. De Laet (ed.) *Acculturation and Continuity in Atlantic Europe*, Dissertationes Archaeologicae Gandenses, Brugge: De Tempel.
—— (1979) *Investigations in Orkney*, London: Society of Antiquaries.
Rowlands, M. J. (1980) 'Kinship, alliance and exchange in the European Bronze Age', in J. Barrett and R. Bradley (eds) *Settlement and Society in the British Late Bronze Age*, Oxford: British Archaeological Reports British Series 83.
Saxe, A. A. (1970) 'Social dimensions of mortuary practices', Ph.D. Dissertation, University of Michigan.
Schmidt, G. (1930–6) *Steinzeitliche Siedelungen in Federseemoor*, Augsburg and Stuttgart.
Shanks, M. and Tilley, C. (1982) 'Ideology, symbolic power and ritual communication: a reinterpretation of Neolithic mortuary practices', in I. Hodder (ed.) *Symbolic and Structural Archaeology*, Cambridge: Cambridge University Press.
Shennan, S. (1982) 'Ideology, change and the European Early Bronze Age', in I. Hodder (ed.) *Symbolic and Structural Archaeology*, Cambridge: Cambridge University Press.
Sherratt, A. (1981) 'Plough and pastoralism: aspects of the secondary products revolution', in I. Hodder, G. Isaac and N. Hammond (eds) *Pattern of the Past*, Cambridge: Cambridge University Press.
—— (1982) 'Mobile resources: settlement and exchange in early agricultural Europe', in C. Renfrew and S. Shennan (eds) *Ranking, Resource and Exchange*, Cambridge: Cambridge University Press.
Sielman, B. (1972) 'Die frühneolithische Besiedlung Mitteleuropas', in J. Lüning (ed.) *Die Anfänge des Neolithikums vom Orient bis Nordeuropa* 5a, Köln: Fundamenta.
Soudsky, B. (1969) 'Etude de la maison neolithique', *Slovenská Archeologia* 17, 5–96.
Sprockhoff, E. (1938) *Die Nordische Megalithkultur*, Berlin and Leipzig.
Srejovic, D. (1972) *Europe's First Monumental Sculpture: New Discoveries at Lepenski Vir*, London: Thames and Hudson.
Startin, W. (1978) 'Linear pottery culture houses: reconstruction and manpower', *Proceedings of the Prehistoric Society* 44, 143–59.
Startin, W. and Bradley, R. (1981) 'Some notes on work organisation and society in prehistoric Wessex', in C. L. N. Ruggles and A. W. R. Whittle (eds)

Astronomy and Society in Britain During the Period 4000–1500 BC, Oxford: British Archaeological Reports British Series 88.

Tilley, C. (1981) 'Conceptual frameworks for the explanation of socio-cultural change', in I. Hodder, G. Isaac and N. Hammond (eds) *Pattern of the Past*, Cambridge: Cambridge University Press.

Waterbolk, H. T. and Van Zeist, W. (1978) *Niederwil, eine Sidelung der Pfyner Kultur*, Berne and Stuttgart.

Whittle, A. W. R. (1977) *The Earlier Neolithic of Southern England and its Continental Background*, Oxford: British Archaeological Reports Supplementary Series 35.

Woodburn, J. (1980) 'Hunters and gatherers today and reconstruction of the past', in E. Gellner (ed.) *Soviet and Western Anthropology*, London: Duckworth.

Part II

SOME IMPLICATIONS OF THE NEW IDEAS

5

POST-PROCESSUAL
ARCHAEOLOGY

PROCESS IS TOO IMPORTANT TO BE LEFT TO THE PROCESSUALISTS

On the whole, the work described in the previous chapters was bliss-fully oblivious to the effects of 'our' context on the interpretations of past symbolic meanings. Indeed, as will be seen in Chapter 9, much of archaeology has been able to incorporate a concern with meaning with-out recognising any crisis in the way that we conceive of the discipline.

However, two developments led to a questioning of this complacent view. The first was the recognition of a dilemma in the philosophy of archaeology. This issue was discussed in the paper reprinted here as Chapter 7, but it has been more widely and fully discussed by Wylie (1989). The dilemma existed before any attempt to interpret past symbo-lism, but it was thrown into focus by that attempt. In essence the problem is that archaeologists had espoused first empiricist and then positivist perspectives according to which they could only test hypoth-eses which concerned the observable world. And yet archaeologists want to go beyond their data to make statements about the dynamics of past societies. They want to make statements about behaviour, econ-omic and social structures and so on which go beyond the data and are not themselves observable. Archaeologists felt that they could ignore this dilemma so long as they could argue for deterministic links from the material to the non-material. But the attempt to get at past symbolism undermines any such argument. The very definition of a symbol nor-mally includes some reference to its arbitrary nature. Few people would argue that the symbolic meaning of an artifact, even if it is historically non-arbitrary (see Chapter 2), can be determined cross-culturally. How could a positivist approach possibly deal with the arbitrary nature of the sign?

The dilemma was exacerbated as the notion of material culture as a text began to take clearer form. In the preceding chapters the view that material culture is meaningfully constituted has taken us close to the

83

realisation that the meaning of an artifact does not derive simply from its production but also from its use and perception by others. The main purpose of the claim that in some respects the metaphor of the text is appropriate for material culture, is to move archaeologists away from the notion that the data are a passive record with only one meaning. Different people will have read the 'text' differently (Chapter 2), in different contexts. It is not a large leap from this last statement to the realisation that archaeologists too, in their different and changing contexts, will 'read the past' differently. If the meaning of a text is not equivalent to the intention of the author, or the context of production and use, but includes the readings made by 'them' and by 'us', then how can we know how 'they' were reading the material culture? Is any reading made by archaeologists, and indeed by non-archaeologists, equally valid? The spectre of relativism haunts archaeology, and is expressed in the chapters which follow (Chapters 6–8).

The second important development which heralded a move away from processual archaeology in the early 1980s was the introduction of a broader social theory. Anglo-American archaeology had clung to positivism, functionalism and adaptation long after these perspectives had been critiqued and transformed in neighbouring disciplines such as sociology, social and cultural anthropology, philosophy, geography, and linguistics. Much as archaeology had tried to keep itself hermetically sealed from these post-positivist developments, the new ideas were beginning to seep in. For example, in Cambridge in the late 1970s and early 1980s a new group of research students came together, several of whom had had training in the new radical directions in anthropology or were involved politically as feminists. Others became influenced by the work of Giddens at Cambridge and felt a strong commitment to social and political involvement. To this group of research students, the vision of archaeology as an objective science and the notion of societies adapting to their environments seemed complacent and politically suspect, as well as being theoretically narrow and out-of-step with exciting debates taking place in other disciplines.

Out of these two developments, and out of the social and political concerns which fuelled them, a critique of processual archaeology developed which came to be termed post-processual archaeology (Hodder 1985). The main points of this critique are provided in Chapter 6 (see also Chapter 3). Overall the aim of post-processual archaeology was to break down six oppositions which had been set up by processual archaeology. The first was the opposition between norm and adaptation or situational expediency. Rather than seeing culture as normative, static and invariant, hindering adaptation, post-processual approaches see culture as being the medium through which adaptation occurs and as being transformed in the process. Culture, norm and meaning are processes, not things, integral to all practical action. The second processual dichotomy which needed to be broken down was between materialism and idealism. While post-processual archaeologists do not reject the importance of material constraints on societies and may even emphasise them, they accept the need to incorporate meaning, values, symbolism. They seek the dialectical processes which link the ideal and the material. Third, post-processual archaeologists reject the separation of system and structure. Through the influence of Marxism and structuralism, they search for structures lying behind systems which may incorporate conflict, tension and contradiction. Fourth, many post-processual archaeologists reject any absolute dichotomy between societies and individuals. While they do not expect that archaeologists can 'see' individuals or that the intentions of individuals shaped the course of history, they often seek the relationships between agency and structure. They are concerned with material culture as active, being used meaningfully to further social interests. Fifth, post-processual archaeologists reject the separation of the general and the particular, anthropology versus history. While many would emphasise the specificity of cultural phenomena, most would also accept the need to translate that specificity into the contemporary world through generalisation. Finally, post-processual archaeologists debate the relationship between subject and object rather than seeing any possibility of a radical separation of the two. This issue will be discussed at length in Chapter 11.

In all these ways post-processual archaeologists are open to seeing processes rather than things or categories. Societies and systems are continually being renegotiated from different perspectives and according to conflicting interests. Material culture meanings are continually being reconstituted and reread. They are not fixed but are fluid, varying according to context. Text and context form and transform each other. Agents construct roles in the daily practices of life. Past and present transform each other in the practices of archaeology. In all these ways, post-processual archaeologists seek to break down categories, entities and essences and to embrace a radical notion of process, according to which all aspects of societies are situated, contextual, changing, moving, dialectical. While processual archaeology presaged some of these points in its emphasis on variability and situational expediency, the processualist view of process was highly restricted. Categories were set apart and dichotomised (norm/adaptation, ideal/material, system/structure, subject/object, etc.). Evolutionary stages and societal types were reified. Economic and subsistence systems were divorced from their cultural context. In these and many other ways, the positivism of processual archaeology led to a simplistic and thoroughly unprocessual view. It is certainly the case that the archaeology of process is too important an issue to leave to the processualists alone (with apologies to Renfrew

1982, 23). By breaking down the dichotomies which underpinned processual archaeology a fully processual approach can be attained, ironically by the post-processualists. Post-processual archaeology needs to build on the emphasis on process and expediency in processual archaeology and make it a central part of archaeological theory.

But perhaps the main underlying theme in post-processual archaeology, which explains the types of theories which have been espoused and the types of critiques which have been set up, is value commitment. On the one hand, archaeology seemed to have become increasingly esoteric, scientific, distant. On the other hand, the awareness by the general public of heritage issues and its fascination with the past seemed to be increasing, at least in Britain. Theory seemed divorced from practice in the community. The supposedly value-neutral science of archaeology was shown to be full of androcentric assumptions and biases. Around the world establishment archaeology was being confronted by minority voices with different conceptions of their pasts. Rather than closing the doors to this wider debate, post-processual archaeologists wish to transform the nature of the discipline so as to include other voices. Such an opening up leads to a confrontation particularly with the subject/object divide. But it also opens all essentialism to critique.

DIVERSITY

I have so far talked of post-processual archaeology as if it was unified. Certainly there was a coherence in the aspects of processual archaeology which were seen as most in need of critique. But nearly all the statements made in the last few paragraphs would be disagreed with by one or another self-proclaimed post-processual archaeologist. As post-processual archaeologists have turned from critique to the presentation of social theory and epistemology, the differences and divisions have started to emerge. The clearest and most sustained statement of a post-processual position, by Shanks and Tilley (1987a; 1987b) has been seen by some commentators as being eclectic or contradictory, as has my own writing. Post-processual archaeologists, however, often celebrate this diversity. They are simply post-, and do not need to set up a new dominating paradigm. They emphasise diversity and multiple voices. Even Binford, at the end of a recent book, is led to muse as to whether its title, *Debating Archaeology*, is not more appropriate to a socially embedded science than to one claiming a non-cultural objectivity (Binford 1989, 485).

I would see several strands running through this diversity (see Shennan 1986). The first is Marxism. Since Marxism is itself today highly diverse it is difficult to be precise about its impact on post-processual archaeology.

Certainly in Britain and Scandinavia the influence of structural-Marxism, through the work of Friedman and Rowlands (1977), has been considerable (for example, Bender 1978; Frankenstein and Rowlands 1978; Gledhill 1978; Kristiansen 1981). These approaches placed a new emphasis on internal contradiction and conflict leading to change, and they gave social rather than economic relations a dominant role. But, rather than fitting into aspects of the Marxist tradition which emphasised explanation as being specific and historical and which problematised the relationship between hypotheses and data, the archaeological applications of Althusserian structural-Marxism often retained an evolutionism, materialism and positivism which did little to threaten the processual paradigm. It was, by contrast, the Marxist notions of ideology, however, which did lead to a more fundamental re-evaluation (Miller and Tilley 1984). Rather than restricting ideology to the dominant ideology, it has been possible to see ideology as related to interest. Different groups in society are able to develop competing ideologies. Thus ideology is constructed within relations of domination and is closely connected with power. The influence of Foucault (1977) has been considerable in that power is seen as being part of a power/knowledge/truth network (Shanks and Tilley 1987a; 1987b). Power over others through the control of material resources has to be linked to the valuation, prestige and knowledge allocated to those resources. Even subordinate groups are able to manipulate the meanings of material culture in order to resist and act against oppression. While the contribution of a distinctively Marxist perspective to these ideas is difficult to distinguish, recent publications (e.g. Miller, Rowlands and Tilley 1989; McGuire and Paynter 1991) have shown a close affiliation with post-processual concerns. Kohl (1985, 112) talks of a 'subtler historical materialism along which ideas and materials actively and continuously interact with one another'.

If some western European Marxist archaeology has become blurred as it has contributed to and merged with post-processual archaeology, the same can be said for structuralism. As noted in Chapters 2–4, the initial influence of structuralism was important because, like Marxism, it introduced the notion of structures behind systems. It also provided a method for approaching symbolic codes. But the critique of structuralism (outlined in Chapter 6) was quickly established. Within a contextual archaeology, the emphasis on structured frameworks of meaning is retained, at least in the initial stages of analysis before the transformation of meanings in situated, practical contexts is explored. Post-processual archaeologists may still employ structuralist oppositions in their attempts to reconstruct specific historical contexts. The further transformation of structuralism into post-structuralism provides another strand of post-processual diversity. Opposed to the reconstruction of original contextual meanings, and opposed to the notion of agency, post-structuralist archaeology explores 'floating' chains of signifiers and leads to a radical undermining of the discipline of archaeology (see Chapter 11).

A third strand within post-processual archaeology is that influenced by various forms of critical theory. Associated particularly with the work of Leone (1982; Leone, Potter and Shackel 1987), this approach has emphasised the role of archaeology in furthering the dominant ideologies of capitalism and has explored alternative ways of empowering people to critique these ideologies. Once again these ideas have been absorbed into post-processual archaeology and are difficult to distinguish, although there are certainly differences in the commitments expressed towards science and objectivity.

A fourth strand is feminism. I hesitate to include this component since important differences have emerged between some post-processual writing and gender archaeology (Gero and Conkey 1991). For example, the apparent commitment to some form of relativism and free-play in post-structuralist writing appears insufficiently engaged politically for some feminists, and it undermines their claims concerning the real material oppression of women in society. Nevertheless, I would argue that feminism forms an important component in post-processual archaeology, because of its concern with meaning, other voices, agency, power, process and the past as construction. Indeed, many of the more active early post-processual writers have since spearheaded the introduction of a politically aware gender archaeology (e.g. Moore 1986; Gero and Conkey 1991; Wylie 1991). There is much variation within gender archaeology and some attempts simply to reconstruct what women were doing in the past fit easily into a processual approach (e.g. Ehrenberg 1989). However, a politically active gender archaeology certainly contributes to, as well as confronts, a value-committed archaeology.

It might be argued that, given all the diversity within and outside post-processual archaeology, there is little point in using a common term. This is particularly true when we include the accommodations being made within processual archaeology which will be discussed in Chapter 9. These blur the distinctions between processual and post-processual archaeology. Perhaps the 'post-processual' term is a ploy which attempts to incorporate everything new which is happening in archaeology under one umbrella. Perhaps as divisions occur and compromises are made archaeology will, like other social sciences, simply embrace diversity as part of its mature existence. Post-processual archaeology would then have played its role in opening up the discipline to reflection, criticism and diversity. I would myself be happy to stop using the term. But I will not do so where, as in North America, processual archaeology remains a dominant force. For me, post-processual archaeology represents a political struggle – a struggle against a closed view of science which measures quantities of neutral objects and for an open view which seeks out qualities, values and subjects.

CONCLUSION

In the chapters which follow, I now feel I was too eager in my attempt to redress the balance between science and society. In stressing the other side of what should be dialectical relationships between, for example, subject and object, particular and general, I distorted their complexity and intricacies. It is true that archaeologists had always emphasised the separate, objective nature of their data and the distance between theory and data. This view was taken by empiricists and positivists alike. The former saw facts as self-evident, and the latter, while accepting that the facts were not self-evident and that theory was necessary, still saw the data as objective and some (middle-range) theories as independent (Binford 1989). I wanted to point out that not enough attention had been paid to the subjectivity of the data. This was my post-processual claim, and my strength of feeling on this issue was supported by the debate over the 1986 World Congress (Chapter 8). Here I felt I met exactly the closed, entrenched positions which I had theoretically linked to a positivist science.

But I went too far in statements such as 'theory and data are not opposed and they are never confronted' (Chapter 7). I would argue that this statement is valid if by 'data' we mean our observations and low-level interpretations. But I no longer think the statement valid if it denies the reality of the patterned remains. The data might not be objective but they are real, existing outside our observation of them. Archaeologists do frequently discover unexpected patterns. A dialectic between theory and real data does occur, even if it is not a simple feedback loop (Chapter 7). The notion that theory and data constitute each other will be discussed in Chapter 12.

I would also now no longer support relativism and the rejection of science, unless by science is meant a narrow view of science as positivist. Rather I would argue for a science in the sense of an historical body of knowledge and a debate informed by that knowledge. The events after the 1986 World Congress have produced a rosier picture than could be presented during the writing of Chapter 8. It is widely recognised that the campaign of sanctions against South Africa contributed, in however small a way, to the end of apartheid. A new World Archaeological Congress has been formed (Ucko 1987, and see the first two volumes of the *World Archaeological Bulletin*), a constitution established, and successful conferences held. This active new body is committed to world participation and seems in a very real sense to have broken the stranglehold of Europe and North America on world archaeology. Other voices and other archaeologies are being heard. The impressive list of publications from the 1986 World Congress (Unwin Hyman One World Archaeology series) includes articles by indigenous archaeologists which confront many of the taken-for-granteds of western science. Arbitrarily I would single out a Bolivian archaeologist who presents alternative notions of history, prehistory, time and sequence and situates western conceptions within the context of domination (Condori 1989). It does indeed seem to be the case that archaeology can include rather than dominate alternative voices without losing its disciplinary or scientific coherence.

REFERENCES

Bender, B. (1978) 'Gatherer-hunter to farmer: a social perspective', *World Archaeology* 10, 204–22.

Binford, L. (1989) *Debating Archaeology*, New York: Academic Press.

Condori, C. M. (1989) 'History and prehistory in Bolivia: what about the Indians', in R. Layton (ed.) *Conflict in the Archaeology of living traditions*, London: Unwin Hyman.

Ehrenberg, M. (1989) *Women in Prehistory*, London: British Museum.

Foucault, M. (1977) *Discipline and Punish*, New York: Vintage Books.

Frankenstein, S. and Rowlands, M. J. (1978) 'The internal structure and regional context of Early Iron Age society in south-west Germany', *Bulletin of the Institute of Archaeology* 15, 73–112.

Friedman, J. and Rowlands, M. J. (eds) (1977) *The Evolution of Social Systems*, London: Duckworth.

Gero, J. and Conkey, M. (eds) (1991) *Engendering Archaeology*, Oxford: Basil Blackwell.

Gledhill, J. (1978) 'Formative development in the North American South-West', in D. Green, C. Haselgrove and M. Spriggs (eds) *Social Organisation and Settlement*, Oxford: British Archaeological Reports International Series 47.

Hodder, I. (1985) 'Post-processual archaeology', in M. Schiffer (ed.) *Advances in Archaeological Method and Theory* 8, New York: Academic Press.

Kohl, P. (1985) 'Symbolic cognitive archaeology: a new loss of innocence', *Dialectical Anthropology* 9, 105–18.

Kristiansen, K. (1981) 'Economic models for Bronze Age Scandinavia – towards an integrated approach', in A. Sheridan and G. Bailey (eds) *Economic Archaeology*, Oxford: British Archaeological Reports International Series 96.

Leone, M. (1982) 'Some opinions about recovering mind', *American Antiquity* 47, 742–60.

Leone, M., Potter, P. B. and Shackel, P. (1987) 'Toward a critical archaeology', *Current Anthropology* 28, 251–82.

McGuire, R. and Paynter, R. (1991) *The Archaeology of Inequality*, Oxford: Basil Blackwell.

Miller, D., Rowlands, M. and Tilley, C. (1989) *Domination and Resistance*, London: Unwin Hyman.

Miller, D. and Tilley, C. (eds) (1984) *Ideology, Power and Prehistory*, Cambridge: Cambridge University Press.

Moore, H. (1986) *Space, Text and Gender*, Cambridge: Cambridge University Press.

Renfrew, C. (1982) *Towards an Archaeology of Mind*, Cambridge: Cambridge University Press.

Shanks, M. and Tilley, C. (1987a) *Reconstructing Archaeology*, Cambridge: Cambridge University Press.

—— (1987b) *Social Theory and Archaeology*, Cambridge: Polity Press.

Shennan, S. J. (1986) 'Towards a critical archaeology?' *Proceedings of the Prehistoric Society* 52, 327–56.

Ucko, P. (1987) *Academic Freedom and Apartheid: the Story of the World Archaeological Congress*, London: Duckworth.

Wylie, A. (1989) 'Archaeological cables and tacking: the implications of practice for Bernstein's "Options beyond objectivism and relativism" ', *Philosophy of the Social Sciences* 19, 1–18.

—— (1991) 'Gender theory and the archaeological record: why is there no archaeology of gender?', in J. Gero and M. Conkey (eds) *Engendering Archaeology*, Oxford: Basil Blackwell.

6

THEORETICAL ARCHAEOLOGY: A REACTIONARY VIEW

FUNCTIONALISM AND THE NEW ARCHAEOLOGY

In defining functionalism, a simplified version of Radcliffe-Brown's (1952) account will be used since his approach can be shown to be close to that followed by many New Archaeologists (those who in the 1960s and 1970s were concerned with explanations and approaches of the types outlined by Binford and his associates). Functionalism introduces an analogy between social and organic life. Emile Durkheim (*Règles de la Methode Sociologique* 1895) defined the 'function' of a social institution as the correspondence between it and the needs of the social organism. In the same way that the stomach provides a function for the body as a whole and allows it to survive, so any aspect of a past society can be assessed in terms of its contribution to the working of the whole society. A society is made up of interrelated parts and we can explain one component by showing how it works in relation to other components. But these are all very general statements, and there is room for a great variety of views within these general propositions. Indeed, Radcliffe-Brown (1952, 188) stated bluntly that the 'Functional School does not really exist; it is a myth'. Functionalism often appears to be little more than a 'dirty word' used by the opponents of anthropologists such as Malinowski, Boas and Radcliffe-Brown himself, and it may convey little meaning. So if it is to be used of the New Archaeology, a more specific definition needs to be provided.

The concept of function is closely linked to the notion of system. In the middle of the eighteenth century Montesquieu used a conception of society in which all aspects of social life could be linked into a coherent whole. What Comte called 'the first law of social statics' held that there are relations of interconnection and interdependence, or relations of solidarity, between the various aspects of society. It is possible analytically to isolate certain groups of particularly close interrelationships as systems.

According to the functionalist viewpoint as stated in systems theory, societies reach a healthy organic equilibrium, called homeostasis. Plato, in the Fourth Book of his *Republic*, saw the health of a society as resulting from the harmonious working together of its parts. The Greeks distinguished good order, social health (*eunomia*), from disorder, social illness (*dysnomia*), while the notion of malfunction and social pathology was a central concern of Durkheim. (In recent systems archaeology, pathologies have been listed and their effects examined by Flannery (1972).)

Pathologies occur during periods when the organic unity and equilibrium are upset as a result of maladaptation. A society can only continue to exist if it is well adjusted internally and externally. Three types of adaptation can be distinguished. The first concerns the adjustment to the physical environment, the ecological adaptation. The second is the internal arrangement and adjustment of components of the society in relation to each other. Finally, there is the process by which an individual finds a place within the society in which he lives. It is through these three types of adaptation that societies survive and evolve. Many anthropologists and archaeologists, however, have discussed change largely in terms of ecological adaptation, the meeting of external constraints. It is an ecological functionalism which prevails today in archaeology.

In this chapter the term functionalism refers to the use of an organic analogy and to the viewpoint that an adequate explanation of a past society involves reference to system, equilibrium and adaptation as outlined above. Although functionalism, and specifically ecological functionalism, were mainstays of the theoretical framework of an earlier generation of archaeologists such as Gordon Childe and Grahame Clark, they have become more widely important as a result of the New Archaeology of the 1960s and 1970s. Indeed, processual and systems archaeology is almost by definition a functionalist archaeology. As Leach (1973a, 761–2) pointed out, 'Binford's remark that "behaviour is the by-product of the interaction of a cultural repertoire with the environment" may be proto-typical of the "new" archaeology, but to a social anthropologist it reads like a quotation from Malinowski writing at the time when naive functionalism was at its peak – that is to say about 1935.' This view is too extreme, but Renfrew (1972, 24) also states that to examine connections between subsystems as in systems theory 'is, of course, simply a statement of anthropological functionalism, that different aspects of a culture are all interrelated'.

The degree to which archaeology has adopted a functionalist conception of society and culture is apparent in the writings of the major figures of the 'new' discipline. Although the archaeological contributions of these writers differ, the notions of organic wholes, interrelated systems, equilibrium and adaptation can all be identified most clearly. For example, in Flannery's systems model for the growth of complex societies, the job of self-regulation within the sociocultural system 'is to keep all the variables in the subsystem within appropriate goal ranges – ranges which maintain homeostasis and do not threaten the survival of the system' (1972, 409). According to Binford (1972, 107) 'we can . . . expect variability in and among components of a system to result from the action of homeostatic regulators within the cultural system serving to maintain equilibrium relationships between the system and its environment'. Similarly, for Clarke (1968, 88), 'the whole cultural system is in external dynamic equilibrium with its local environment'. 'Equilibrium is defined as that state in which dislocation amongst the component variety is minimised. . . . Dislocation most frequently arises . . . when different networks independently transmit mutually contradictory information – presenting an anomaly at nodes in the structure of the system. Sociocultural systems are continuously changing in such a way as to minimise the maximum amount of immediate system dislocation' (ibid., 129). According to Hill (1971, 407), a set of variables is only a system if their 'articulation . . . be regulated (maintained in steady-state) by homeostatic processes'.

The importance of maintaining equilibrium with the 'environment' has also been emphasised by Renfrew (1972). Indeed, man's relationship with the environment is seen by him as one of the main aspects of systems theory. 'The whole purpose of utilising the systems approach is to emphasise man–environment interrelations, while at the same time admitting that many fundamental changes in man's environment are produced by man himself' (ibid., 19–20). 'Culture . . . is essentially a homeostatic device, a conservative influence ensuring that change in the system will be minimised. It is a flexible adaptive mechanism which allows the survival of society despite fluctuations in the natural environment' (ibid., 486).

Thus it is thought that human sociocultural systems can be described as if they were adapting to the total social and environmental milieu. Renfrew (1972, 24–5) talks of the 'essential coherence and conservatism of all cultures . . . the society's "adjustment" or "adaptation" to its natural environment is maintained: difficulties and hardships are overcome'. A similar view is expressed by Binford (1972, 20): 'Change in the total cultural system must be viewed in an adaptive context both social and environmental.' Indeed Binford's definition of culture 'as the extrasomatic means of adaptation for the human organism' (ibid., 22) is one of the main tenets of systems archaeologists. 'Culture, from a systemic perspective, is defined . . . as interacting behavioural systems. One asks questions concerning these systems, their interrelation, their adaptive significance' (Plog 1975, 208). 'Culture is all those means whose forms are not under direct genetic control . . . which serve to adjust individuals and groups within their ecological communities. . . . Adaptation is always a local problem, and selective pressures favouring new cultural forms result from nonequilibrium conditions in the local ecosystem' (Binford 1972, 431).

The functionalist and processual emphasis in archaeology aimed objectively to identify relationships between variables in cultural systems. There was a natural link to an empirical and positivist concept of science. 'The meaning which explanation has within a scientific frame of reference is simply the demonstration of a constant articulation of variables within a system and the measurement of the concomitant variability among the variables within the system. Processual change in one variable can thus be shown to relate in a predictable and quantifiable way to changes in other variables, the latter changing in turn relative to changes in the structure of the system as a whole' (ibid., 21). This statement demonstrates the link between functionalism and a conception of explanation as the prediction of relationships between variables. It is thought that the relationships can be observed empirically and quantification can be used to assess the significance of associations. The way is thus open for recovering cross-cultural generalisations, and 'the laws of cultural process' (ibid., 199). Although Binford (1977, 5) appears more recently to have doubted the explanatory value of cross-cultural statistics, the above attitudes to explanation have at times been developed into a rigid hypothetico-deductive method based on a reading of Hempel (e.g. Fritz and Plog 1970; Watson, Leblanc and Redman 1971).

CRITIQUE OF FUNCTIONALISM

I do not intend to examine the problems of applying systems theory in archaeology (Doran 1970), or whether systems theory has really aided archaeologists in their functionalist aims (Salmon 1978). Rather, I want to consider the criticisms of functionalism itself. Martins (1974, 246) describes the critique of functionalism as an initiation *rite de passage* into sociological adulthood, and I have suggested elsewhere (Hodder 1981) the need for a wider debate in archaeology concerning the various critiques of and alternatives to ecological functionalism.

Many of the problems and limitations of the organic analogy as applied to social systems have long been recognised. Radcliffe-Brown (1952, 181) noted that while an animal organism does not, in the course of its life, change its form, a society can, in the course of its history, undergo major organisational change. Other problems are not inherent to the approach but result from the particular emphasis that is given by archaeologists, perhaps as a result of the limitations of their data. For example, a systems approach which assumes that homeostatic equilibrium is the natural state of things results in the notion that all change ultimately has to derive from outside the system. Negative feedback occurs in reaction to outside stimuli, and positive feedback and deviation amplifying processes need initial external kicks. According to Hill (1977, 76) 'no system can change itself; change can only be instigated by outside sources. If a system is in equilibrium, it will remain so unless inputs (or lack of outputs) from outside the system disturb the equilibrium.' The result of this view has been to place great emphasis on the impact of supposed 'independent' variables from outside the sociocultural system under study. The favourite external variables have been environmental factors (e.g. Carneiro 1968), long-distance trade (Renfrew 1969), and population increase (Hill 1977, 92), although it is not often clear why the latter is assumed to be an independent variable. Little advance has been made in the study of factors within societies that affect the nature of change (see, however, Friedman and Rowlands 1977). But Flannery (1972) has shown how the systems approach can be extended to include internal forces of change and those forms of internal adaptation within the organic whole which have been described above.

A more fundamental limitation of the functionalist viewpoint centres on the inadequacy of function and utility in explaining social and cultural systems, and on the separation made between functional utility and culture. All aspects of culture have utilitarian purposes in terms of which they can be explained. All activities, whether dropping refuse, developing social hierarchies, or performing rituals, are the results of adaptive expedience. But explanation is sought only in terms of adaptation and function. The problem with such a viewpoint is not so much the emphasis on function since it is important to know how material items, institutions, symbols and ritual operate, and the contribution of the New Archaeology to such studies is impressive. It is rather the dichotomy which was set up between culture and adaptive utility which restricted the development of the approach.

In archaeology the split between culture and function took the form of an attack on what was termed the 'normative' approach. In Binford's (1965) rebuttal of the 'normative school', he referred to American archaeologists such as Taylor, Willey and Phillips, Ford, Rouse and Gifford who were concerned with identifying cultural 'wholes' in which there was an ideational basis for the varying ways of human life within each cultural unit. Such archaeologists aimed at identifying the normative concepts in the minds of people now dead. Binford more specifically criticised the normative studies which tried to describe the diffusion and transmission of cultural traits. It is not my concern here to identify whether the normative paradigm, as characterised by Binford, ever existed. Certainly, as will be shown below, European archaeologists such as Childe were already able to integrate a concern with cultural norms and a notion of behavioural adaptability. But in Binford's view, the normative approach emphasising homogeneous cultural wholes contrasted with the study of functional variability within and between cultural units. The normative school was seen as historical and descriptive, not allowing explanation in terms of functional process. So he moved to an opposite extreme where culture, norms, form and design had only functional value in, for example, integrating and articulating individuals and social units into broader corporate entities. In fact Binford suggested that the different components of culture may function independently of each other. Functional relationships could thus be studied without reference to cultural context, and regular, stable and predictable relationships could be sought between variables within social systems. As a result, an absolute gulf was driven between normative and processual studies. 'An approach is offered in which culture is not reduced to normative ideas about the proper ways of doing things but is viewed as the system of the total extrasomatic means of adaptation' (Binford 1972, 205). More recently (1978a) Binford has still more clearly separated the study of norms from the study of process. He has attacked the historical and contextual emphasis of Kroeber and Kluckhorn (ibid., 2). On the one hand (ibid., 3), artifacts are the reflections of the mental templates of the makers and these ideas in the minds of people cannot adapt intelligently to new situations. On the other hand, cultural variability is simply the result of adaptive expedience. He could ask (ibid., 11) 'do people conduct their ongoing activities in terms of invariant mental templates as to the appropriate strategies regardless of the setting in which they find themselves?' Indeed, his Nunamiut ethnoarchaeology is introduced as an attempt to identify whether faunal remains could be studied as being 'culture-free'. Cultural bias can only be identified (ibid., 38) when an anomaly occurs; when the adaptively expedient expectations are not found.

The dichotomy set up between culture and function limits the development of archaeological theory because 'functional value is always relative to the given cultural scheme' (Sahlins 1976, 206). All actions take place within cultural frameworks and their functional value is assessed in terms of the concepts and orientations which surround them. That an item or institution is 'good for' achieving some end is partly a cultural choice, as is the end itself. At the beginning of this chapter Durkheim's definition of the function of a social institution as the correspondence between it and the needs of the social organism was described. But the needs of the society are preferred choices within a cultural matrix. It follows that function and adaptation are not absolute measures. All daily activities, from eating to the removal of refuse, are not the results of some absolute adaptive expedience. These various functions take place within a cultural framework, a set of ideas or norms, and we cannot adequately understand the various activities by denying any role to culture. An identical point is made by Deetz (1977) in his comparison of cultural traditions in two historical periods in North America.

The above discussion is particularly relevant to the functionalist view

97

of material items. As already noted, Binford assumes that culture is man's extrasomatic means of adaptation. According to David Clarke (1968, 85) 'culture is an information system, wherein the messages are accumulated survival information'. In this way material culture is seen as simply functioning at the interface between the human organism and the social and physical environment in order to allow adaptation. It has a utilitarian function (Sahlins 1976). The result of this view is that cultural remains are seen as *reflecting*, in a fairly straightforward way, what people *do*. Even work on deposition and post-depositional processes (Schiffer 1976), while adding complexity to the situation, still assumes that material culture is simply a direct, indirect or distorted reflection of man's activities. This is a continuation of earlier views of material culture as 'fossilised action'. As Fletcher (1977b, 51–2) has pointed out, material culture is seen simply as a passive object of functional use; a mere epiphenomenon of 'real' life. But there is more to culture than functions and activities. Behind functioning and doing there is a structure and content which has partly to be understood in its own terms, with its own logic and coherence. This applies as much to refuse distributions and 'the economy' as it does to burial, pot decoration and art.

Linked to the separation of function and culture has been the decreased emphasis on archaeology as an historical discipline. If material items and social institutions can be explained in terms of their adaptive efficiency, there is little concern to situate them within an historical framework. The evolutionary perspective has emphasised adaptive relationships at different levels of complexity, but it has not encouraged an examination of the particular historical context. However, it is suggested here that the cultural framework within which we act, and which we reproduce in our actions, is historically derived and that each culture is a particular historical product. The uniqueness of cultures and historical sequences must be recognised. Within the New Archaeology there has been a great concern with identifying variability. But in embracing a cross-cultural approach, variability has, in the above sense, been reduced to sameness. Diachronic sequences are split into phases in which the functioning of systems can be understood in synchronic terms as instances of some general relationship. The dichotomy between diachrony and synchrony is linked to the split between culture and history on the one hand and function and adaptation on the other. The resolution of the culture/function dichotomy which is sought in this book (Hodder 1982c) will also reintroduce historical explanation as a legitimate topic of concern in archaeology.

Another limitation of the functionalist perspective of the New Archaeology is the relationship between the individual and society. The functional view gives little emphasis to individual creativity and intentionality. Individual human beings become little more than the means to achieve the needs of society. The social system is organised into subsystems and roles which people fill. The roles and social categories function in relation to each other to allow the efficient equilibrium of the whole system. In fact, however, individuals are not simply instruments in some orchestrated game and it is difficult to see how subsystems and roles can have 'goals' of their own. Adequate explanations of social systems and social change must involve the individual's assessments and aims. This is not a question of identifying individuals (Hill and Gunn 1977) but of introducing the individual into social theory. Some New Archaeologists have recognised the importance of this. 'While the behaviour of the group, of many individual units, may often effectively be described in statistical terms without reference to the single unit, it cannot so easily be *explained* in this way. This is a problem which prehistoric archaeology has yet to resolve' (Renfrew 1972, 496). The lack of resolution is inherent in the functionalist emphasis in archaeology.

Further criticism of functionalist archaeology concerns the emphasis on cross-cultural generalisations. After an initial phase in which ethnoarchaeology was used largely to provide cautionary tales and 'spoilers' (Yellen 1977), the concern has been to provide cross-cultural statements of high predictive value. Because of the preferred hypothetico-deductive nature of explanation, it became important to identify rules of behaviour and artifact deposition which were used regardless of cultural context. As already noted, such an approach was feasible because the particular historical and cultural dimensions of activity were denied. Different subsystems were identified, such as subsistence, exchange, settlement, refuse disposal and burial, and cross-cultural regularities were sought. Since the role of cultural and historical factors was not examined, it was necessarily the case that the resulting generalisations either were limited to mechanical or physical aspects of life or were simplistic and with little content. Some aspects of human activity are constrained by deterministic variables. For example, it is difficult for humans to walk bare-footed on spreads of freshly knapped flint, or to work or sit in or near the smoke of fires (Binford 1978b; Gould 1980). Certain types of bone do hold more or less meat or marrow, and they fracture in different ways (Binford 1978a; Gifford 1978). The seeds sorted by wind during winnowing depend partly on wind velocity and seed density (Jones, pers. comm.). Smaller artifacts are more difficult for humans to hold and find than large artifacts and so the patterns of loss may differ (Schiffer 1976). Cross-cultural predictive laws or generalisations can be developed for these mechanical constraints on human behaviour, and ethnoarchaeology has been most successful in these spheres, but attempts to extend this approach to social and cultural behaviour have been severely criticised as is shown by the debate over the hypothesis put forward by Longacre (1970), Deetz (1968), and Hill (1970) (e.g. Allen and Richardson 1971; Stanislawski 1973), and the result has been the frustration implied by Flannery's (1973) characterisation of Mickey Mouse laws. As soon as any human choice is involved, behavioural and functional laws appear simplistic and inadequate because human behaviour is rarely entirely mechanistic. The role of ethnoarchaeology must also be to define the relevant cultural context for social and ecological behaviour.

Linked to the emphasis on cross-cultural functional laws is the idea of 'predicting the past' (Thomas 1974). The percentages of modern societies in which women make pots (Phillips 1971) or in which size of settlement is related to post-marital residence (Ember 1973) are difficult to use as measures of probability for the interpretation of the past because modern societies are not independent nor do they comprise a random or representative sample of social forms. More important, however, is the lack of identity between prediction and understanding. It is possible to predict many aspects of human behaviour with some accuracy but without any understanding of the causal relationships involved. Equally, a good understanding of a social event may not lead to an ability to predict the outcome of a similar set of circumstances. Levels of probability and statistical evidence of correlation are no substitute for an understanding of causal links and of the relevant context for human action. The use of mathematical and statistical formulae which provide good fits to archaeological data leads to little understanding of the past. My own involvement in spatial archaeology, a sphere in which statistical prediction has been most successful, has shown most clearly that prediction has little to do with explanation.

The embrace of the hypothetico-deductive method and prediction in relation to interpretation of the past has allowed the definition of independent levels of theory. A distinct 'middle-range theory' has been identified because it has been assumed that objective yardsticks or instruments of measurement can be obtained for the study of past systems and their archaeological residues (Binford 1978a, 45). We have general theories of social development and lower-level theories concerning the formation of the archaeological record. Similarly, Clarke (1973) suggested that pre-depositional, depositional, post-depositional, analytical and interpretive theories could be distinguished despite the existence of overall controlling models. This separation of levels or types of theory is partly possible because of a model of man which separates different functional activities and sets up predictive relationships between them. Thus, depositional theory can be separated from interpretive theory because artifact deposition is adaptively expedient and can be predicted without reference to wider social theories. The hypotheses concerning social institutions and social change are thought to be different in nature from the hypotheses concerning the relationship between society and material culture. But both material items and their deposition are actively involved in social relations and we cannot separate independent levels of theory. Frameworks of cultural meaning structure all aspects of archaeological information. Leone (1978) has shown most clearly how data, analyses and interpretations are inextricably linked. The different theoretical levels should be congruent, and beyond natural processes there can be no instruments of absolute measurement.

The aim of the New Archaeology was to show the rationality of institutions with respect to their environments. The main criticisms of this general approach as described above are as follows. (1) The dichotomy set up between cultural form and objective functional expedience is misleading, and material items are more than tools holding survival information. (2) The functionalist viewpoint is unable to explain cultural variety and uniqueness adequately. (3) Social systems become reified to such an extent that the individual contributes little. (4) The cross-cultural generalisations which have resulted from functionalist studies by archaeologists have been unable to identify valid statements about social and cultural behaviour because the relevant context is insufficiently explored. (5) Different levels or types of hypothesis have been identified, but in fact all hypotheses are and should be integrated within a coherent social and cultural theory. This volume seeks to respond to these criticisms by developing alternative approaches. I wish to begin by considering various definitions of 'structure'.

STRUCTURE AS SYSTEM, PATTERN AND STYLE

In the preceding discussion of functionalism, reference has been made to the adaptive utility of material items and institutions within social and cultural systems. Subsystems (pottery, settlement, social, economic, etc.) can be identified and discussed in cross-cultural perspective. Within each socio-cultural system a particular set of systemic relationships is produced in order to meet local needs at particular moments in time. In the analysis of such systems, the words 'system' and 'structure' are interchangeable. The system (or structure) is the particular set of relationships between the various components; it is the *way* the interrelationships are organised. Within New Archaeology, then, structure is the system of observable relations. Structure is the way things are done and it, like individual items and institutions, is explained as the result of adaptive expedience.

The functionalist view of structure is apparent in discussions of social organisation, social relations or social systems, none of which are distinguished from social structure. The term social structure is used by New Archaeologists to refer to bands, tribes, chiefdoms, states, as well as to reciprocal, redistributive and prestige transactions. Social structure is observed directly in burial and settlement patterns where the visible differentiation in associations and forms is seen as reflecting roles and activities organised in relation to each other. The structure of social relations as a whole is organised so as to allow adaptation to such factors as the distribution of environmental resources (uniform or localised), the availability of prestige items or valued commodities, and the relationships with neighbouring social groups.

In such systemic studies the close relationship between the terms 'structure' and 'pattern' is apparent. In identifying social and economic structures various patterns are analysed. These patterns include the distributions of settlements of different sizes and functions across the landscape, the distributions of artifacts and buildings in settlements, the distributions of resources, the distributions of artifacts among graves in cemeteries, the regional distributions of exchanged items and the regional distributions of artifacts in interaction or information exchange spheres or 'cultures'. These various patterns are 'objective' and are immediately susceptible to statistical manipulation, quantification and computerisation. The concern with pattern allows the legitimate use of a wide range of scientific software, including numerical taxonomy and spatial analysis.

The identification of pattern and the implementation of 'analytical archaeology' is extended to studies of arrangements of attributes on individual artifacts, where 'pattern' is often equivalent to 'style'. The analysis of pottery and metal decoration, and of the form of artifacts, leads to the definition of 'types' based on the association of attributes. Artifact styles are interpreted as having utilitarian or non-utilitarian functions; they are technomic, sociotechnic or ideotechnic (Binford 1972). Style is involved in the support of group solidarity (Hodder 1979) and the passing on of information (Wobst 1977).

In functionalist archaeology, structure is examined as system, organisation, distribution, pattern, or style. It is produced by people attempting to adapt to their environments. Like any artifact, structure is a tool for coping. If culture is a tool acting between people and the environment, and if the term 'culture' describes the particular adaptive organisation produced in each environmental context, then structure is also similar to culture. A culture is seen as the way material bits and pieces are assembled and associated in a geographical area in order to allow human adaptation.

STRUCTURE AS CODE

In this chapter I wish to distinguish between system and structure (Giddens 1979), by defining structure not as system, pattern or style, but as the codes and rules according to which observed systems of interrelations are produced. Several archaeological studies have made a contribution to the analysis of structure as code, and some examples are discussed here.

Within studies of Palaeolithic cave art, Leroi-Gourhan (1965) has made specific interpretations of signs as male or female and has suggested various codes for the combination and relative placing of the signs within the caves. Marshak (1977) identified specific interpretations of symbols as dangerous and he related the structure associated with the meander in cave art to the general flow and participation in daily life. Conkey (1977) identified general aspects of the rules of organisation of Upper Palaeolithic art, such as 'the non-differentiation of units', and did not attempt to provide a specific meaning in terms of social organisation. All these analyses were concerned to identify codes or rules, but the nature of the interpretation of these structures and of their relationship to social structures varied.

Studies of later artifact and pottery design have often tended towards a still more formal emphasis in that little attention is paid to the social context in which structures are produced. The linguistic model has been developed most fully by Muller (1977) in his analysis of the grammatical rules of design. His work, and Washburn's (1978) definition of different types of symmetry, do not result in any attempt at translating cultural meaning and symbolism. Rather, Washburn uses symmetry simply as an additional trait for the discovery of population group composition and interaction spheres. Such analyses can be, and have been, carried out without any major change in functionalist theories of society.

Some of the work on the identification of settlement structures has also involved little criticism of the New Archaeology. Clarke's (1972, 828 and 837) identification of structural transformations (bilateral symmetry relating to male/female) in the Iron Age Glastonbury settlement appears as a peripheral component of a systems analysis. A clear link is made between the generative principles of the settlement design and the social system. Isbell's (1976) recognition of the 3000-year continuity in settlement structure in the South American Andes, despite major discontinuities in social and economic systems, raises more fundamental problems for systemic studies since structure is seen to continue and lie behind adaptive change. Fritz's (1978) interesting account of prehistoric Chaco Canyon in northwestern New Mexico shows that the organisation of houses, towns, and regional settlement can be seen as transforms of the same underlying principle in which west is symmetrical to east, but north is asymmetrical to south. This study is concerned to link the organisation of social systems to underlying structures. The structuralist analysis of a Neolithic cemetery by Van de Velde (1980) has related aims. Fletcher's (1977a) work on the spacing between 'entities' – posts, walls, door posts, pots and hearths – in settlements is concerned less with social strategies and more with ordering principles which carry long-term adaptive value. Hillier *et al.* (1976) have identified a purely formal logic for the description of all types of arrangement of buildings and spaces within settlements.

The above examples are drawn from prehistoric archaeology but structural studies have an important place in historical archaeology (Frankfort 1951; Deetz 1967; Glassie 1975; Ferguson 1977; Leone 1977). While many of the prehistoric and historic archaeology studies explain structure in terms of social functions and adaptive values, they also introduce the notion that there is more to culture than observable relationships and functional utility. There is also a set of rules, a code, which, like the rules in a game of chess, is followed in the pursuit of survival, adaptation and socio-economic strategy. In an ethnographic analysis of the Nuba in Sudan, it has been shown that all aspects of material culture patterning (burial, settlement, artifact styles) must be understood as being produced according to sets of rules concerned with purity, boundedness and categorisation (Hodder, 1982a). Individuals organise their experience according to sets of rules. Communication and understanding of the world result from the use of a common language – that is, a set of rules which identify both the way symbols should be organised into sets, and the meaning of individual symbols in contrast to others. Material culture can be examined as a structured set of differences. This structured symbolising behaviour has functional utility, and it must be understood in those terms. But it also has a logic of its own which is not directly observable as pattern or style. The structure must be interpreted as having existed partly independently of the observable data, having generated and produced those data.

The concern with material culture as the product of human categorisation processes is described by Miller (1982). It is sufficient to emphasise here that the various structuralist analyses of codes can be clearly distinguished from functionalist studies of systems. Both structuralists and functionalists are concerned with relationships and with the way things and institutions are organised. In other words, both are concerned with 'structure' if that word is defined in a very general way. But there is a difference in that the logic analysed by functionalists is the visible social system (the social relations) which exists separately from the perceptions of people. For Leach (1973b; 1977; 1978), structure is an ideal order in the mind. For Lévi-Strauss (1968), it is an internal logic, not directly visible, which is the underlying order by which the apparent order must be explained. But for Lévi-Strauss, the structure often appears to lie outside the human mind (Godelier 1977). Structuralists, including Leach and Lévi-Strauss, claim that adequate explanation of observed patterns must make reference to underlying codes.

CRITICISMS OF STRUCTURALISM

The problems and limitations of the different types of structuralism are discussed by, for example, Giddens (1979), and in this chapter only those criticisms will be examined which are particularly relevant to the themes to be debated in this book (Hodder, 1982c). A major problem concerns the lack of a theory of practice (Bourdieu 1977). The structuralism of Saussure, which uses a linguistic model, separates *langue* as a closed series of formal rules, a structured set of differences, from semantic and referential ties. The formal set of relationships is distinct from the practice of use. Similarly, Lévi-Strauss identifies a series of unconscious mental structures which are separated from practice and from the ability of social actors to reflect consciously on their ideas and create new rules. In both linguistic and structural analyses it is unclear how the interpretation and use of rules might lead to change. How an individual can be a competent social actor is not clearly specified. As in functionalism, form and practical function are separated.

The failure within structuralism and within structuralist analyses in archaeology to develop a theory of practice (concerning the generation of structures in social action) has encouraged the view within functionalist archaeology that structuralism can only contribute to the study of norms and ideas which are epiphenomenal. The gulf between normative and processual archaeology has been widened since, on the one hand, structuralist approaches could be seen as relating to ideas divorced from adaptive processes while, on the other hand, it was thought by processualists that social change could be examined adequately without reference to the structure of ideas. Some of the structuralist studies identified above, such as those by Muller and Washburn, make little attempt to understand the referential context. The notion of a 'mental template' can be criticised in a similar vein because it envisages an abstract set of ideas or pictures without examining the framework of referential meaning within which the ideas take their form. In other, more integrated studies, such as those by Fritz and Marshak, the social and ecological contexts of the structures identified are examined, but the link between form and practice is insecure and no relevant theory is developed. On the other hand, work such as that of Flannery and Marcus (1976), which fits better into the functionalist mould, relates all form to function and structural analysis is limited. Few archaeological studies have managed to provide convincing accounts of the relationship between structure as code and social and ecological organisation.

Other limitations of structuralism can be related to the above. As in functionalism, the role of the individual is slight. In functionalism the individual is subordinate to the imperatives of social co-ordination. In the structuralism of Lévi-Strauss the individual is subordinate to the organising mechanisms of the unconscious. The notion of a 'norm' in traditional archaeology implies a structured set of cultural rules within which the individual plays little part.

The dichotomy between synchrony and diachrony, statics and dynamics, exists in structuralism as it does in functionalism. Structural analyses can incorporate time as a dimension for the setting up of formal differences, but the role of historical explanation is seen to be slight in the work of Lévi-Strauss, and there is little attempt to understand how structural rules can be changed. Structures often appear as static constraints on societies, preventing change. Structuralism does not have an adequate notion of the *generation* of change.

While the main concern of reactions to structuralism is to develop an adequate theory of practice (Piaget 1971; 1972; Bourdieu 1977; Giddens 1979), other criticisms have concentrated on the methods of analysis. Structures, because they are organising principles, are not observable as such, and this is true whether we are talking about anthropology, psychology or archaeology. They can only be reached by reflective abstraction. Thus, structures of particular kinds could be said to emerge because the analyst is looking for them, trying to fit the data into some expected and hypothetical structural pattern. But how can such hypotheses ever be falsified (Pettit 1975, 88)? For structuralism to be a worthwhile pursuit, it must be possible to disprove a weak hypothesis. However, Pettit feels that rejection of structuralist hypotheses is impossible, at least in regard to myths, for a number of reasons (ibid., 88–92). For example, the initial hypothesis in structuralist analysis often is necessarily vague so that the analyst can give himself room to shift the hypothesis to accommodate the new transformations. Also, because there are few rules on the way in which structures are transformed into different realities, one can make up the rules as one goes along. By using sufficient ingenuity, any two patterns can probably be presented as transformations of each other.

Thus the structural method of Lévi-Strauss 'is hardly more than a licence for the free exercise of imagination in establishing associations' (ibid., 96). There is certainly a danger that archaeologists may be able to select arbitrary aspects of their data and suggest a whole series of unverifiable transformations. These criticisms are discussed in detail by Wylie (1982). Here I wish to note that Pettit's attack is directed at those formal and structural analyses which take little account of the referential context of social action. Within a structuralism in which a theory of practice has been developed, Pettit's criticisms have less force because the structural transformations must 'make sense' as part of a changing and operating system. Abstract formal analysis must be shown to be relevant to a particular social and historical context, and it must lead to an understanding of the generation of new actions and structures through time.

All the above criticisms of structuralism have concerned the need to examine the generation of structures within meaningful, active and changing contexts. The criticisms of both functionalism and structuralism centre on the inability of the approaches to explain particular

historical contexts and the meaningful actions of individuals constructing social change within those contexts. Archaeology in particular has
moved away from historical explanation and has tried to identify cross-
cultural universals concerning either the functioning of ecological systems or (rarely) the human unconscious. There is a need to develop a
contextual archaeology which resolves the dichotomy evident in functionalism and structuralism between cultural norm and societal adaptation.

ARCHAEOLOGY AS A CULTURAL SCIENCE

The approaches developed by the majority of the authors in this volume (Hodder 1982c) are not structuralist in that they take account of
the criticisms of the work of, for example, Leach and Lévi-Strauss,
made by various 'post-structuralist' writers (Ardener 1978; Harstrup
1978). Yet the insights offered by structuralism must be retained in any
adequate analysis of social processes, and it is for this reason that I
have not deleted the term structuralism from the papers in this book
(e.g. Wylie (1982); see also the term 'dialectical structuralism' used by
Tilley (1982)). Even if structuralism as a whole is generally rejected, the
analysis of structure has a potential which has not been exhausted in
archaeology.

Structural analyses involve a series of approaches described by Miller
(1982). Important concepts which can be retained from structuralism
include syntagm and paradigm. Syntagm refers to rules of combination,
and to 'sets' of items and symbols. In burial studies it may be noted, for
example, that particular 'costumes' can be identified which are associated with particular sub-groups within society. The rules of combination
describe the way in which items or classes of item (e.g. weapons) placed
on one part of the body are associated with other classes of item on other
parts of the body. Similarly, sets of items may be found to occur in
settlements. Syntagmatic studies can also be applied to the combination
of attributes on artifacts, and Hodder (1982d) describes rules for the
generation of Dutch Neolithic pottery decoration. Paradigm refers to
series of alternatives or differences. For example, in the burial study, a
brooch of type *A* may be found worn on the shoulder in contrast to a pin
or a brooch of type *B* placed in the same position on other skeletons.
Each alternative may be associated with a different symbolic meaning.

But in all such structural analyses the particular symbol used must not
be seen as arbitrary. 'High structuralist' analyses are directed towards
examinations of abstract codes, and the content or substance of the
symbol itself often appears arbitrary. However, the symbol is not arbitrary, as is seen by, for example, the placing of a symbol such as a
crown, associated with royalty, on the label of a bottle of beer in order to
increase sales. The crown is not chosen arbitrarily in a structured set of

differences. Rather, it is chosen as a powerful symbol with particular evocations and connotations which make its use appropriate within the social and economic context of selling beer in England. The content of the sign affects the structure of its use. Barth (1975) has demonstrated elegantly that material symbolisation cannot be described simply as sets of categories and transformations, however cross-cutting and complex one might allow these to be. Culture is to be studied as meaningfully constituting – as the framework through which adaptation occurs – but the meaning of an object resides not merely in its contrast to others within a set. Meaning also derives from the associations and use of an object, which itself becomes, through the associations, the node of a network of references and implications. There is an interplay between structure and content.

The emphasis on the symbolic associations of things themselves is not only a departure from purely formal and structuralist analyses. It also breaks with other approaches in archaeology. In processual analyses of symbol systems, the artifact itself is rarely given much importance. An object may be described as symbolising status, male or female, or social solidarity, but the use of the particular artifact class, and the choice of the symbol itself, are not adequately discussed. Similarly, traditional archaeologists use types as indicators of contact, cultural affiliation and diffusion, but the question of which type is used for which purpose is not pursued. The symbol is seen as being arbitrary. In this book (Hodder 1982c) an attempt is made by some of the authors to assess why particular symbols were used in a particular context. For example, the shape of Neolithic burial mounds is seen as having been appropriate because the shape itself referred back to earlier houses, and such references and evocations had social advantage in the context in which the tombs were built (Hodder 1982d).

The structural and symbolic emphases lead to an awareness of the importance of 'context' in interpretations of the use of material items in social processes. The generative structures and the symbolic associations have a particular meaning in each cultural context and within each set of activities within that context. Although generative principles such as pure/impure, or the relations between parts of the human body (see Shanks and Tilley 1982), may occur widely, they may be combined in ways peculiar to each cultural milieu, and be given specific meanings and associations. The transformation of structures and symbols between different contexts can have great 'power'. For example, it has been noted elsewhere (Hodder and Lane 1982) that Neolithic stone axes in Britain and Brittany frequently occur in ritual and burial contexts, engraved on walls, as miniatures or as soft chalk copies. The participation of these axes in secular exchanges would evoke the ritual contexts and could be used to legitimate any social dominance based on privileged access to these items. In a study of the Neolithic in Orkney (Hodder 1982a) it has been suggested that the similarities between the spatial structures in burial, non-burial ritual, and domestic settlement contexts were used within social strategies to legitimise emerging elites.

So far, it has been suggested that material items come to have symbolic meanings as a result both of their use in structured sets and of the associations and implications of the objects themselves, but that the meanings vary with context. It is through these various mechanisms that material items and the constructed world come to represent society. But what is the nature of representation in human culture? In particular, how should social relations be translated into material symbols? For New Archaeologists these questions are relatively unproblematic since artifacts (whether utilitarian, social or ideological) are simply tools for adaptive efficiency. Symbols are organised so as to maximise information flow and there is no concept in such analyses of the *relativity of representation*. It is in studies of representation that concepts of ideology play a central role, and although there is considerable divergence of views within this book (Hodder 1982c) on the definition and nature of ideology, it is at least clear that the way in which structured sets of symbols are used in relation to social strategies depends on a series of concepts and attitudes that are historically and contextually appropriate. I have demonstrated elsewhere (Hodder 1982b), for example, that social ranking may be represented in burial ritual either through a 'naturalising' ideology in which the arbitrary social system is represented as occurring in the material world, or through an ideology in which social dominance is denied and eradicated in artifacts and in the organisation of ritual. This example demonstrates two extremes in the representation and misrepresentation of social relations, but it serves to indicate that all material patterning is generated by symbolic structures within a cultural matrix.

Burial pattern, then, is not a direct behavioural reflection of social pattern. It is structured through symbolically meaningful codes which can be manipulated in social strategies. Archaeologists must accept that death and attitudes to the dead form a symbolic arena of great emotive force which is employed in life. Similar arguments can be made in relation to other activities in which material culture is involved (Hodder 1982a). Throwing away refuse and the organisation of dirt are used in all societies as parts of social actions (see, for example, the use by Hippies of dirt and disorder in the 1960s and 1970s in western Europe and North America). Equally, the preparation of food, cooking and eating have great symbolic significance in forming, masking or transforming aspects of social relations. Pottery shapes and decoration can be used to mark out, separate off or conceal the social categories and relationships played out in the context of food preparation, storage and consumption. There is no direct link between social and ceramic variability. Attitudes to food and the artifacts used in eating activities play a central role in the construction of social categories (as is seen, for example, in the use by Hippies and Punks of natural 'health' and unnatural 'plastic' foods in contemporary western Europe). Similar hypotheses can be developed for the wearing of ornaments on the body, the organisation of the production of pottery and metal items, and the organisation of space within settlements and houses. Before archaeology can contribute to the social sciences, it must develop as a cultural science. The concern must be to examine the role of material culture in the ideological representation of social relations. Excavated artifacts are immediately cultural, not social, and they can inform on society only through an adequate understanding of cultural context.

Material symbolisation is not a passive process, because objects and activities actively represent and act back upon society. Within a particular ideology, the constructed world can be used to legitimise the social order. Equally, material symbols can be used covertly to disrupt established relations of dominance (see Braithwaite 1982). Each use of an artifact, through its previous associations and usage, has a significance and meaning within society so that the artifact is an active force in social change. The daily use of material items within different contexts recreates from moment to moment the framework of meaning within which people act. The individual's actions in the material world reproduce the structure of society, but there is a continual potential for change. The 'power' of material symbols in social action derives not only from the transformation of structures between different contexts or from the associations evoked by particular items or forms. It resides also in the ambiguous meanings of material items. Unlike spoken language, the meanings of material symbols can remain undiscussed and implicit. Their meanings can be reinterpreted and manipulated covertly. The multiple meanings at different levels and the 'fuzziness' (Miller 1982) of material symbols can be interpreted in different ways by different interest groups and there is a continuing process of change and renegotiation. It is essential to see material symbols as not only 'good to think', but also 'good to act'. Artifacts, the organisation of space and ritual are embedded in a 'means-to-end' context. The effects of symbols, intended and unintended, must be associated with their repeated use and with the 'structuration' of society. Symbolic and structural principles are used to form social actions, and they are in turn reproduced, reinterpreted and changed as a result of those actions.

The dichotomy between normative and processual archaeology is thus by-passed by the notion that symbolic structures are in a continual state of reinterpretation and change in relation to the practices of daily life. Because of the emphases on context and on the continual process of change which is implicated in material practices and symbolisation, archaeological enquiry is of an historical nature. Artifacts and their organisation come to have specific cultural meanings as a result of their use in particular historical contexts. The examples of the crown and the Neolithic barrows have been provided above. The enquiry is also historical because the intended and unintended consequences of action affect further action. They form a setting within which future actors must play.

The approaches explored in this book (Hodder 1982c) are neither idealist nor materialist. They attempt to bridge the gap between these extremes. On the one hand, it is hoped that the major criticisms of structuralism, as outlined above, are avoided. The aim is not to identify cognitive universals. It is not intended to encourage the notion that material items are simply reflections of categories of the mind, or to develop abstract linguistic analyses of material symbolism. Archaeology is seen as an historical discipline concerned with the active integration of cultural items in daily practices. Structures are identified in relation to meaning, practices and change. Verification is aided by the use of models concerning the ways in which structures are integrated in action. The models identify the components which make up cultural contexts. They suggest relevant causal relationships within adaptive systems.

On the other hand, attempts are made to answer the various criticisms of functionalism described earlier in this chapter. It is clear that the approaches outlined here can be described as extensions of the New Archaeology in that there is a continued concern with social processes and with the use of material items in those processes. Since processual studies in archaeology have been so closely linked to functionalism it is necessary to indicate that the suggestions made here can avoid the various criticisms of that school. A significant development is that the culture/function and statics/dynamics dichotomies are denied since meaning and ideology are inextricably tied to daily practices. In addition attempts are made to locate the individual as an active component in social change, since the interests of individuals differ and it is in the interplay between different goals and aims that the rules of the society are penetrated, reinterpreted and reformed. The cross-cultural generalisations which are to be developed are concerned less with statistical levels of association in summary files of modern societies and more with careful considerations of relevant cultural contexts. Finally, all aspects of archaeological endeavour become infused with the same social and cultural theories, the same models of man. Theories concerning the relationship between material residues and the non-material world are placed within overall theories of society and social change.

THE HISTORICAL CONTEXT OF A SYMBOLIC AND STRUCTURAL ARCHAEOLOGY

While the ideas put forward here can be seen to provide an extension of the New Archaeology, an asking of additional questions, it would be misleading to claim that the aims of a contextual or cultural approach are altogether new. The views are reactionary in the sense that they have certain similarities to the attitudes of an older generation of British prehistorians. Writers such as Childe, Clark, Daniel and Piggott placed a similar emphasis on archaeology as an historical discipline, they eschewed cross-cultural laws, and they saw material items as being structured by more than functional necessities. They saw artifacts as expressions of culturally framed ideas and they were concerned primarily with the nature of culture and cultural contexts.

Many traditional archaeologists acknowledged that artifacts were ultimately expressions of ideas specific to each cultural and historical context. These archaeologists were 'normative' in the sense described by Binford. But British prehistorians often found it difficult to apply their aims in practice since the ideational realm was seen as being unrelated to the practical necessities of life. Daniel (1962, 129) asserted that, although prehistory used scientific methods, it was a humanity (an art or human science) partly because it was concerned with man as a cultured animal, with a transmittable body of ideas, customs, beliefs and practices dependent on the main agent of transmission, language. Thus artifacts such as Acheulian handaxes 'are cultural fossils and the product of the human mind and human craftsmanship' (ibid., 30). On the other hand, archaeologists have access only to the 'cutlery and chinaware of a society' (ibid., 132), not to its ideals, morals and religion. Since 'there is no coincidence between the material and non-material aspects of culture' (ibid., 134–5), prehistorians cannot speak of social organisation or religion. It is this belief in the lack of integration between the different aspects of society and culture which prevented a development of the humanistic aims that Daniel had set up. There was no theory according to which the structure and cultural form of all actions within each context could be considered.

Similar problems were accepted by many British archaeologists. Piggott (1959, 6–11) agreed with Hawkes (1954) that it was difficult for archaeologists to find out about past language, beliefs, social systems and religion. He used megalithic burial in western Europe as an example of the limitations of archaeological data (Piggott 1959, 93–5). An archaeologist can reconstruct the ritual such as successive burials, making fires at entrances to the tombs, the offerings of complete or broken pots placed outside the tomb, the exposure of the corpse before interment, the moving aside of old bones. But having reconstructed the ritual, noted its distribution, and suggested that the dispersal could indicate a common religion, 'it is at this point that we have to stop' (ibid., 95). While it is certainly true that the detailed beliefs connected with the ritual are unlikely to be recoverable archaeologically, it is not the case that no further inference can be made about the place of the described megalithic ritual in Neolithic society. The chapters by Shanks and Tilley, Shennan and Hodder in the last part of this volume (Hodder 1982c) use generalisations from ethnographic and anthropological studies to link Neolithic megalithic ritual into other aspects of archaeological evidence. Piggott was prevented from following his historical and humanistic aims by a lack of theory linking idea to action.

The difficulties encountered by Hawkes, Piggott and Daniel in their pursuit of an historical and humanistic discipline concerned with culture and ideas resulted from a lack of theory concerning the links between different aspects of life – the technological, economic, social and ideological rungs of Hawkes' (1954) ladder. Grahame Clark and Gordon Childe had similar aims, but also employed theories concerning the relationships between the different subsystems. Their work could less easily, I think, be described as 'normative' in Binford's sense.

By 1939 Clark was already employing an organic analogy for society which has continued into his more recent writings. In 1975 material items were described as parts of organic wholes adjusting within an environment. Every aspect of archaeological data 'forms part of a working system of which each component stands in some relationship, usually reciprocal, to every other' (Clark 1975, 4). Man and his society could be seen as the products of natural selection in relation to the natural environment. But this ecological and functional stance has, throughout Clark's writings, been coupled, sometimes uncomfortably, with an awareness of the importance of cultural value within historical contexts. He was at pains to emphasise that the economic organisation of prehistoric communities was not conditioned by, but was adjusted to available resources, and could not be understood outside the social and 'psychic' context (1975). 'Most biological functions – such as eating, sheltering, pairing and breeding, fighting and dying – are performed in idioms acquired by belonging to historically and locally defined cultural groups . . . whose patterns of behaviour are conditioned by particular sets of values' (ibid., 5). Clark's greater willingness to discuss social and 'psychic' aspects of archaeological data is consonant with, but also contradicts, his use of a functional theory. Unlike Daniel, for example, he saw the material and non-material worlds as functionally related. On the other hand, it was difficult to see how a generalising and functionalist approach could be used to interpret specific historical contexts and cultural values.

Clark, like Daniel and Piggott, accepted that artifacts were not only tools of man, extensions of his limbs, 'they were also projections of his mind and embodiments of his history' (ibid., 9). Gordon Childe was prone to make similar statements. Also, and again like Clark, he began with a functionalist view of the relationship between ideas and economies. But during his life he questioned whether an anthropological functionalist approach based on general laws of adaptation could be used to explain particular historical sequences.

In the 1920s, Childe had already espoused the view that culture was an adaptation to an environment. By 1935 and 1936 he could state clearly that culture could be studied as a functioning organism with material culture enabling communities to survive. Material innovations increased population size and so aided selection of successful communities. Magic, ideas and religion could be assessed in terms of their adaptive value (1936). But Childe also criticised natural and organic models, and he acknowledged the importance of cultural styles and values. In his earliest work particular patterns of behaviour were seen simply as innate characteristics of specific peoples. Thus in Germany there had been a 'virile' Stone Age, European cultures had 'vigour and genius', and 'stagnant' megalithic cultures were not European (Trigger 1980, 51).

But in *Man Makes Himself* (1936) Childe began to give more careful consideration to the structure of ideas and its relationship to social action. He noted (ibid., 238) that the achievements of societies are not automatic responses to environments, and that adjustments are made by specific societies as a result of their own distinctive histories. The social traditions and rules, shaped by the community's history, determine the general behaviour of the society's members. But these traditions can themselves be changed as men meet new circumstances. 'Tradition makes the man, by circumscribing his behaviour within certain bounds; but it is equally true that man makes his traditions' so that man makes himself. Yet at times in *Man Makes Himself* ideas act only as a constraint on social change. A functional/non-functional dichotomy is set up and ideas do not take a full part in the practice of economic and social actions.

In later writings Childe further resolved some of the contraditions between an ecological functionalist stance and a concern with the form and content of cultural traditions. In *Social Worlds of Knowledge* (1949) he emphasised that different conceptions of the world framed archaeological evidence in different terms. He began by saying that the meaning that is given to the outside world, and one's perception of it, is socially and culturally determined. The environment of man is not the same as the environment of animals since it is perceived through a system of conventional symbols (ibid., 7). Man acts in a world of ideas (ibid., 7) collectively built up over thousands of years and which helps to direct the individual's experience (ibid., 8). If the environment of man can only be understood by reference to his mind, so too must past 'laws' of logic and mathematics be studied as part of culturally variable worlds of knowledge. Geometrical pattern in space and concepts of space vary in different societies, and 'any society may be allowed its own logic' (ibid., 18).

Even basic distinctions between mind and matter, society and nature, subject and object were seen by Childe as having varied through time. In Neolithic Europe these distinctions were not made. For example, the ritual burial of animals and the use of miniature axes and amulets were seen as suggesting mental attitudes which did not separate society and nature, practice and ritual (ibid., 20). The conceptual separation of man from nature was envisaged (ibid., 20) as being first apparent in the writings of Egyptian, Sumerian, and Babylonian clerks. But nature was still personal; it was an I–thou not an I–it relationship. Social relations were projected onto nature. It was only with the arrival of the machine age that causality could become fully depersonalised and mechanistic; our own distinctions and views are part of this latest stage.

Thus, 'environments to which societies are adjusted are worlds of ideas, collective representations that differ not only in extent and content, but also in structure' (ibid., 22). While it could be claimed that Childe never developed these various components of a general theory so that they could be used successfully in archaeology, and while he never developed structural analyses, never gave the individual sufficient place in social theory and never gave an adequate account of the recursive relationship between norm and practice, he did, more than any other archaeologist, recognise the contextual nature of social action and material culture patterning. He tried to develop a non-functionalist conception of man and his culture by emphasising the relative nature of functional value and by concerning himself with historical contexts. 'Whether Childe saw beyond the New Archaeology or mere mirages in the Promised Land remains to be determined' (Trigger 1980, 182). While there are clear differences between the work of Childe and the viewpoints put forward in this volume (Hodder 1982c), the papers do develop many of the themes he espoused.

Whatever the other differences between traditional British prehistorians, all claimed archaeology as an historical discipline. 'Archaeology is in fact a branch of historical study' (Piggott 1959, 1). 'Prehistory is . . . fundamentally historical in the sense that it deals with time as a main dimension' (Clark 1939, 26). In both these quotations archaeology is referred to as historical simply because it is concerned with the past. Daniel, however, gave additional reasons why prehistory should be viewed as part of history (1962, 131). Prehistory suffers from all the problems found in historical method – the difficulty of evaluating evidence, the inability of writing without some form of bias, and the changing views of the past as the ideas and preconceptions of prehistorians alter.

But the term 'historical' can be used to refer to more than the study of the past or the subjective assessment of documents. Prehistoric archaeology and history are idiographic studies which provide material for generalisations about man (Radcliffe-Brown 1952). Historical explanation describes an institution in a society as the end result of a sequence of events forming a causal chain. Of course, generalisations are used in this type of explanation, but the particular and novel structure of the cultural context is emphasised (Trigger 1980). Within such a viewpoint there is no absolute dependence on cross-cultural generalisations and laws, and Childe did not see archaeological inference as a deductive process.

Childe was wary of the use of cross-cultural laws and he rarely referred to ethnographic generalisations. Daniel (1962, 134) also doubted the possibility of identifying immutable laws concerning man, his culture and society and he denied the deterministic use of ethnographic data. Indeed the only traditional British prehistorian who has frequently used ethnographic data, Grahame Clark, is the one scholar who has accepted most readily the functionalist stance and has referred to cross-cultural laws of adaptation and selection.

If archaeology was to be accepted as being concerned with historical explanation, the viewpoint of most traditional archaeologists that cross-cultural ethnographic correlations should be used with caution was correct. But ethnographic analogies could be used if the relevant context for the comparison could be specified. Childe did use ethnographic analogies when he though that the total context was comparable (Trigger 1980, 66) and in his later writings he emphasised the importance of close links between archaeology and ethnography. But the general paucity of detailed studies of particular ethnographic contexts severely hampered the development of historical explanation by traditional prehistoric archaeologists. There were few analogies and little general theory concerning the use of material symbols in social action and within different ideologies. It will be possible to reuse the traditional definition of archaeology and prehistory as history if contextual ethno-archaeology continues to expand and if a general theory of practice is further developed. The use of analogies associated with an emphasis on a general understanding of the nature of the links between structure, symbolism and action allows the idiographic aspect of historical explanation to be retained, in line with the viewpoints of traditional archaeologists, without accepting the existence of immutable behavioural, ecological or functional laws.

There is some evidence that the contextual and cultural archaeology proposed here and some traditional British prehistorians have a common direction, as least in comparison with the deterministic functional laws and positivism of much of the New Archaeology. But traditional prehistorians such as Childe found difficulty in pursuing their aims, partly because the careful collection of large amounts of primary archaeological data and the resolution of chronological issues had only just begun. But their work was also hampered by the lack of an adequate theory of social practice wherein the role of material culture in the relation between structure, belief and action could be described. In pulling archaeology 'back into line', it is necessary greatly to expand, alter and develop the earlier approaches.

CONCLUSION

The theory discussed in this chapter is reactionary in that it accepts that culture is not man's extrasomatic means of adaptation but that it is meaningfully constituted. A contextual or cultural archaeology is also reactionary in that it sees archaeology as an historical discipline. Man's actions and his intelligent adaptation must be understood as historically and contextually specific, and the uniqueness of cultural forms must be explained. It is only by accepting the historical and cultural nature of their data that archaeologists can contribute positively to anthropology, the generalising study of man. The papers in this volume (Hodder 1982c) also react against the rigid logico-deductive method that has become characteristic of much New Archaeology. Explanation is here not equated solely with the discovery of predictable law-like relationships but with the interpretation of generative principles and their co-ordination within relevant cultural contexts.

In this chapter I have attempted to demonstrate that archaeology could profitably explore the notion that the severe and absolute rejection by some New Archaeologists of many traditional emphases hampered the development of a mature discipline. In particular, the dichotomies set up by Binford and various of his associates between culture and function, norm and adaptation, history and process, altogether impeded an adequate understanding of the very aim of their enquiry – social and economic adaptation and change. I have tried to show that the New Archaeology can be extended by a reconsideration of the issues outlined by traditional and historical archaeologists, and that culture, ideology and structure must be examined as central concerns.

REFERENCES

Allen, W. L. and Richardson J. B. (1971) 'The reconstruction of kinship from archaeological data: the concepts, the method, and the feasibility', *American Antiquity* 36: 41–53.

Ardener, E. (1978) 'Some outstanding problems in the analysis of events', in E. Schwimmer (ed.) *The Yearbook of Symbolic Anthropology* 1, London: Hurst.

Barth, F. (1975) *Ritual and Knowledge among the Baktaman of New Guinea*, Oslo: Universitetsforlaget.

Binford, L. R. (1965) 'Archaeological systematics and the study of cultural process', *American Antiquity* 31: 203–10.

—— (1972) *An Archaeological Perspective*, New York: Seminar Press.

—— (1977) 'General introduction', in L. R. Binford (ed.) *For Theory Building in Archaeology*, New York: Academic Press.

—— (1978a) *Nunamiut Ethnoarchaeology*, New York: Academic Press.

—— (1978b) 'Dimensional analysis of behaviour and site structure: learning from an Eskimo hunting stand', *American Antiquity* 43: 330–61.

Bourdieu, P. (1977) *Outline of a Theory of Practice*, Cambridge: Cambridge University Press.

Braithwaite, M. (1982) 'Decoration as ritual symbol: a theoretical proposal and an ethnographic study in southern Sudan', in I. Hodder (ed.) *Symbolic and Structural Archaeology*, Cambridge: Cambridge University Press.

Carneiro, R. (1968) 'Cultural adaptation', in D. Sells (ed.) *International Encyclopaedia of the Social Sciences* 3: 551–4.

Childe, V. G. (1935) 'Changing aims and methods in prehistory', *Proceedings of the Prehistoric Society* 1: 1–15.

—— (1936) *Man Makes Himself*, London: Collins.

—— (1949) *Social Worlds of Knowledge*, Oxford: Oxford University Press.

Clark, J. G. D. (1939) *Archaeology and Society*, London: Methuen.

—— (1975) *The Earlier Stone Age Settlement of Scandinavia*, Cambridge: Cambridge University Press.

Clarke, D. L. (1968) *Analytical Archaeology*, London: Methuen.

—— (1972) 'A provisional model of an Iron Age society and its settlement system', in D. L. Clarke (ed.) *Models in Archaeology*, London: Methuen.

—— (1973) 'Archaeology: the loss of innocence', *Antiquity* 47: 6–18.

Conkey, M. (1977) 'Context, structure and efficacy in Palaeolithic art and design', Paper presented at the Burg Wartenstein Symposium, 74.

Daniel, G. E. (1962) *The Idea of Prehistory*, Harmondsworth: Penguin.

Deetz, J. (1967) *Invitation to Archaeology*, New York: Natural History Press.

—— (1968) 'The inference of residence and descent rules from archaeological data', in S. R. Binford and L. R. Binford (eds) *New Perspectives in Archaeology*, Chicago: Aldine.

—— (1977) *In Small Things Forgotten*, New York: Anchor Books.

Doran, J. (1970) 'Systems theory, computer simulations and archaeology', *World Archaeology* 1: 289–98.

Ember, M. (1973) 'An archaeological indicator of matrilocal versus patrilocal residence', *American Antiquity* 38: 177–82.

Ferguson, L. (ed.) (1977) *Historical Archaeology and the Importance of Material Things*, Society for Historical Archaeology, Special Series Publication 2.

Flannery, K. V. (1972) 'The cultural evolution of civilisations', *Annual Review of Ecology and Systematics* 3: 399–426.

—— (1973) 'Archaeology with a capital S', in C. Redman (ed.) *Research and Theory in Current Archaeology*, New York: Wiley.

Flannery, K. V. and Marcus, J. (1976) 'Formative Oaxaca and the Zapotec Cosmos', *American Scientist* 64: 374–83.

Fletcher, R. (1977a) 'Settlement studies (micro and semi-micro)', in D. L. Clarke (ed.) *Spatial Archaeology*, New York: Academic Press.

—— (1977b) 'Alternatives and differences', in M. Spriggs (ed.) *Archaeology and Anthropology*, Oxford: British Archaeological Reports Supplementary Series 19.

Frankfort, H. (1951) *The Birth of Civilisation in the Near East*, London: Ernest Benn.

Friedman, J. and Rowlands, M. (eds) (1977) *The Evolution of Social Systems*, London: Duckworth.

Fritz, J. M. (1978) 'Paleopsychology today: ideational systems and human adaptation in prehistory', in C. Redman *et al.* (eds) *Social Archaeology Beyond Dating and Subsistence*, New York: Academic Press.

Fritz, J. M. and Plog, F. T. (1970) 'The nature of archaeological explanation',

American Antiquity 35: 405–12.

Giddens, A. (1979) *Central Problems in Social Theory*, London: Macmillan Press.

Gifford, D. P. (1978) 'Ethnoarchaeological observations of natural processes affecting cultural materials', in R. A. Gould (ed.) *Explorations in Ethnoarchaeology*, Albuquerque: University of New Mexico Press.

Glassie, H. (1975) *Folk Housing in Middle Virginia: a Structural Analysis of Historical Artifacts*, Knoxville: University of Tennessee Press.

Godelier, M. (1977) *Perspectives in Marxist Anthropology*, Cambridge: Cambridge University Press.

Gould, R. (1980) *Living Archaeology*, Cambridge: Cambridge University Press.

Harstrup, K. (1978) 'The post-structuralist position of social anthropology', in E. Schwimmer (ed.) *The Yearbook of Symbolic Anthropology* 1, London: Hurst.

Hawkes, C. (1954) 'Archaeological theory and method: some suggestions from the Old World', *American Anthropologist* 56: 155–68.

Hill, J. N. (1970) *Broken K Pueblo: Prehistoric Social Organisation in the American Southwest*, Anthropological Papers of the University of Arizona 18.

——— (1971) 'Report on a seminar on the explanation of prehistoric organisational change', *Current Anthropology* 12: 406–8.

——— (ed.) (1977) *The Explanation of Prehistoric Change*, Albuquerque: University of New Mexico Press.

Hill, J. N. and Gunn, J. (eds) (1977) *The Individual in Prehistory*, New York: Academic Press.

Hillier, B., Leaman, A., Stansall, P. and Bedford, M. (1976) 'Space syntax', *Environment and Planning B* 3: 147–85.

Hodder, I. R. (1979) 'Social and economic stress and material culture patterning', *American Antiquity* 44: 446–54.

——— (1981) 'Towards a mature archaeology', in I. Hodder, G. Isaac and N. Hammond (eds) *Pattern of the Past*, Cambridge: Cambridge University Press.

——— (1982a) *Symbols in Action*, Cambridge: Cambridge University Press.

——— (1982b) 'The identification and interpretation of ranking in prehistory: a contextual perspective' in C. Renfrew and S. Shennan (eds) *Ranking, Resource and Exchange*, Cambridge: Cambridge University Press.

——— (ed.) (1982c) *Symbolic and Structural Archaeology*, Cambridge: Cambridge University Press.

——— (1982d) 'Sequences of structural change in the Dutch Neolithic', in I. Hodder (ed.) *Symbolic and Structural Archaeology*, Cambridge: Cambridge University Press.

Hodder, I. R. and Lane, P. (1982) 'Exchange and reduction' in J. Ericson and T. Earle (eds) *New Approaches to Exchange Studies in Prehistory*, New York: Academic Press.

Hymes, D. (1970) 'Comments on Analytical Archaeology', *Norwegian Archaeological Review* 3: 16–21.

Isbell, W. H. (1976) 'Cosmological order expressed in prehistoric ceremonial centres', Paper given in Andean Symbolism Symposium Part 1: Space, time and mythology, International Congress of Americanists, Paris.

Leach, E. (1973a) 'Concluding address', in C. Renfrew (ed.) *The Explanation of Culture Change*, London: Duckworth.

——— (1973b) 'Structuralism in social anthropology', in D. Robey (ed.) *Structuralism: an Introduction*, Oxford: Clarendon Press.

——— (1977) 'A view from the bridge', in M. Spriggs (ed.) *Archaeology and Anthropology*, Oxford: British Archaeological Reports Supplementary Series 19.

——— (1978) 'Does space syntax really "constitute the social" ', in D. Green, C. Haselgrove and M. Spriggs (eds) *Social Organisation and Settlement*, Oxford: British Archaeological Reports British Series 47.

Leone, M. P. (1977) 'The new Mormon temple in Washington DC', in L. Ferguson (ed.) *Historical Archaeology and the Importance of Material Things*, Society for Historical Archaeology, Special Series Publication 2.

—— (1978) 'Time in American archaeology', in C. Redman *et al.* (eds) *Social Archaeology Beyond Subsistence and Dating*, New York: Academic Press.

Leroi-Gourhan, A. (1965) *Préhistoire de l'Art Occidental*, Paris: Mazenod.

Lévi-Strauss, C. (1968) *Structural Anthropology*, London: Allen Lane.

Longacre, W. (1970) 'Archaeology as anthropology', Anthropological Papers of the University of Arizona 17, Tucson.

Marshak, A. (1977) 'The meander as a system: the analysis and recognition of iconographic units in upper Palaeolithic compositions', in P. J. Ucko (ed.) *Form in Indigenous Art*, London: Duckworth.

Martins, H. (1974) 'Time and theory in sociology', in J. Rex (ed.) *Approaches to Sociology*, London.

Miller, D. (1982) 'Artefacts as products of human categorisation processes', in I. Hodder (ed.) *Symbolic and Structural Archaeology*, Cambridge: Cambridge University Press.

Muller, J. (1977) 'Individual variation in art styles', in J. Hill and J. Gunn (eds) *The Individual in Prehistory*, New York: Academic Press.

Pettit, P. (1975) *The Concept of Structuralism: a Critical Analysis*, Dublin: Gill and Macmillan.

Phillips, P. (1971) 'Attribute analysis and social structure of Chassey – Cortaillod – Lagozza populations', *Man* 6: 341–52.

Piaget, J. (1971) *Structuralism*, London: Routledge and Kegan Paul.

—— (1972) *The Principles of Genetic Epistemology*, London: Routledge and Kegan Paul.

Piggott, S. (1959) *Approach to Archaeology*, Harvard: McGraw Hill.

Plog, F. T. (1975) 'Systems theory in archaeological research', *Annual Review of Anthropology* 4: 207–24.

Radcliffe-Brown, A. R. (1952) *Structure and Function in Primitive Society*, London: Cohen and West.

Renfrew, C. (1969) 'Trade and culture process in European prehistory', *Current Anthropology* 10: 151–69.

—— (1972) *The Emergence of Civilisation*, London: Methuen.

—— (1973) *Social Archaeology*, Southampton: Southampton University Press.

Sahlins, M. (1976) *Culture and Practical Reason*, Chicago: University of Chicago Press.

Salmon, M. H. (1978) 'What can systems theory do for archaeology?', *American Antiquity* 43: 174–83.

Schiffer, M. B. (1976) *Behavioural Archaeology*, New York: Academic Press.

Shanks, M. and Tilley, C. (1982) 'Ideology, symbolic power and ritual communication: a reinterpretation of Neolithic mortuary practices', in I. Hodder (ed.) *Symbolic and Structural Archaeology*, Cambridge: Cambridge University Press.

Stanislawski, M. B. (1973) 'Review of Archaeology as anthropology: a case study by W. A. Longacre', *American Antiquity* 38: 117–22.

Thomas, D. H. (1974) *Predicting the Past*, New York: Holt, Rinehart & Winston.

Tilley, C. (1982) 'Social formation, social structures and social change', in I. Hodder (ed.) *Symbolic and Structural Archaeology*, Cambridge: Cambridge University Press.

Trigger, B. (1980) *Gordon Childe: Revolutions in Archaeology*, London: Thames and Hudson.

Van de Velde, P. (1980) *Elsloo and Hienheim: Bandkeramik Social Structure*, Analecta Praehistorica Leidensia 12.

Washburn, D. K. (1978) 'A symmetry classification of Pueblo ceramic designs', in P. Grebinger (ed.) *Discovering Past Behaviour*, New York: Academic Press.

Watson, P. J., Leblanc, S. A. and Redman, C. L. (1971) *Explanation in Archaeology: an Explicitly Scientific Approach*, London: Columbia University Press.

Wobst, H. M. (1977) 'Stylistic behaviour and information exchange', *University of Michigan Museum of Anthropology, Anthropological Paper* 61: 317–42.

Wylie, M. A. (1982) 'Epistemological issues raised by a structuralist archaeology', in I. Hodder (ed.) *Symbolic and Structural Archaeology*, Cambridge: Cambridge University Press.

Yellen, J. (1977) *Archaeological Approaches to the Present*, New York: Academic Press.

7

ARCHAEOLOGY IN 1984

... the lie passed into history and became truth. 'Who controls the past', ran the Party slogan, 'controls the future: who controls the present controls the past.' And yet the past, though of its nature alterable, never had been altered. Whatever was true now was true from everlasting to everlasting.

(George Orwell, *Nineteen Eighty-Four*, Penguin, p. 31)

Recently there has been an increased interest in the archaeological recovery of past ideas, reconstrucing the minds of humans long dead (Leone 1982; Renfrew 1982b). The notion that archaeologists study artifacts made by man which were 'the product of the human mind and human craftsmanship' (Daniel 1962, 30) and 'projections of his mind and embodiments of his history' (Clark 1975, 9; see also Childe 1949) is of course not new and is emphasised in Collingwood's (1956) contribution to the idealist view of history. Yet in the ladder of inference outlined by Hawkes (1954) the ideational realm was seen as being the most difficult to grasp and for many 'New Archaeologists', at least initially, attempts at getting into prehistoric people's heads were decried as palaeopsychology (Binford 1965, 203–10) and for Binford (1982, 162) archaeological reconstruction of mental phenomena is still deemed inappropriate. As Leone (1982) has cogently argued, the renewed attempts at reconstructing mind take varied paths from the symbolic functionalism of, for example, Wobst (1977), Fritz (1978), Hall (1977), Flannery and Marcus (1976) and Friedel (1981), to the structuralism of Leroi-Gourhan (1967), Deetz (1977) and Glassie (1975), the cognitive accounts of Kehoe and Kehoe (1973) or Muller (1977), the various materialist studies of ideology (Rowlands 1980; Tilley 1981; Shennan 1982) or of archaeological interpretations as ideology (Leone 1978; Meltzer 1981). Often, however, these studies appear to side-step important epistemological issues raised by the 'archaeology of mind'. In particular, how can a scientific archaeology devoted to the testing of theories against data cope with verifying statements about ideas in prehistoric people's heads?

While the reconstruction of past ideas brings such a question to the fore it can be claimed that the dilemma has always been present, if not fully recognised, in 'scientific' archaeology. All statements about the past involve adding to archaeological data in the process of interpretation. It is always a question of saying more than is actually there, from the stage of interpreting colours and textures on a trench wall in an archaeological excavation to reconstructing social systems. Leaps of faith are necessarily made since much of what archaeologists reconstruct is unobservable. This is particularly clear in much recent 'processual' archaeology. As Binford (1982, 162) has commented, the frequent references by social archaeologists to prestige systems, status, display, rank or conspicuous consumption, for example in burial studies, involve notions of values in the heads of prehistoric individuals. Equally, within ecological archaeology, assumptions of minimising effort, least risk, and maximising resources cannot in themselves be verified in archaeological data. The implications of such assumptions can, of course, be 'tested' in archaeological data, in the same way that most ideas in the mind have effects on the material world. The effects can be tested but to do so is tautological and self-fulfilling, and the values and ideas themselves remain beyond observation.

The re-emergence of an interest in past ideas thus brings to the fore an ever-present problem which the archaeological emphasis on objectivity and the separation of theory and data, evident from Childe (1925) to Renfrew (1982a), rarely faced (see, however, Childe 1949). It is altogether remarkable that, without any ability adequately to test their reconstructions of the past, archaeologists have come to reach agreement and consensus on many issues. It may be helpful to refer to an example of this process.

A major arena of recent archaelogical research has been the exchange of prehistoric artifacts. Basic texts of the reconstruction of the social mechanisms involved in exchange have been written (Earle and Ericson 1977; Ericson and Earle 1982) and general theories of exchange have been built (Sahlins 1972; Pryor 1977). Much of the interest in archaeology has centred on prehistoric Europe where the scientific armoury has been thrown at the sourcing of, for example, obsidian, pottery, stone axes, shells (Renfrew, Dixon and Cann 1968; Peacock 1969; 1977; Shackleton and Renfrew 1970; Cummins 1979). Statistical techniques have been applied to the interpretation of fall-off curves, and the debate has spread widely with numerous articles written (for example, Hodder 1974; Renfrew 1977; Sidrys 1977; Clark 1978; McBryde 1978; Ammerman 1979; McVicar 1982). Much of the work in Europe has taken an early article by Renfrew (1969) as a starting point, and the underlying assumption has been throughout that artifacts were passed from person to person across wide areas. This idea was initially encouraged by Grahame Clark's (1965) acquaintance with Australian ethnographic material, and the exchange of prehistoric artifacts has continually been supported by ethnographic models. All the work on the movement of prehistoric artifacts in Europe assumes that exchange occurred. A large literature has been built on an unverifiable assumption. It is simply impossible to test whether prehistoric artifacts moved from source to destination by exchange from person to person or whether, on the other hand, individuals went directly to the source. Recently I thought such a test would be possible in relation to British neolithic stone axes and it was suggested (Hodder and Lane 1982) that if axes were exchanged from person to person, being used and resharpened through time, they should get smaller with increasing distance from the source. This 'test' was successful since axes did prove to get smaller with increasing distance from their source, but in the end it is apparent that the assumption of exchange itself has not been tested. If axes were obtained directly from the source it is possible that individuals farther from the source would make the journey less frequently than individuals nearer the source, they would use and resharpen their axes for longer before replacing them, so that, once again, the sizes of axes would decrease with increasing distance from the source. Certainly other, more ingenious 'tests' will be suggested, but ultimately the hypothesis of prehistoric exchange is about the unobservable. It involves 'adding to' that which is observed. The amount of analytical, computer and research time that has been spent on questions of prehistoric exchange is enormous. It has been possible to spend so many resources because of a consensus in the archaeological community which accepts, somewhat mysteriously, not to question a particular assumption. As far as I am aware no-one in the literature has suggested that prehistoric exchange did not occur.

It is not my concern here to examine the process of reaching consensus, why some assumptions are accepted and others rejected by archaeologists, nor to account for the sociology and self-maintenance of a discipline. But I do wish to emphasise further that archaeologists need to face squarely the notion that archaeological hypotheses are not tested on archaeological data and that theory and data do not confront each other within an objective science of archaeology. Renfrew (1982a, 143) has restated 'the old relationship betwen theory and data' as:

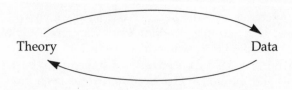

Figure 14 Renfrew's suggested relationship between theory and data

Examples such as the following appear to support such a picture of the way archaeologists work. Imagine that an archaeologist has an hypothesis that a particular unexcavated site had a hunter-gatherer economy. This hypothesis may have been suggested because of the type of soil around the site and because of various theories concerning resource utilisation. The site is then excavated in order to test the theory through examination of the faunal remains. Imagine that the excavator recovers few wild animal bones but that the bones of domesticated cattle, sheep, goat and pig are well represented. Numerous carbonised cereal grains are recovered as well as querns and other artifacts of a farming economy. Surely here a theory has been proposed, tested against the data, proved false, leading to change in the theory? The confrontation and objective testing of theory against data is here apparent. Or is it?

Closer examination shows that the hunter-gatherer hypothesis has not been tested against archaeological data, but against an edifice of auxiliary theories and assumptions which archaeologists have agreed not to question. There is only space here to refer to a few of these assumptions. First, there are theories concerning stratigraphical relationships and the nature of archaeological sites and layers. The discussion of economies assumes that the interpretation of soil and colour changes, associations of artifacts, are correct. Second, it is assumed that an 'assemblage' in a 'layer' represents 'an economy' whereas, for example, it is possible that the 'closed assemblage' is a palimpsest, representing the activities of different groups or individuals with a variety of different economies. Third, there are problems in the definition of wild or domestic animals. What is meant by 'domesticated? Different criteria can be used to specify domestication and the choice of method is theory-dependent. Fourth, domesticated resources on the site could have been obtained by exchange while dependence on wild resources may be underrepresented because wild animals were processed off sites or at subsidiary sites. To examine all such assumptions would involve writing a text of archaeological theory and method but I hope that enough has been said to demonstrate that archaeological theories are 'tested', not on archaeological data, but on other archaeological theories. As in the exchange example, assumption is built upon assumption and a consensus is reached, but ultimately statements about the past are about the unobservable and they are unverifiable.

Within processual or systems archaeology the problem of testing theories about the unobservable was usefully discussed in relation to the incomplete and very large Black Box (Clarke 1968, 59–62). Leach (1973) stated how difficult it was for archaeologists to look into the box with anything more than guesswork, but systems analysis suggested that correlations could be observed between inputs and outputs and the predictability of such relationships in the past and present could be used to test ideas about the contents of the box (Clarke 1979, 51). Much of the New Archaeology was characterised by a 'certainty' in the reconstruction of the past as long as scientific methods were pursued. The optimism of Binford's (1962) view that archaeological assemblages present a picture of the total extinct cultural system is distinctive. More recently, it might be suggested, doubts are increasing: Flannery's (1973) 'young fogeys' abound, mistrustful of complex social interpretations of the past.

In view of the discussion above it might be appropriate to replace the Black Box by a much less certain box, the appearance of which depends on the point of view of the observer (Figure 15). The problem to be faced by archaeologists is that the objects or systems they observe depend on the theories they are supposedly testing. The boundaries and nature of the systems have to be specified by the analyst. Theory and data are not opposed and they are never confronted. Rather, data are observed within interpretation and theory.

It might be countered that surely archaeologists can count 'things', showing similarities and differences across space and time in archaeological assemblages. But the 'things' one counts are always classes of things constructed by the observer. Before we can count we need to define classes or types. As David Clarke noted (1968, 15), there are perhaps limitless numbers of different attributes to measure on objects, and the classes or types of object that are produced depend on what attributes one thinks relevant. For example, we may have a theory that matrilocal residence leads to localised styles of pottery within a site (Longacre 1970). To 'test' this theory in prehistory it is thought necessary to use the decoration or shapes of pots. But depending on how we describe and 'observe' the sherds, different types and degrees of spatial clustering within sites will emerge. All sherds are similar in some respects but different in others. We cannot measure everything, so what are we to emphasise in the analysis? There can be no independent theory which allows us to decide what to measure or count since the choice of such a theory is itself theory-dependent. In any case, 'indepen-

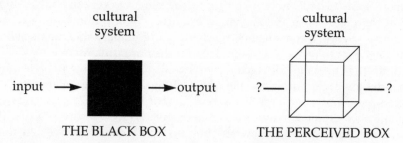

Figure 15 The incomplete Black Box of systems theory compared with the subjectively perceived box of interpretation theories

dent' or 'middle-range' theories are themselves based, in ethnoarchaeological studies of present-day societies, on moving beyond the data to cultural inferences. Once again, archaeologists can only work by consensus, building up assumption upon assumption.

Similar problems of verification are faced in most disciplines, and the issues raised have been widely discussed (for example, Kuhn 1962; Berger and Luckmann 1967; Feyerabend 1975; Gregory 1978), but the example of archaeology is of interest because it presents the problems in a particularly acute form. The leaps of faith that have to be made in interpreting archaeological data are great because so little is known and yet so much is said. It might be hoped that difficulties encountered in other disciplines can be squarely faced and resolutions sought in archaeology.

To summarise, the dilemma apparent for archaeologists is that there is a widespread desire for science and objective tests, a fear of speculation and the subjective, and yet we want to say something about the past. In particular, in recent years it has become clear that if we want to say anything interesting about the past, we must include statements about prehistoric ideas. Yet to say anything about the past, and about past ideas, involves moving beyond the data to interpret them, and there can be no testing of these interpretations because the data themselves are formulated within and are part of the same argument as the theories. Speculation and the subjective are therefore part of the 'scientific' process.

However, the dilemma only occurs if archaeology is seen as a (pure) science. The 'problem' is of the archaeologists' own making. If archaeology is seen properly as a cultural and social product, the 'problem' dissolves. The data of the past are observed and have meaning within a present social and cultural context. Archaeology is a discipline with specified methods, rigorously defined, and theories of its own. It is a science in the general sense of using explicit and repeatable procedures. It contributes to debates about the nature of humankind. But it is not a science if by that is meant a discipline in which objective truth can be provided or approached. Rather, archaeology does and must continue to play an active social role in the various cultures in which it is produced. In the west scientific archaeology has, if anything, had the danger of removing archaeology from any ability to make a relevant contribution to the modern world, both because of the neutral, apolitical aura which it has claimed as a science, and because of the scientific terminology and specialisation with which it has surrounded itself. Yet changing interpretations of the past can be seen to be linked to the changing expectations and attitudes of archaeologists and contemporary society (Leone 1978; Trigger 1980; Meltzer 1981).

The notion that the past is an active product of the present, however, raises problems and dilemmas of its own. In particular, if archaeologists cannot be seen as providing neutral information for the public, what social responsibilities are involved? The questions that come to the fore include: what type of past do people want, should archaeologists provide a past that supports (legitimates) or disturbs present outlooks, which sections of society do archaeologists write for, and what are the implications of western archaeologists working in developing countries? Such questions seem particularly important today when archaeology, as a peripheral non-school subject, is under heavy pressure as either a soft science or an expensive humanity. In Britain, at least, the call for accountability requires academic archaeologists to consider more carefully their relationship with the public.

Yet how are archaeology and archaeologists viewed by the public and what is the role of the distant past in modern western society? Such questions have been asked in developing countries (for example, Miller 1980). In Britain many archaeologists probably feel that they have a good impression of public attitudes from adult education classes, from the popularity of *Horizon* and the *Mary Rose* (although see Parker Pearson 1983), from talking to the public at the side of excavation trenches, or from perusing the pages of *Popular Archaeology*. Yet as producers we are probably not ideally placed to assess the product. It is probably the case that most professional archaeologists come from a fairly limited range of social backgrounds. The past that interests them (us) may not be of such interest to others.

For varied reasons, then, it would be of value to examine how different views of the past and of archaeologists relate to social and cultural backgrounds. At present a number of surveys are being carried out in England[1] in order to obtain a fuller picture of the place of archaeology and the distant past in contemporary English society. A small pilot study has already been undertaken by an independent research group[2] in Cambridge and I will briefly refer to the type of result that is emerging.

In general, the survey suggests that professionals with university or other higher education tend to be more interested in archaeology, to think that people need a distant past and that spending money on archaeology is worthwhile. Individuals in unskilled employment and who have left school at an early age are more likely to feel that people do not need a distant past, and that archaeology is 'generally useless' and a 'complete waste of money'. Other differences between social groups in definitions of archaeology and in the aspects of the past that *are* found interesting were also noted. Whatever the reasons, educational, cultural or social, for such differences, it is clear that we cannot assume that the stories we are writing are socially neutral. There is a need to examine carefully the effects of the past we reconstruct.

An example of the assumptions that archaeologists make without regard to social differences can be taken from the publicity produced by

STOP, the campaign against the plundering of Britain's past. This national movement against treasure hunting is supported by most of the major archaeological bodies such as the CBA, the Museums Association, Rescue, the Association of County Archaeological Officers and the Standing Conference of Unit Managers. Under the heading 'the purpose of archaeology' the publicity pamphlet claims: 'we all need the stability which comes from a thorough knowledge of our own heritage', and further, 'the results of archaeologists' work . . . increase our understanding of the past and . . . deepen our sense of belonging in the present'. While this may be the view of certain groups in society, and it may be the consensus of archaeologists themselves, it is not a natural truth that can be taken for granted. At least the type of archaeology that archaeologists write may not be easily justified to many sections of society. A notion of social responsibility, brought to the fore by disillusion with the vision of archaeology as an objective science, implies that archaeologists should achieve some general understanding of the social and cultural context of the past they write.

It might even be claimed that widely circulated statements such as that provided by STOP have the danger of adding to social divisions within our society. While metal detectors and treasure hunters are at times described as 'rapists of the national heritage', an alternative viewpoint is expressed in the pages of the magazine *Treasure Hunting*. 'Professional archaeologists are university trained academics. With a few notable exceptions, they are, by preference, totally out-of-touch with the general public. During the past 20 years they have made it their business to *complicate* the story of Britain's ancient history . . . with the intention of securing the futures of their own academic careers. . . . The media's files are full of bumph which perpetuates the myth that every newly-qualified professional archaeologist gets a brightly polished halo with his university degree, along with a licence to "salvage the nation's heritage", whereas the crime of "people's archaeologists" is that "they have no academic qualifications and . . . therefore no right to an interest in British history" ' (*Treasure Hunting* 1982, 9). Perhaps some of us academics may be feeling our haloes a bit tarnished and may be wondering, without the comfort of 'objective science' to hide behind, how archaeology could play a more active part in society. The quotes from STOP and *Treasure Hunting* seem infused with differences in attitudes that have a social and cultural basis and which can be linked to mistrust and contempt glimpsed throughout a broad social arena. The survey of attitudes to archaeology and the past referred to above is a first stage in the process of understanding such differences and their social contexts so that, whatever political stance a particular archaeologist takes, (s)he can at least have a clearer, if not more responsible, idea of the social impact of the past (s)he reconstructs.

CONCLUSION

I have argued elsewhere (Hodder 1982) that interpretations of the past should take greater account of meaning, the individual, culture and history. These claims for a 'post-processual' or 'contextual' archaeology have been argued for 'academic' reasons to do with the construction of explanations, the inadequacy of the concepts of system and adaptation, the importance of culture in human nature, the central role of intentionality and so on. The stance is also taken because as an historical and, only in a broad sense, scientific discipline, archaeology is best able to contribute its data on long sequences of cultural change within local areas to general understanding of the relationships between historical and cultural contexts and social change. Yet ultimately the claims for developments in archaeology are political in origin in three respects.

First, at its worst the scientific 'New Archaeology' raised an image of man the passive and efficient animal controlled by laws which cannot be usurped. A timeless past was produced in which all societies could be described in terms of their 'technologistical' control over nature. The human past legitimated and made universal the principles of the technocratic west. In contrast, the past can be used to emphasise the historical contextuality of rationality and to engender respect for the individual, actively and meaningfully negotiating and creating social position.

Second, the emphases on science and cross-cultural generalisation have been associated with an ever-increasing split between theory and practice, between interpretation and excavation. Field archaeology is devalued and decried as technique, while theoretical archaeology is viewed from the outside as suspicious and remote. Popular interest which derives from 'digging up pots and bones' is divorced from ivory-tower ponderings about the meaning of the past. There are individuals who successfully cross the divide, but alienation is widespread. Yet if data are seen as dependent on theory, then excavation must be valued as an interpretive experience rather than a technique. We are all theoreticians. Equally, cross-cultural behavioural and evolutionary theories involve seeing the data from the past, such as the great civilisations of Egypt and the Indus, and the hunter-gatherers of Scandinavia, as mere examples of general social processes such as segregation, centralisation and hypercoherence. The emphasis on cultural context advocated here relocates the objects from the past in the historically specific rather than in the theoretically abstract. The unique cultural achievement of Egyptian civilisation is seen as having an interest in its own right. In this way there is a potential for the popular interest in the past through the experience of the concrete to be retained in the forming of abstract theories. We are all theoreticians but we also deal in data. This is not to claim that the data are independent of theory, but to state that our theories must be better moulded to the historically specific data.

Third, the notion of 'archaeology as science' legitimated the professional theoretician in the provision of neutral knowledge. Even if such knowledge might be used in planning the future, examples such as Hiroshima encouraged a separation of scientific theory and its social use. The split between theory and data described above is linked to that between knowledge and social process. The academic prehistorian hands out professional qualifications in the manipulation of abstract knowledge and his/her position depends on maintaining the aura of the specialist. In fact, however, such control of knowledge can amount to a form of hidden social control, in which one view of the past is seen as correct, in objective terms. The interests of one social class are seen as universal and the implications of Orwell's statement, quoted at the beginning of this article, loom before us. We have seen that there is no external, objective basis for saying that any one theory, well argued and coherent internally and 'fitting' to the data, is any better than another theory, equally well argued but based on different assumptions. The result of this relativism is not anarchy, if by that is meant that an endless series of arbitrary pasts will be produced. Rather, different pasts will be constructed within different but limited sets of social interests. There are signs that groups other than white, Anglo-Saxon, protestant, male, middle-class intellectuals want to write their own pasts. Other social groups in England, women in England and America, ethnic minorities and archaeologists in less-developed countries are beginning to make claims to their own archaeology. They should be encouraged to develop their own observational, methodological and historical theories for reconstructing the past so that their social and cultural experiences in archaeology can be actively involved in social debate. If these different but coherent viewpoints can be discussed openly, then the past will play a role in unearthing and objectifying alternative viewpoints and social dispositions, contributing to social change. The past is everybody's past and by releasing it the dangers of Orwell's totalitarianism are lessened and the central role of the past is assured. But what this strategy implies for professional archaeology as an institution is not clear. From one point of view, the concerns of alternative social groups will increasingly force the western professional archaeologist to be involved with and supported by a restricted set of social interests. From this angle, communication of the past by archaeologists, leading to wider popular appeal, will result in appropriation of the past by other social interests so that western professional archaeologists serve a diminishing public. On the other hand, it remains possible that flexible training and understanding can be engendered in an archaeological community motivated, not by fears of anarchy and attacks on the control of neutral knowledge, but by the vision of the past as an arena for the playing out of different social values and interests.

NOTES

1 These surveys in several British cities are being co-ordinated by Peter Stone (Southampton), Mike Parker Pearson and the author (Cambridge).
2 The pilot study was carried out by the Cambridge Research Co-operative for Mike Parker Pearson and the author. Informants were drawn at random from the electoral register.

REFERENCES

Ammerman, A. (1979) 'A study of obsidian exchange networks in Calabria', *World Archaeology* 11, 95–110.

Berger, P. and Luckmann, T. (1967) *The Social Construction of Reality*, Harmondsworth.

Binford, L. R. (1962) 'Archaeology as anthropology', *American Antiquity* 28, 217–25.

—— (1965) 'Archaeological systematics and the study of culture process', *American Antiquity* 31, 203–10.

—— (1982) 'Meaning, inference and the material record', in C. Renfrew and S. Shennan (eds) *Ranking, Resource and Exchange*, Cambridge.

Childe, V. G. (1925) *The Dawn of European Civilisation*, London.

—— (1949) *Social Worlds of Knowledge*, Oxford.

Clark, J. G. D. (1965) 'Traffic in stone axe and adze blades', *Economic History Review* 18, 1–28.

—— (1975) *The Earlier Stone Age Settlement of Scandinavia*, Cambridge.

Clark, J. R. (1978) 'Measuring changes in the ease of trade with archaeological data: an analysis of coins found at Dura Europus in Syria', *Professional Geographer* 30, 256–63.

Clarke, D. L. (1968) *Analytical Archaeology*, London.

—— (1979) *Analytical Archaeologist. Collected Papers of David Clarke*, London.

Collingwood, R. (1956) *The Idea of History*, Oxford.

Cummins, W. A. (1979) 'Neolithic stone axes: distribution and trade in England and Wales', in T. H. McK. Clough and W. A. Cummins (eds) *Stone Axe Studies*, CBA Research Report 23.

Daniel, G. E. (1962) *The Idea of Prehistory*, Harmondsworth.

Deetz, J. (1977) *In Small Things Forgotten*, Garden City.

Earle, T. K. and Ericson, J. E. (1977) *Exchange Systems in Prehistory*, New York.

Ericson, J. E. and Earle, T. K. (1982) *Contexts for Prehistoric Exchange*, New York.

Feyerabend, P. (1975) *Against Method*, London.

Flannery, K. V. (1973) 'Archaeology with a capital S', in C. L. Redman *et al.* (eds) *Research and Theory in Current Archaeology*, New York.

Flannery, K. V. and Marcus, J. (1976) 'Formative Oaxaka and the Zapotek cosmos', *American Scientist* 64, 374–83.

Friedel, D. A. (1981) 'Civilisation as a state of mind', in G. Jones and R. Kautz (eds) *Transformations to Statehood*, Cambridge.

Fritz, J. M. (1978) 'Palaeopsychology today: ideational systems and human adaptation in prehistory', in C. Redman *et al.* (eds) *Social Archaeology*, New York.

Glassie, H. (1975) *Folk Housing of Middle Virginia*, Knoxville.

Gregory, D. (1978) *Ideology, Science and Human Geography*, London.

Hall, R. L. (1977) 'An anthropocentric perspective for eastern United States prehistory', *American Antiquity* 42, 499–518.

Hawkes, C. (1954) 'Archaeological theory and method: some suggestions from the Old World', *American Anthropologist* 56, 155–68.

Hodder, I. (1974) 'Regression analysis of some trade and marketing patterns', *World Archaeology* 6, 172–89.

—— (1982) 'Theoretical archaeology: a reactionary view', in I. Hodder (ed.) *Symbolic and Structural Archaeology*, Cambridge.

Hodder, I. and Lane, P. (1982) 'A contextual examination of neolithic axe distribution in Britain', in J. E. Ericson and T. K. Earle (eds) *Contexts for Prehistoric Exchange*, New York.

Kehoe, A. B. and Kehoe, T. F. (1973) 'Cognitive models for archaeological interpretation', *American Antiquity* 38, 150–4.

Kuhn, T. (1962) *The Structure of Scientific Revolutions*, Chicago.

Leach, E. (1973) 'Concluding address', in C. Renfrew (ed.) *Explanation of Culture Change*, London.

Leone, M. P. (1978) 'Time in American archaeology', in C. Redman *et al.* (eds) *Social Archaeology*, New York.

—— (1982) 'Some opinions about recovering mind', *American Antiquity* 47, 742–60.

Leroi-Gourhan, A. (1967) *The Art of Prehistoric Man in Western Europe*, London.

Longacre, W. (1970) 'Archaeology as anthropology', *Anthropological Papers of the University of Arizona* 17, Tucson.

McBryde, I. (1978) 'Wil-im-ee Moor-ring. Or where do axes come from?', *Mankind* 11, 354–82.

McVicar, J. (1982) 'The spatial analysis of axe size and the Scottish axe distribution', *Archaeological Review from Cambridge* 1, 30–45.

Meltzer, D. J. (1981) 'Ideology and material culture', in R. A. Gould and M. B. Schiffer (eds) *Modern Material Culture, the Archaeology of Us*, New York.

Miller, D. (1980) 'Archaeology and development', *Current Anthropology* 21, 709–26.

Muller, J. (1977) 'Individual variation in art styles', in J. Hill and J. Gunn (eds) *The Individual in Prehistory*, New York.

Parker Pearson, M. (1983) ' "Roses" are read, my love, when violence is news . . .', *Royal Anthropological Institute Newsletter* 55, 5.

Peacock, D. P. S. (1969) 'Neolithic pottery production in Cornwall', *Antiquity* 43, 145–9.

—— (1977) *Pottery and Early Commerce*, London.

Pryor, F. L. (1977) *The Origins of the Economy*, New York.

Renfrew, A. C. (1969) 'Trade and culture process in European prehistory', *Current Anthropology* 10, 151–69.

—— (1977) 'Alternative models for exchange and spatial distribution', in T. K. Earle and J. E. Ericson (eds) *Exchange Systems in Prehistory*, New York.

—— (1982a) 'Discussion: contrasting paradigms', in A. C. Renfrew and S. Shennan (eds) *Ranking, Resource and Exchange*, Cambridge.

—— (1982b) *Towards an Archaeology of Mind*, Cambridge.

Renfrew, A. C., Dixon, J. E. and Cann, J. R. (1968) 'Further analyses of Near Eastern obsidians', *Proceedings of the Prehistoric Society* 34, 319–31.

Rowlands, M. J. (1980) 'Kinship, alliance and exchange in the European Bronze Age', in J. Barrett and R. Bradley (eds) *Settlement and Society in the British Later*

Bronze Age, British Archaeological Reports British Series 83.

Sahlins, M. D. (1972) *Stone Age Economics*, Chicago.

Shackleton, N. and Renfrew, C. (1970) 'Neolithic trade routes re-aligned by oxygen isotope analysis', *Nature* 228, 1062–5.

Shennan, S. (1982) 'Ideology, change and the European Early Bronze Age', in I. Hodder (ed.) *Symbolic and Structural Archaeology*, Cambridge.

Sidrys, R. (1977) 'Mass-distance measures for the Maya obsidian trade', in T. K. Earle and J. E. Ericson (eds) *Exchange Systems in Prehistory*, New York.

Tilley, C. (1981) 'Conceptual frameworks for the explanation of sociocultural change', in I. Hodder, G. Isaac and N. Hammond (eds) *Patterns of the Past*, Cambridge.

Trigger, B. G. (1980) 'Archaeology and the image of the American Indian', American Antiquity 40, 662–76.

Wobst, M. (1977) 'Stylistic behaviour and information exchange', *University of Michigan Museum of Anthropology, Anthropological Paper* 61, 317–42.

8

POLITICS AND IDEOLOGY IN THE WORLD ARCHAEOLOGICAL CONGRESS 1986

In rather crude terms one can distinguish two views about ideology in recent archaeological literature. On the one hand, ideology represents the interests of the dominant group in society. The dominant perspective becomes absorbed and 'taken for granted'. We become mystified and duped. On the other hand, ideology can be seen as enabling as well as misrepresenting. This second position is the one that I have adopted – it suggests that society is made up of different interest groups, with varying ideologies, and that social change comes about through the practice of social debate. This is a more optimistic and active view of the individual in society. Indeed, I have felt that the role of archaeology and the past in society should be to encourage debate about the present through debate about the past. I have felt that archaeology and the past could play an active role in contributing to change in the present. The dominant ideology can be criticised and changed. I believed, through social action, including social debate.

Which of these two views seems more relevant to the World Congress debate – ideology as duping or ideology as socially active?

In answering this question it is first necessary to examine the main ideological themes running through the World Congress debate. Since the banning of South Africa from the Congress, I have received many resignation letters from intending participants and have read much of the articles and letters in the press and in journals. These are the data for my ethnographic analysis.

The dominant theme in all the letters, pronouncements and discussions has been academic freedom. There is reference to 'the ethos of free communication and movement among scholars', 'the free flow of information', the 'free pursuit of knowledge unaffected by any national, religious or political interests [which] is an absolute condition for the preservation of a free society', 'keeping the Congress open to all', 'free speech', 'scholars' rights to participate in . . . exchange, regardless of ideas and individuals . . . of scholarly information'. Professor Tobias for example has suggested that the greatest casualty of the ban on South

Africa 'is the principle of freedom in scientific communication, irrespective of race, national origin, political stance, gender or any variable other than the status of the individual as a *bona fide* scholar'. Finally, to quote from the 9 December 1985 statement from the SAA Executive Committee to its members, 'the SAA has upheld, and will continue to uphold, the principles of freedom of research and the freedom of scholars from all nations to meet and exchange ideas'.

So, for most people, the World Congress has raised the dominant issue of individual academic freedom. This idea is frequently linked to the non-political nature of archaeological science. More quotes: the 'dangerous precedent for the further politicisation of international scientific meetings', 'politicisation of the Congress', 'the dangers to the archaeological profession of involving its members in political debate', making 'the congress a political pawn'. For many, then, science, including archaeological science, should be 'above politics', and 'open to all'. There is also reference to the 'universality of science'.

The notion that science can be neutral and non-political has deep roots within the western world, and the critique of western science as ideology is well developed within critical theory. The vision of scientists as above politics, neutral analysts, masks the ideological component of their endeavour and assures them a permanent place within capitalist society. Science, neutralised and objective, can be bought and sold as a commodity in the market-place. Within capitalism, and particularly in high-technology capitalism, science is the basis of industrial success. It is thus an important component of weath, prestige and social status. Yet, within western democracies, it is also free, open to all – the neutral basis for social competition.

Whether one agrees with such analyses or not, it is clear that the notion that science should be 'open to all' is a *belief* about the way the world should be. That *belief* becomes *ideological* when it is linked to certain social *interests*. These social interests are not difficult to find within the ideology of 'academic freedom' as it is used in archaeology. I am talking to a room now in which there are few, if any, black American or American Indian archaeologists. In England, there are still pitifully few professional women archaeologists, at least at higher levels, and few women archaeological writers. In England, archaeology has always been linked to the upper-middle class, to the better educated and wealthier members of society. The interests of black Americans, American Indians, women and the working class are not well represented in archaeological discourse. The archaeological science that is conducted represents dominant social interests. It is therefore ideological. I wish further to suggest that the 'academic freedom' argument used in the World Congress debate is part of this dominant ideology.

Indeed, in my view, this point is especially clear in relation to the

World Congress, since few would claim that academic freedom exists for black South Africans. The views of this subordinate group are not well represented in scientific debate. For example, black South African leaders and the ANC have expressed opinions in favour of an academic boycott on South Africa, and the Pan African Congress (now the African Association for Prehistory and Related Studies) has a policy of 'censorship of colleagues and institutions maintaining links with South African institutions'. Yet such views are disregarded by the dominant western perspective which is against any curtailing of 'academic freedom'. Similarly, large parts of the Third World and the Eastern Block countries would appear to be in favour of a ban on South African participation at the World Congress. Indeed many would not have attended if South Africa had been present. The UISPP is in name international, but in practice it is dominated by Europe. It has a permanent council which normally meets only at the Congress which has only once been held outside Europe. Through the recent debate it did not take an adequate vote of the opinion of world members. As a result, the dominant European view held sway in favour of 'academic freedom' and in favour of South African participation. As a result, UISPP dissociated itself from the Southampton World Congress and plans to set up an alternative Congress with South Africa present, in Mainz in 1987.

If there is still doubt about whether the notion of academic freedom is itself ideological and political, we can focus on the implication of sticking to the supposedly neutral ideal that the Southampton Congress should be open to all. Following this ideal, the ban on South African participation would be lifted. There is clear evidence that, as a result, large numbers of archaeologists, particularly from the Third World, Eastern Block, and Scandinavian countries would either have absented themselves in protest, or would have been prevented from coming by their governments.

Thus the main people present at a conference theoretically 'open to all' would have been the existing dominant groups – Europeans and American, western and white archaeologists, including some South Africans. The supposedly neutral ideal of academic freedom would lead in practice to a political boycotting of the conference and to a political reinforcement by the west of its own dominant position. The 'academic freedom' would be the academic freedom of a dominant few.

How does the ideology of academic freedom regenerate itself as the dominant ideology? Answering this question is perhaps the most helpful way in which we can use the World Congress data. I will make six points. The first is that we all seem to be able to see freedom as an ideal to strive for, while accepting that the present imperfections or curtailment of academic freedom will one day be ironed out. Thus we may accept that female or Third World archaeologists are not able to express

137

their ideas easily but that the academic freedom ideal assures their right to do so. We have already seen that in practice the open interchange of archaeological knowledge is not enhanced by sticking to the ideal of academic freedom, since large parts of the world would not attend a conference at which the South Africans were present. Yet we manage to overlook curtailments in holding to our future ideal.

This ability to overlook inconsistences in our argument leads to a second point about the process by which ideologies remain dominant. We clearly are able to overlook contradictions that do not relate to our own interests. For example, in protesting against the boycott of South Africans, many people have resorted to a boycott of the Southampton Congress. The ideal of academic freedom is expressed in relation to South Africa, but in order to achieve that end, the academic freedom of individuals to attend the Conference is restricted. For example, in Britain many bodies have withdrawn funds from the conference. In the United States, the SAA and the American Council of Learned Societies decided not to support proposals for travel funds so that Americans who want to attend the Southampton Congress now find it extremely difficult to do so. Pressures of all types on young academics have been particularly severe, and a number of young archaeologists have said to me that they resigned because they were worried about future blackballing. Their academic freedom has in practice been curtailed.

This ability to overlook internal contradictions within an argument is selective. For example, in North America and increasingly in Britain many public and private bodies have long followed a policy of Affirmative Action. I take this policy to involve temporary curtailment of open access to jobs and opportunities by, for example, white males, in order to allow for the rights of, for example, blacks and women. Affirmative Action is precisely the policy being followed by the Southampton Congress. In order to allow the Third World a say in world archaeology, and in order to establish the rights of black South Africans, a temporary curtailment of the opportunities open to white South Africans is suggested. Yet that is not how many of the western archaeologists see the issue. Many may accept Affirmative Action in relation to women and minority groups in the west, even though it contradicts the ideal of an open society. But in relation to the rest of the world, we do not accept Affirmative Action and we hold to our abstract ideal.

A third, and again related strategy by which the dominant ideology is continued, is the strategy of silence. It is interesting to look at what salient issues are not talked about. For example, the Southampton Congress Executive Committee has repeatedly noted that to lift the ban on South Africa would lead to withdrawal by participants from Third World and the Eastern Block countries. This point was made in a summary of events by the UISPP President, circulated on 22 October 1985, and again in a letter to proposed participants on 26 November 1985. The reaction of the rest of the world has been emphasised in more recent circulars. Yet this point is not even mentioned in, for example, the SAA statement of 9 December 1985. Indeed I have found that many people in England and the US are unaware of the proposed resignations from the rest of the world. A silence surrounds issues that contradict or embarrass the dominant view of 'academic freedom' and no-ban-on-South Africa.

On the other hand, as a fourth strategy, the dominant viewpoint focuses on the weaknesses in alternative viewpoints, bringing them into the limelight in order to discredit them. For example, much of the recent debate has avoided the main issues and focused on the initial reluctance of the British Executive Committee to take a clear moral stance in relation to South Africa. Other issues such as the legality of the British decision, or the anti-apartheid contributions made by the South African archaeologists, or the notion that it was made without adequate consultation, have also been brought in.

A fifth strategy is the control of communication. The British Executive's viewpoint was not well presented initially in the press and in academic journals. It could be argued that the refusal by the SAA to allow the British Executive Committee members, some of whom are actually SAA members, to speak as discussion leaders in the debate tomorrow was another example of the control of ideology through control of communication channels.

The sixth and final way in which, in this case, the dominant ideology of 'academic freedom' is reproduced is also the most subtle and difficult to deal with. The dominant ideology becomes the terms on which all discussion, including critical discussion, takes place. Since it is the framework of discussion, it is never open to criticism itself. In the World Congress debate all the varied shades of opinion use the same language and the same ideal of academic freedom – that concept itself is rarely criticised. Those who argue *against* the ban on South Africa are concerned about the freedom of speech and access to academia of *black* South Africans. Those, like me, who emphasise the need for the ban to break down West–East, North–South barriers, are concerned with the freedom of speech of *non-western* societies. We all appear to use the same underlying assumption that academic freedom is a paramount virtue. That ideology is therefore continued, beyond criticism and beyond debate.

In this paper I have argued that, in the same way that all critical theory analyses are themselves ideological and political, so all standpoints in archaeology, including the idea that archaeological science is not political, are themselves ideological and political. I have also shown six mechanisms by which a dominant ideology is maintained. It should also be stressed that in trying to become dominant, subordinate ideologies try to use very similar tactics.

Returning to my original questions about the nature of ideology, it is possible to be optimistic and embrace my view – that ideology can be socially active, revealing rather than masking, enabling rather than repressing. After all, I have been able to make my case today from within the subordinate position, and certainly my own awareness of world issues has been increased by the debate. It is possible to argue that levels of consciousness about South Africa, the Third World and the political nature of archaeology have been raised. And the World Congress *will* take place in Southampton without South Africa and with many successful and exciting sessions. Also, there are plans to discuss setting up a permanent world archaeological organisation dedicated to a broader world participation. World conferences in other disciplines are beginning to take the same stand as the World Archaeological Congress. All this is positive in that it shows how the dominant view can be eroded and how the existing system can be changed through critical action and debate. Critical debate can thus have an active role.

On the other hand, it is possible to take an extremely pessimistic position in which dominant ideologies are seen as duping and unchanging, beyond debate. It is possible to argue that debate about the past merely reflects and reinforces current ideologies. Very few people seem to have changed their minds during the debate about the World Congress – most people seem to start from one position, manipulating, 'reading' what they see in terms of their own interests. We can see this clearly by looking at the world-wide pattern of resignations from the World Congress over the South African ban. I have current figures on resignations by letter, which may have little relationship with the actual numbers intending to withdraw. However, the relative proportion resigning from each country does give an indication of where the major feelings against the ban are centred. Well at the top of the list of resignations come the US and Israel. Of the 625 US citizens who had filled in application forms to attend the conference, 22 per cent (140) have resigned because of the South African ban. I do not include in the figures those who have withdrawn for other reasons. Of the 30 Israelis intending to come 23, that is 77 per cent, have resigned over the ban (small sample). As we move into western Europe the numbers begin to drop off. Of the 437 British participants 10 per cent (47) have resigned and in the rest of western Europe 7 per cent (66) of the total 878 have resigned. The picture in the rest of the world is different. Of 160 intending participants from eastern Europe (including Russia) 2 people (1 per cent) have resigned and only 3 people have resigned from the whole of the Third World, including South America, India and Africa.

These figures suggest the same picture that can be obtained from other means. While the American and British Foundations such as the American Council for Learned Societies, Wenner Gren, The British Society of Antiquaries and so on have withdrawn their financial or other sponsorship, so African, Indian and other agencies have added theirs.

It is of course mainly Eastern Block and Third World groups, such as the OAU, and even the Commonwealth and EEC that have argued for cultural, as well as economic, sanctions against South Africa. The archaeological reaction around the world to the banning has thus mirrored more or less exactly the positions of various governments towards South Africa. Where there is more public and government criticism of South Africa, and less economic involvement in that country, there is more willingness to accept an archaeological ban. But where there is closer involvement in South Africa there is more rejection of the archaeological ban. It is in the west that the cry of academic freedom as a universal priority is raised in support of maintaining links with South Africa. This ideology is adhered to even if it involves restriction on the participation of Third World countries at the conference. The archaeological traditions and interests of non-western countries are ignored or played down.

So the figures I gave you of current resignations from the Congress on the South African issue in different parts of the world, seem similar to the divisions between the west and the east, north and south, that we see reproduced daily in world politics, including reactions to Libya or invasions of the Falklands, including world economic systems and world political alliances.

So what I find depressing in the recent archaeological discussion is not simply that few people seem to change their views. Rather, it suggests that debate has little ability to change the dominant ideologies. How you act and how I respond seem stereotyped. I want to believe that we can break out of our entrenched ideologies. But even in our criticisms of each other, and in our debates, we make certain common assumptions which seem themselves beyond criticism. As a result western science and notions of free speech do indeed appear universal. My greatest sadness and disillusion occurs when it is realised that intellectuals themselves in America and England who might be expected to be able to provide a critical position, only reproduce the dominant ideologies of their own governments and countries. Unwittingly they establish ideology as truth, the arbitrary as universal. We do indeed seem duped by our own ideologies, caught passively within systems of ideas that we cannot change, because we do not even see them.

Part III

DEBATE AND RE-EVALUATION

9

THE PROCESSUAL REACTION

Unsurprisingly, the reaction of processual archaeology to the papers reprinted above and to *Reading the Past* (Hodder 1986) and the two books by Shanks and Tilley (1987a; 1987b) concentrated on their most undermining feature – the attack on the objectivity and neutrality of archaeology as a science. Watson (1986) was concerned about the scepticism involved and claimed that I did not believe the real past was accessible (see also Bintliff 1990, 18). If this was so, and if the voices of 'the other', the marginal, the 'fringe', the subordinate were to be allowed, what would happen to the integrity of archaeology as a discipline? How would we be able to retain science funding if we admitted a political involvement? Surely post-processual really meant post-archaeology.

I will return to this issue and show that processual archaeology was full of contradictions and could no longer claim a coherent position on objectivity, independence and hypothesis testing. But the often violent debate about subjectivity obscures the fact that in most other realms of the post-processual critique, movement was already taking place. Either independently or as a reaction to the post-processual attack, processual archaeology began to accommodate and absorb many of the more salient points.

Already in the 1970s, processual archaeology saw internal reactions against the extremes of the early New Archaeology. The law-and-order emphasis was softened by a systemic approach which recognised the local complexity of behaviour (Flannery 1973). A disillusion with neo-evolutionism set in as research like that conducted by Earle (1977) on Hawaiian chiefdoms began to question some of the expected correlates. A social, rather than an ecological or materialist archaeology was defined (Renfrew 1973). The importance of historical factors was long stressed by Trigger (1978), and this has been more widely accepted recently (e.g. Deetz 1988). Flannery and Marcus (1976; 1983) incorporated culture-historical dimensions into their work. Inductive reasoning was early recognised to be as valid as deductive. Even those such as

Schiffer (1976) who retained a deductive, law-and-order view, showed that surviving material culture was not a direct reflection of past behaviour – it had to be understood in its archaeological context.

As another example of movement beyond the early processual position, in 1982 Renfrew argued for an 'archaeology of mind' which he has since developed into a 'cognitive processual' archaeology (Renfrew 1989). According to this view, 'mind' is 'the formulated concepts and the shared ways of thought which, within any specific cultural matrix, are the common inheritance of all its citizens as participants' (Renfrew 1982, 26). In common with other processual approaches, this is a highly normative and non-processual perspective, but it does emphasise that the concepts which affect artifact patterning are to some degree historically particular and contextual. Similarly, Flannery and Marcus (1976; 1983) have inferred an 'ethic' which underlay ritual, society and economy through long periods in Mesoamerica. These processual accounts of symbolism and meaning, then, do not just concern the functions of symbols. They move from a strict adaptive view and argue that cultural meanings can be the framework for, rather than the tools of, adaptation. And to some degree they accept the particular, contextual and arbitrary nature of these meanings.

Another clear example of convergence is presented by Earle and Preucel (1987) in their attempt to build a behavioural archaeology. For them, the important aspects of the post-processual critique were already being dealt with in processual archaeology. The aspects of post-processual archaeology which they accept are the importance of symbolism, the importance of history (although mainly in a neo-Darwinian sense), the incorporation of the individual within a less normative and less mechanistic social theory, and some form of Marxism. While they accept the need to consider the relevance of archaeology to a modern world, they do not seem to want to move very far in their questioning of the epistemological basis of the 'scientific method'.

Renfrew (1989), in addition to incorporating cognitive issues, has accepted the critique of functionalist/adaptationist arguments, the need to consider conflict and contradiction in cultural change, and the need to consider and evaluate rigorously structuralist forms of analysis. He has also argued for the need to consider the social production of archaeological knowledge. This latter aim is to some degree compromised by his continued commitment to value-free, objective science (see below, p. 151).

A number of people (e.g. Mithen 1989) have noted apparent similarities between modern evolutionary biology and post-processual archaeology. In discussing such an approach, Mithen accepts the following aspects of post-processual archaeology: the importance of the active individual, of cognition, of creative thought, and of history. He accepts the notion of knowledgeable human actors monitoring the intended and unintended consequences of their actions within unique historical contexts. Differences of course remain, and Mithen prefers cost-benefit analyses to interpretations of symbolism, and he does not problematise the past/present, object/subject relationships.

Both Bintliff (1990) and Renfrew and Bahn (1991) have thus argued for a new synthesis in which the difficulties in processual archaeology exposed by the post-processual critique are accepted so that the critique can be turned towards the improvement of the discipline. It is perhaps the case that many Anglo-American archaeologists today would accept the first five of the six post-processual critiques discussed in Chapter 5. Thus, they would accept that cultural meanings are enabling, that material culture is meaningfully constituted as well as being materially grounded, that structures are incorporated within systems, that agents and material culture are active rather than passive, and that history is important. They may well have drifted to these points of view despite, rather than because of, the post-processual critique. A real convergence has somehow occurred. It is perhaps a minor issue whether the resulting synthesis is closer to processual archaeology (as Renfrew would claim) or post-processual archaeology (as I would claim). The giving of labels is largely political in this context.

Despite the movements towards a new synthesis, an important area of difference which remains is that which concerns method and verification. At first sight, even the sixth point of the post-processual critique would appear to be accepted by some processual archaeologists. Flannery (1973; 1982) has long been critical of the law-and-order approach. Renfrew and Bahn (1991, 432) reject the formulation of 'laws of culture process' as in physics and they argue that 'an extreme "positivist" view of the philosophy of science can no longer be sustained: "facts" can no longer be viewed as having an objective existence independent of theory' (ibid.). Indeed, taken at face value, such statements (see also Binford and Sabloff 1982) might lead one to believe that there are no differences remaining between the two 'camps'.

In fact, however, we cannot yet claim a happy compromise, because processual archaeologists remain somewhat confused over method and epistemology. Many processual archaeologists had gradually come to accept that their knowledge was socially constructed (Trigger 1984). This realisation came from a number of sources. Particularly influential was the recognition that the supposedly 'pristine' cultures which archaeologists had been using as objective correlates for past societies had probably all been affected to some degree by contact with technologically more advanced societies prior to ethnographic study. For example, the Bushmen of southern Africa had been influenced by Bantu and Hottentot farmers and herders (Schrire 1980). Neutrality, objectivity and universalism were thus undermined by history. Peoples who had been described as 'other' (Fabian 1983) or as 'without history' (Wolf 1982) were gaining a new voice. But some processual archaeologists were not ready to face the implications of the social construction of knowledge. They wished to retain the comfort of a positivist label. I wish to show that by retaining a positivist approach to method while at the same time accepting the theory-dependence of data and the other parts of the post-processual position, processual archaeologists have landed themselves in a hopeless contradiction. The only way that a coherent position can be maintained is to abandon a narrow view of science and embrace the type of approach that will be described in Chapter 12. For the moment, I wish only to explore the contradiction within the processual position.

A HOPELESS PROCESSUAL DILEMMA

I noted at the beginning of Chapter 5 that positivist archaeologists committed to the testing of theories against objective data are faced with the problem of how to test theories about unobservable parts of past cultural systems. This is a difficulty which affects all types of theorising in archaeology (Wylie 1989a). However, it is exacerbated by consideration of symbolism and mind since symbolic meanings are historically arbitrary. By definition, therefore, universal instruments of measurement will not on their own allow us to test theories about past symbolic meanings.

The dilemma is clearly expressed by Watson in her 1986 review of archaeological interpretation. Binford (1981; Binford and Sabloff 1982) accepts that the past is perceived within a social and cultural matrix. He accepts that the archaeological record is dependent on our observations of it. He therefore reaches the incredibly pessimistic and negative conclusion that 'we cannot use either the archaeological record or the inferred past to test our premises or assumptions' (1981, 29). 'The testing of theories was thus an illusion' (Binford and Sabloff 1982, 138). Instead, we need to test our theories in the present, using 'actualistic' studies to build middle-range theories which are in some sense independent of our paradigms. Thus middle-range theories can be used to test 'objectively' between paradigms (ibid.).

Apart from severely limiting the role of the archaeologist, this view is undermined by two of its features (Wylie 1989b). First, as Watson (1986) also argues, our actualistic ethnoarchaeology is also paradigm-related. Ethnographers as well as archaeologists face the problem that the way they construct 'the other' is embedded in social and cultural relations. Middle-range theory cannot be independent of our paradigms.

Second, Watson (1986) shows the contradictory nature of Binford's position. Binford has noted that since observation is not independent of our explanations, theories and paradigms, there is a danger of 'affirming

148

the consequent', or of assuming that which one should be trying to prove. His solution is to develop very well-confirmed laws and regularities about behavioural correlates in present-day societies. Watson recognises that even if we could find such regularities, we still have to 'affirm the consequent' when we choose which correlates are relevant to a particular case. Binford claims that middle-range theory concerns those things which the present shares with the past. These common things provide the basis for a comparison between times (past and present). But, Watson asks (1986, 448), how can we decide with any certainty which things the present shares with the past? 'We must always affirm the consequent if we are to do any meaningful interpretation at all' (ibid.).

This last statement by Watson is extremely important. It states with clarity the hermeneutic position which will be explored in Chapter 12. Watson is making the obvious hermeneutic point that no interpretation is possible until interpretation has begun. We cannot even begin to make sense of the archaeological material until we make some assumptions about it. We cannot know what universals and correlates and regularities are relevant to the data until we have made some assumptions about what the data mean. As an extreme example, we cannot apply theories of exchange to stone objects we think of as thunderbolts! We do not think theories of indigenous development and social complexity are relevant to the data if we think observed cultural changes are the product of movements of people. A more appropriate example today is that Schiffer (1987) pays scant attention to social theory because he does not think that the notion that material culture is meaningfully constituted is relevant to discard behaviour.

Processual archaeologists have thus got themselves into a terrible mess. They have come to accept that the data are theory-laden. In essence, therefore, they accept the hermeneutic circle. But they cling to the idea that they can get out of the circle according to which subjectivity is accepted as part of science and verification. So they engage in some fast foot-work and wool-pulling. But the hoped-for solution of independent middle-range theory is undermined by their own assertion that the data are theory-laden. Middle-range theories too must be within the subjective hermeneutic circle. And by stating that middle-range theory has to share something with the past in order to make it relevant to the past, processual archaeologists also prove that all their work is enmeshed in a priori assumptions. We have to start interpreting the archaeological record before we can explain it. Our interests guide what we look at, how we look at it, what theories and regularities we call upon, and so on.

I will argue in Chapter 12 that these realisations do not lead to relativism (Wylie 1989b) and a denial of science. I will argue that an alternative based on hermeneutics and dialectics provides a better account of archaeological methodology. For the moment, I simply wish to document the extraordinary confusions and contradictions that are now expressed in processual archaeological writing, resulting from an attempt to retain both positivism and hermeneutics at the same time. It simply is not possible to retain a positivist commitment to objective and independent science while at the same time accepting that the data and our theories are always already interpretations. Wylie (1989a) has put the point well. Hempelian positivism emphasises the testing of observables. But even by 1977, Binford, for example, had come to see that observations are theory-dependent. His interest thus shifted to building more secure theory in the present. But the use of secure theories about necessary causal relationships and processes, developed in the contemporary world, is profoundly non-positivistic. According to Wylie, the positivist emphasis is on testing, not on secure theory. Processual archaeology thus claims positivism in theory, but in practice undermines it. A processual archaeology which clings to objective testing cannot deal with the paradigm-dependence of observation in the modern world and of observation of archaeological data. Many processual archaeologists do not seem to have realised this hopeless confusion. They live on, blind to the contradictions they are writing.

For example, in his collection of papers entitled *Debating Archaeology*, Binford (1989) argues repeatedly that it is possible to reveal the external world 'in terms of itself' (ibid., 69) or 'in its own right' (ibid., 67 and 71). He aims to show that it is possible to 'make others aware of their own uncritical acceptance of an unevaluated set of assumptive views about the world' (ibid., 486). He argues that we must combat the self-appointed authorities who proclaim what we are like and who then use such alleged knowledge to create pasts consistent with their beliefs (ibid., 68). Binford writes that paradigm-dependence never bothered him and that it does not seem to be a general or necessary problem for scientists (ibid., 37). We can step outside culture and history and know the external world in terms of itself. 'The archaeologist . . . is outside history in the participant sense' (ibid., 52).

But in the same book there are statements which contradict the above views. 'Do we really expect scientists to be "outside" their culture? That, of course, is impossible' (ibid., 46). At several points in the 1989 volume, Binford accepts that archaeologists are caught within their own cultural milieu and that they cannot see reality 'objectively'. Our task is not the objective approximation of truth but the investigation of our culturally bound ignorance. 'All archaeological data are generated by us in our terms' (ibid., 57). He also seems to recognise (ibid., 162) that there are problems inherent in making observations on a living system and that his presence as an ethnographer affected what he was observing. In fact, his own account of his ethnoarchaeological work expresses a richly

150

textured and personal involvement. Thus at least some of his ethno-archaeological work 'is not intended as a demonstration of secure knowledge' (ibid., 255). And as for knowing in advance what matters are relevant to the past, he makes his position clear by stating a number of a priori generalisations. For example, 'intentional acts were not the causal force standing behind history' (ibid., 20). 'Cultural systems are not closed ideological structures. They are thermodynamic systems' (ibid., 53). Binford provides an excellent example of an archaeologist caught within culture and history. In this way he is the same as all of us, even if he does not realise it.

Similar tensions can be found in the work of other, less extreme processual archaeologists who have accepted many of the post-processual arguments. As a final illustration I will take some of the recent writing by Renfrew. Here, the contradictions are again clearly stated. 'Today, no one claims that data can in an absolute sense be "objective": they are not formulated other than by human activity and are not independent of that process' (Renfrew 1989, 38). Indeed, he accepts that practising scientists use both the criteria of coherence and correspondence in evaluating theories. In other words, he puts a hermeneutic position. He accepts that the data are theory-laden (ibid., 36). But he then veers away from coherence and puts all his faith in objective data. 'The material record of the past, the actual remains, may indeed be claimed as "value-free" and lacking in observer-induced bias', so that the data 'alone can validate or falsify our own (subjectively produced) hypotheses' (ibid., 39). The direct contradictions between these sets of statements cannot be avoided by any practising archaeologist. Rather than ignoring them and pretending that the contradictions do not exist, we need to see the contradiction as a dialectic between subject and object which forms the building block of our science. This hermeneutic view will be put in Chapter 12.

Renfrew's work is of particular interest since he develops his ideas in the context of an attempt to build a cognitive processual archaeology (1982; 1989). As already noted, when positivism is extended to symbolism and mind, the contradictions become more severe because of the partly arbitrary nature of the sign. On the one hand, Renfrew (1982) argues that each culture has its own historical trajectory. The development of ideas, he says, will be different in each context. Each history will have its own cognitive phylogeny. It is simply not possible to square these views with the notion of value-free data which alone can validate or falisify our subjectively produced hypotheses. The views are contradicted by the claim (ibid.) that we can develop general theories which will allow us to infer cognitive processes without making intuitive (interpretive) leaps. Perhaps there are some aspects of psychology and cognition and perception which are universal and not culturally variable. But even if we manage to build secure knowledge of this type, it will still be necessary, as Watson argued in relation to Binford's claims, to decide to what aspects of the archaeological record such general knowledge might be relevant. Once again, interpretation will only be possible once interpretation has begun.

In his interpretation of a Bronze Age Aegean sanctuary or shrine, Renfrew (1985) provides us with a clear example of how his positivist, hypotheses-testing approach can be applied to issues of symbolism. Renfrew wants to break away from the vicious circle according to which shrines are identified in the Aegean because they look like other shrines in the Aegean. This is of course necessary, but Renfrew thinks that the answer is to build a general theory about religion, based on anthropological writing, and then to make various predictions about what a sanctuary should look like in the archaeological record. He develops a check-list of behavioural correlates for religious ritual. The list includes such things as 'attention-focusing devices', 'gestures of adoration' and cult images, symbolism and iconography of omnipotent powers and deities (ibid., 19). But in order to identify the items on the check-list, we have to interpret the meanings of the objects involved. We have to enter 'their' minds and say that a platform was 'attention-focusing', or that a figurine was perceived as a deity or that the upraised arms of a human figurine represent a 'gesture of adoration'. No universal criteria are offered to do this. Indeed, Renfrew's own arguments indicate that universal criteria for identifying 'their' meanings could not be provided, since each history has its own cognitive phylogeny. Renfrew's attempt at developing a universalist, objective hypothesis-testing procedure has been contradicted by his own need to say what the past means. In the end, he has to accept that he needs evidence and interpretations from other shrines in the Aegean in order to support his interpretation of a particular building as a shrine. In the end, then, he has to accept a hermeneutic position. We will see later, in an applied example, that it is possible to avoid the viciousness of the hermeneutic circle by other means (Chapter 15).

In conclusion, the unacknowledged contradictions evident in recent processual archaeology writing have always been there. They are a necessary part of any positivist approach, at least when applied in the humanities and social sciences. To accept subjectivity while claiming objectivity just won't wash. The limitations of a view which grasps universal measuring devices, independence and value-free data are particularly acute when applied to symbolic matters. Few would argue that symbolic meanings are not partly historically and subjectively constructed. The arbitrary and the subjective simply cannot be made to cohere with the universal and the objective. The resulting contradictions which I have shown are blatant in a considerable body of processual archaeological writing, have become gradually more evident as people have tried to do two opposite things at one and the same time. In the end, processual archaeology would probably have undermined itself without any prompting from post-processual archaeology. But the processual dilemma has become more hopeless often in response to the post-processual critique. As more and more evidence of the extent to which our science is socially embedded has emerged, the difficulties of a simple objectivist or falsification position have become more stark. We need a different epistemology.

REFERENCES

Binford, L. (1977) *For Theory Building in Archaeology*, New York: Academic Press.
—— (1981) *Bones: Ancient Men and Modern Myths*, New York: Academic Press.
—— (1989) *Debating Archaeology*, New York: Academic Press.
Binford, L. and Sabloff, J. (1982) 'Paradigms, systematics and archaeology', *Journal of Anthropological Research* 38, 137–53.
Bintliff, J. (1990) 'Foreword', in J. Bintliff (ed.) *Extracting Meaning from the Past*, Oxford: Oxbow Books.
Deetz, J. (1988) 'History and archaeological theory: Walter Taylor revisited', *American Antiquity* 53, 13–22.
Earle, T. (1977) 'A reappraisal of redistribution: complex Hawaiian chiefdoms', in T. Earle and J. Ericson (eds) *Exchange Systems in Prehistory*, New York: Academic Press.
Earle, T. and Preucel, R. (1987) 'Processual archaeology and the radical critique', *Current Anthropology* 28, 501–38.
Fabian, J. (1983) *Time and the Other*, New York: Columbia University Press.
Flannery, K. (1973) 'Archaeology with a capital S', in C. Redman (ed.) *Research and Theory in Current Archaeology*, New York: Wiley.
—— (1982) 'The golden Marshalltown: a parable for the archaeology of the 1980s', *American Anthropologist* 84, 265–78.
Flannery, K. V. and Marcus, J. (1976) 'Formative Oaxaca and the Zapotec cosmos', *American Scientist* 64, 374–83.
—— (1983) *The Cloud People*, New York: Academic Press.
Hodder, I. (1986) *Reading the Past*, Cambridge: Cambridge University Press.
Mithen, S. (1989) 'Evolutionary theory and post-processual archaeology', *Antiquity* 63, 483–94.
Renfrew, A. C. (1973) *Social Archaeology*, Southampton: Southampton University Press.
—— (1982) *Towards an Archaeology of Mind*, Cambridge: Cambridge University Press.
—— (1985) *The Archaeology of Cult*, London: Thames and Hudson.
—— (1989) 'Comments on "Archaeology into the 1990s" ', *Norwegian Archaeological Review* 22, 33–41.
Renfrew, A. C. and Bahn, P. (1991) *Archaeology*, London: Thames and Hudson.
Schiffer, M. (1976) *Behavioural Archaeology*, New York: Academic Press.
—— (1987) *Formation Processes of the Archaeological Record*, Albuquerque: University of New Mexico Press.
Schrire, C. (1980) 'An inquiry into the evolutionary status and apparent identity of San hunter gatherers', *Human Ecology* 8, 9–32.
Shanks, M. and Tilley, C. (1987a) *Re–constructing Archaeology*, Cambridge: Cambridge University Press.
—— (1987b) *Social Theory and Archaeology*, Cambridge: Polity Press.
Trigger, B. G. (1978) *Time and Traditions*, Edinburgh: Edinburgh University Press.

—— (1984) 'Archaeology at the crossroads: what's new?', *Annual Review of Anthropology* 13, 275–300.

Watson, P. J. (1986) 'Archaeological interpretation, 1985', in D. Meltzer, D. Fowler, and J. Sabloff (eds) *American Archaeology Past and Future*, Washington DC: Smithsonian Institution Press.

Wolf, E. (1982) *Europe and the People without History*, Berkeley: University of California Press.

Wylie, A. (1989a) 'The interpretive dilemma', in V. Pinsky and A. Wylie (eds) *Critical Traditions in Contemporary Archaeology*, Cambridge: Cambridge University Press.

—— (1989b) 'Archaeological cables and tacking: the implications of practice for Bernstein's "Options beyond objectivism and relativism" ', *Philosophy of the Social Sciences* 19, 1–18.

10

TOWARDS RADICAL DOUBT:
A DIALOGUE

What I found particularly interesting in the way processual archaeologists reacted to my writing was that they did not respond to what I
said, but to what they wanted me to say. In other words, they had
already begun their interpretation of my work before they read it. They
were following classically hermeneutic procedures, but it was none the
less annoying. Archaeologists had absorbed stereotypical oppositions
between objective and subjective, materialism and idealism, the general
and the particular, science and relativism. Even though I wrote that I
wanted to break down these divides, processual archaeologists claimed
that I was being idealist, that I rejected generalisations, that I took a
relativist position. As is clear from Chapter 3, I tried not to take such a
one-sided view. Yet my work was read in terms of the old expectations. I
was set up as a 'straw man' so that I could be knocked down.

*Wait a minute. Are you not being just a little hypocritical? You said yourself
in the last chapter that processual archaeologists such as Flannery and Renfrew
were already moving in post-processual directions and taking more nuanced
positions. They had already accepted the importance of history, the individual,
active material culture, symbolism and meaning and so on. You simply set up a
straw processual archaeologist to serve your own purposes. And you are doing
the same here.*

I agree there may be some truth to that. I have been, at least subcons-
ciously, career-mongering. But some processual archaeologists did initially react in a stereotypical way. At least I did try to set up my straw
persons correctly. Some of the processual criticisms, such as those by
Yengoyan (1985) and Chapman (1990) simply had not understood the
issues, while others misrepresented my work.

*Why do you mind? Surely any reading is as good as any other? In your reply
to Bell's (1987) review of* Reading the Past, *you wrote: 'I do not want to argue
that my interpretation of "my own" book is right and that Bell is wrong. The
book is divorced from me. Its meaning does not depend on the author but on the
reading of it that is given. I do not wish for any authority in relation to the text'
(Hodder 1987, 91). And in your edited volume* The Meanings of Things

155

(Hodder 1989) you tried to undermine the authority of western archaeological writing by placing it on an equal basis to the writing of indigenous writers. Surely you should accept the 'death of the author' and delight in the different readings of your texts? What right do you have to say that certain interpretations of your work are wrong?

I can't surrender all responsibility for what I write. Take, for example, the reaction of younger Spanish archaeologists to post-processual archaeology (Rodriguez, Chapa and Zapatero 1988; Marcen and Risch 1990; Ruiz and Nocete 1990). In Spain, the critique of New Archaeology serves to create links with traditional archaeology. In the Spanish context, post-processual archaeology supports the reactionary emphasis on norm, historical particularism, intuition, the rejection of scientific research designs and techniques, and the rejection of theory. I had to respond (Hodder 1990) in order to correct their understanding of my work and show that I accepted the need for scientific rigour in field methods, generalisation and theory-building. Otherwise my work would have a reactionary rather than an enlightening effect in Spain.

Poor deluded fool. No-one has taken much notice of your response in Spain. People will read your texts as they want to. You can't be responsible for how your work is understood. You can't control meaning, without embracing Stalinism.

It's true that I do feel in a real dilemma. Sometimes, as in my response to Bell or in *The Meanings of Things*, I have no sense of being 'an author' because I have accepted the need to listen to others and to relativise my own arbitrary position. I live in a post-modern world. I feel fragmented, consumerised, sound-bitten. I accept multiple voices, versioning and mixing. My kids introduce me to 'virtual reality' machines. But on the other hand, as a parent I feel certain duties and I believe in certain moral truths. As a member of society I feel strongly about the underprivileged and I am idealistic, romantically hopeful about alleviating the condition of the disadvantaged. As an archaeologist I believe that the past should be saved or that Spanish archaeology should break out of an atheoretical empiricism. How can I believe all these things and yet be full of post-modern doubt?

Yes, you really are confused. You think you believe in post-processual archae-ology because it helps to construct a better world in which people in their different and particular historical conditions are taken seriously. You think you believe in a radical humanism, that you can 'change the world' for the better. But in fact you believe in nothing except your own interests. You have simply flitted opportunistically from theory to theory. You have pretended this is not so, both to yourself and to others. This book is perhaps the worst example of your duplicity. So far you have been constructing a neat developmental history of your ideas. But there has been no coherent growth. What you said in the preface was nonsense. You said there that you would show the developmental coherence of your 'œuvre' (how pretentious!). That it was guided by big questions. But as you did your work there was little sense of coherence.

But I really do believe in the dangers of scientism and in the dangers of claims to objectivity and neutrality. Look at terrible cases such as children being wrenched from their parents because 'science had shown', wrongly as it turned out, that the children had been sexually abused. Or look at how the problems and domination of the Third World have so often been exacerbated by the imposition of 'universal' but inappropriate policies. We need to be sensitive to people, culture, history, context. And I really do believe that processual archaeology, in however small a way, contributed to the disregard of such issues. I know that people were moving in a post-processual direction anyway, but without recognising it. The political impact was thus being ignored. The social statement was being neutralised and appropriated.

I'm afraid that just won't wash. Where were all these high political ideals when you were doing your spatial analysis work? You seemed conveniently to have forgotten them then, as you did all that objective science and as you simulated people in computer models (Hodder and Orton 1976; Hodder 1978). In fact, your emphasis on social responsibility and the new post-processual theories largely came about because of disciplinary politics. You wanted to make a mark. It was also largely accidental, dependent on the students who happened to come to Cambridge. You didn't point out in that totally false Chapter 2 that the 'discovery' of the view that material culture is meaningfully constituted was contingent. It resulted from what you happened to come across amongst the Nuba, what you happened to have read such as Mary Douglas, and so on. You made that chapter sound as if some universal truth had been uncovered. All this social idealism you are now claiming came about contingently and it suited your interests. In fact it was all opportunistic.

But I really did feel more of a 'whole person' once I gave up spatial analysis. I had felt split between my 'objective' spatial analytical work and my beliefs as a member of society. It was only as a post-processual archaeologist that I felt my research and my convictions were working in the same directions. I am someone who really believes in these new directions.

What's all this 'I am . . .' and 'whole person' stuff? The 'you' that is now speaking has been constructed contingently and opportunistically. It has grown out of the dialogue with your critics. You have written a lot and it is confused and contradictory. There is no coherent œuvre and no 'you' which is not situated in the moment of debate.

It is true that I have written contradictory things, but I was searching for something, trying out different directions to find out what 'I' wanted. There was an underlying purpose. What is the point of doing research unless you change your mind, learning through experience? Through dialogue and through archaeology I came to see what 'I' wanted to do. My conclusions may be historically contingent, but surely they are real?

The notion of a 'real' cause, condition, principle or whatever assumes some universal way of evaluating the world. You know that is not possible. Your whole emphasis on context and history undermines the notion that there is one reality to social life.

I suppose you are right. You know, I always find these conversations exhausting. I really prefer to write in my ivory garret. I find the real world of debate (especially spoken debate) and practice difficult to control. I prefer writing. I can control theory and words within the boundaries of a text. I feel comfortable and safe within the academic cannon. I suppose I should stick to my writing and not worry about how people react.

Yes.

And you know another thing? It is to my advantage to argue for multiple readings of my texts, the death of the author and all that. My writing is polysemous, contingent. I keep changing my mind and con-tradicting myself, moving to new positions. I do not want to be categor-ised because I realise that I can then be controlled, labelled, dismissed, closed off. I want to remain on the margins of everything, always criticising but never able to be tied down and subjected to a disabling and final criticism myself. You can't hit a moving target. It is in my interest to be ambiguous, contradictory, with no faith, no *oeuvre*, no 'I'. I obtain power and authority through irony and critique. I float, disaggre-gated, between positions. No-one can touch me. It doesn't matter if I don't believe anything. I'm above all that, on a higher plane. Doubt makes me feel good.

Yes, you've got it.

REFERENCES

Bell, J. (1987) 'Rationality versus relativism: a review of "Reading the past" ', *Archaeological Review from Cambridge* 6(1), 75–86.

Chapman, R. (1990) *Emerging Complexity*, Cambridge: Cambridge University Press.

Hodder, I. (ed.) (1978) *Simulation Studies in Archaeology*, Cambridge: Cambridge University Press.

—— (1987) 'Reading Bell reading "Reading the Past" ', *Archaeological Review from Cambridge* 6(1), 87–91.

—— (ed.) (1989) *The Meanings of Things*, London: Unwin Hyman.

—— (1990) 'El debate Espanol sobre la arqueologia contextual', *Trabajos de Prehistoria* 47, 379–82.

Hodder, I. and Orton, C. (1976) *Spatial Analysis in Archaeology*, Cambridge: Cambridge University Press.

Marcen, P. G. and Risch, R. (1990) 'Archaeology and historical materialism: outsiders' reflections on theoretical discussions in British archaeology', in F. Baker and J. Thomas (eds) *Writing the Past in the Present*, Lampeter: St David's University College.

Rodriguez, A. R., Chapa, T. and Zapatero, G. R. (1988) 'Contextual archaeology: a critical review', *Trabajos de Prehistoria* 45, 11–17.

Ruiz, A. and Nocete, F. (1990) 'The dialectic of the past and the present in the construction of a scientific archaeology', in F. Baker and J. Thomas (eds) *Writing the Past in the Present*, Lampeter: St David's University College.

Yengoyan, A. A. (1985) 'Digging for symbols: the archaeology of everyday material life', *Proceedings of the Prehistoric Society*, 51, 329–34.

11

THE POST-PROCESSUAL
REACTION

As seen in Chapter 9, the processual reaction to post-processual archaeology, while accepting most of its aspects, was worried about verification. The knowledge claims of archaeologists seemed to be
undermined by the post-processual emphasis on contextuality. If interpretations could not be based on universal theories and instruments
of measurement, and if they could not be tested on objective neutral
data, how could we distinguish between 'real' and 'fringe' archaeology?
I have shown that in fact these problems were being raised within
processual archaeology. Binford and Sabloff's (1982, 138) statement that
'the testing of theories was thus an illusion' was as radical as anything I
or Shanks and Tilley have written. However, these unsettling tendencies were identified with post-processual views. They were seen as too
dangerous to admit into the core of the processual discipline.

My reaction to the processual critique concerning verification was to
argue that we can reject an absolute objectivism while still recognising
that our theories can be fitted to the data to see which theories fit best.
Thus, as shown in Chapter 2, I 'tested' my theory that tombs meant
houses against eight aspects of the evidence, and as further data were
collected they supported my interpretation. There is no finality, and my
interpretation is only a moment in a moving dialectic, but it is nevertheless grounded in the patterned material remains. This is a more optimistic view than that offered by Binford and Sabloff.

The reaction to my work within post-processual archaeology has been
the opposite. Here I have been criticised for not being radical enough. I
have been criticised for still clinging to the past as real, for wanting to
find out what really happened. My work has been shown to be contradictory because it accepts the past as subjective, but tests theories
against data. The notion that one can test theories against data is said to
be an illusion, a naked attempt to retain authority and scientific privilege. There is in fact a remarkable convergence between Binford's views
and the post-processual critique, as noted by Watson (1986). Both
appear to reject an ability to approach the real past, and place their

emphases on the present. There are, of course, many differences between the two sets of views. For example, post-processual archaeologists would claim to be socially active in the present. But it is perhaps
ironic, given Binford's view, that post-processual archaeologists claim I
have not been sufficiently radical.

The problem develops in the following way. I claimed in Chapters 2
and 3 that material culture is meaningfully constituted. I understood this
to mean that there are ideas and concepts embedded in social life which
influence the way material culture is made, used and discarded. As a
result, it was realised that archaeologists work with a double hermeneutic. They do not simply deal with a physical, 'fossil' record, organised by
universal, non-cultural processes. Rather, they deal with the meanings
constructed by other people, with another realm of meaning. They have
to deal not only with 'our' meanings ('our' hermeneutic), but also with
'their' meanings ('their' hermeneutic). In this way, as Patrik (1985) has
shown, the archaeological data can be compared less with a fossil record
and more with a text. A text is written to mean something. It has to be
understood within a framework of meaning. It has to be translated from
'their' into 'our' meanings.

Initially (as in Chapter 3) I assumed that everyone in a cultural 'whole'
would give the same meanings to an object conceived as text. But this
view was discarded when it was realised that different people in societies, with different social lives, would view the world and material
culture differently (Hodder 1986). This notion that different people in
the past and present would give different meanings to the same object
places an emphasis on the reading of texts. The meaning of a text, or of
material culture, lies less in its production and intention, and more in its
interpretation from different points of view. The object has no meaning
until it has been 'read'.

Yates (1990a; 1990b), for example, notes that the main aim of the text
analogy is to move away from notions of an absolute passive identity of
the past, the past as a record. Instead the material remains are seen as
being actively read by the archaeologist. The meaning of the material
culture is constructed by placing it within a network of differences, a
network of signifiers. Each signifier functions because of its differences
from other signifiers. Material culture is read as having different meanings as it is placed in relation to different chains of signifiers in the
present.

The radical post-structuralist position, therefore, is that we cannot get
to any original meaning in the past. We certainly cannot get at what
material culture meant in the past to 'them'. This is because, even in the
past, material objects did not have any singular meaning, any meaning
'in themselves'. Both in the past and the present, the meanings of
objects depended on how the objects were read. The objects were and

are placed in relation to an ever-shifting flow of difference. Yates (1990a) places the emphasis on chains of differences in the present, on horizontality in the present rather than on depth (the return back to the 'arche'). 'There is only and always difference' (ibid., 169). This is equivalent to Derrida's famous statement that 'there is nothing outside the text' (see Yates 1990b). Olsen (1990) argues in a similar vein that the desire to get at the original meaning, at what the 'author' of material culture meant, is deluded (see also Moran and Hides 1990).

These post-structuralist views are certainly at odds with my own position. Even in starting with the idea of 'text', I start with an 'origin', with a starting point which I accept unquestioningly. And certainly I argue that there is real patterning in the material remains and that Neolithic tombs meant houses, to 'them'. But how can I make such claims while adopting the text analogy for material culture? Surely I must see that a text can be read in endless new ways. An object's meaning was and is diffused along countless chains of signification.

My response to the notion of the free flow or play of signification is context. In order to stop meaning running away down chains of signifiers, people in the past and present use context. Subjective readings of the world are translated into objective material actions, written into the material remains. In situated material contexts, stable and definable relationships are set up which allow the reader to recognise and understand meaning. As Yates (1990a) notes in a useful review, the notion of context operates to close down the chains of signifiers and to forestall the unsettling effects of the loose play of difference. In particular, as Barrett (1987) has argued, archaeologists deal with a material context which restrains and channels possible meanings. Our readings of material texts are constrained by material possibilities and by the material associations, similarities and differences in the evidence.

But as Yates (1990a; 1990b) points out, I run into difficulties here. I argue that terms and materials must be understood contextually. And yet my 'context' is beyond the system of differences. It is not itself contextually defined. What defines the context? The term, in my writing, becomes transhistorical. How do I define what to put into the context and what to exclude? Is not the context itself an interpretation? Since meaning depends on context, I have to start by defining past contexts. But in imposing a context I have to have decided before I start what the past was like. I exclude from my analyses a whole series of starting points which I bring from outside.

My response to this conundrum has been again to say that we do not simply impose our ideas on the material evidence. The real material similarities and differences form a basis for defining sites, regions, cultures and other types of context. While we do read the material texts in changing ways, the interpretations are influenced by real material patterning. The contexts we impose interact with real contexts left as material traces. Thus the past, in my view, has a relative autonomy from the present.

But surely, argues Bapty (1990), you (Hodder) are glossing over another contradiction here. The notion of context contains two components: there is the context of the present and the context of the past. Material culture is meaningfully constituted and patterned in past contexts. But those contexts are also the results of situated production of the past in the present. You have argued that our interpretations need to be reflexive and critically aware. So you argue for interpretations which reflect and acknowledge the past–present relationship but are not completely subsumed by the interests of the present. Is this not a contradiction? Your contextual archaeology produces the past through the ironic mode of a sustained *double entendre*, observing the past but admitting that it is not completely observable.

I will argue in Chapter 12 that the duality of the past as constructed yet real is not duplicit. I will argue that past and present, object and subject, text and context constitute each other and bring each other into existence. We need to chart a way between objectivism and subjectivism (Rowlands 1984). One of the reasons that I have taken this more moderate stance, which I will outline more fully in Chapters 12 and 13, is my response to the post-structuralist position. There are two particular limitations of post-structuralist archaeology which I see. The first is the danger of being locked into the present, with the past effectively negated. The second is that archaeology loses any political agency by being committed to a particular view of plurality and multivocality.

PRESENTISM AND VALUE-COMMITMENT

Post-structuralists (Bapty and Yates 1990; Baker and Thomas 1990; Tilley 1990b) deny the possibility of getting back to original meanings in the past. Instead, they focus on chains of difference in the present. They wish to undermine archaeological 'truths' by showing that they are nothing more than arbitrary points in the free flow of signifiers. Our origins, causes, material bases, all our taken-for-granteds (from culture and society to text and context) can be deconstructed by showing how they derive their meaning not from any essence, but from other terms in chains of signifiers. Terms such as Neolithic, technology, period, state, past derive their meaning from a contingent and situated disciplinary tradition. From Foucault and Derrida (see Tilley 1990b), the claim is made that we cannot enquire about truth, only about how the effects of truth come about.

I certainly agree that one of the main positive aspects of post-processual archaeology has been to focus attention on the social construction of the past in the present. The contribution of critical theory (e.g. Leone, Potter and Shackel 1987) and gender archaeology (Gero and

Conkey 1991), as well as the impact of non-western peoples has been considerable in this regard. The particular contribution of post-structuralist archaeology has been to point to language and writing as vehicles for unacknowledged vested interests. There has been a shift from reading the past to writing the past. How archaeologists write their texts has rightly become a focus of analysis (see Chapter 18). Writing has been studied as being part of a discourse of power–knowledge–truth, as being underpinned by a politics of truth (Tilley 1990a).

A critical component is essential in archaeology as I argue in Chapter 13. But it is dangerous to claim that the past is only constructed in the present. Shanks and Tilley (1987a; 1987b) have put the case for a value-committed archaeology well. But for them, the material remains from the past are merely networks of resistances to our theories. On the whole, they see a value-committed present imposed on a relatively malleable past. As a result, the archaeological remains play a minimal role. The attention switches to writing, the production of archaeological texts and their political impact. Archaeology becomes a power play of theoretical positioning in the present. I do not deny the existence of such power plays, but I do find that they become abstracted from archaeological data and thus come to be manipulated within an elite academic discourse. Argument must be through rather than over the data if it is to be informed by something more than vested interest. If we do not try and read a relatively autonomous material past and try to understand it in its own terms, then we can be doing no more than reproducing ourselves in a mirror of self-interest. In fact, however, the mirror of the materially patterned past reflects back a distorted picture of ourselves which can help us to see ourselves in a different light. We may go to the data with politically motivated questions and assumptions, but we return from the past data often with unexpected results and discoveries which force us to rethink our positions. If archaeologists are to contribute to rather than reproduce contemporary debates, they need to relate their value-commitment to a partly autonomous past.

If we put all our eggs in the basket of value-commitment, we do not really have to bother with archaeological data any more. The data become mere 'quotes' which we use to write our texts in the present for political purposes. In this way the discipline is entirely undermined. There is no longer any platform or specialism from which the archaeologist can speak. The authority of archaeologists, that they know the data and what it 'really' means, is undercut by the commitment to politically motivated reconstruction. An argument is correct because it contains the right values. The only way that the discipline can retain power and authority is thus through a Stalin-like policing of what is or is not 'acceptable' archaeology (Thomas 1990).

Political misuse of the past needs to be open to evaluation in relation to the data. For example, claims that southern Africa was 'empty' when whites arrived can be countered by evidence showing that 'it was not like that'. The objectivity of the data can be emancipating. Land claims of minority groups in the present can be supported by showing that their ancestors 'really' were there. Of course, an uncritical and atheoretical belief in objectivity is just as prone to political misuse as is a belief in subjectivity and the past as myth. We need to be critically aware and value-committed in the present at the same time as recognising the reality of the patterning of archaeological data.

PLURALISM AND MULTIVOCALITY

The second limitation I see with the post-structuralist position concerns its attitude to pluralism and multivocality. Shanks and Tilley (1987a, 192) argue that my work 'comes close to a disabling relativism', in the spirit of liberal pluralism. They argue that I put my faith on debate in an open society, on civilised and liberal discussion. They ask whether a contextual archaeology will ever change anything. They point out that the system only *allows* certain people to do and write archaeology. They are dubious that critical reflection and debate can achieve change. Instead, they prefer the Marxist tradition and the Frankfurt school emphasis on the situated conditions of communication. They argue for a multiplicity of voices concerned not just with interpreting the past in new ways, but also with changing interpretations of the past in relation to social reconstruction in the present.

As already noted, I accept the importance of a critical tradition and of the understanding and transformation of the relationships between power, knowledge and truth. I also accept that archaeology should be value-committed and socially and politically aware, that it should try to use the past to form a better present. But I do not accept that it should be only value-committed. I do not accept that the only grounds for discriminating between different archaeologies should be political or social. Rather, I would argue that a critical, value-committed archaeology, on its own, becomes a new form of elite interest which is not reflexive. It has to be opposed by and integrated with a commitment to understanding the objective reality of other contexts. This involves embracing hermeneutic procedures and the reality of data patterning.

The whole aim of the contextual approach is indeed to encourage pluralism and multivocality. But it is not adequate simply to 'let a thousand flowers bloom' since, as Shanks and Tilley note, not all flowers have the chance to bloom. We do need to focus on present contexts of power which enable people to write and speak about their pasts. But we also need to integrate such interests with a commitment to past contexts. The trouble with the Shanks and Tilley position is that it appears to reject the possibility of learning about the present through experiencing the past. Plurality and multivocality represent only the war waged by competing interests in the present. There is little notion that different perspectives and interests in the present can be enabled by or transformed by archaeological evidence.

The example of feminist archaeology is instructive in this regard. The framework of a politically motivated pluralism undermines any attempt made by gender archaeologists to argue that the past can be shown to demonstrate the subordination of women. Such demonstrations would simply be dismissed as special pleading by vested interests, and therefore as unsound. Feminist archaeologists do in fact argue their cases in relation to the data (examples in Gero and Conkey 1991). They do not argue for 'anything goes as long as it is politically correct'. They try to persuade that women really were fulfilling certain roles in the past. In other words, the political direction of this 'other' voice is enhanced by an appeal to evidence.

CONCLUSION

Thus I reject the open-ended and purely political plurality argued for by post-structuralists such as Bapty and Yates and by writers such as Shanks and Tilley. While the contextual approach argues for multivocality, the different voices which are released will have no authority, except perhaps through the exercise of naked power, unless related to data. Of course, a commitment to the testing of theories against data might weaken arguments made in relation to contemporary vested interests. After all, the data might not support the arguments that are made. But this is precisely the point. It is by opening contemporary concerns to the possibility of rejection in the past that the past becomes active. It is not difficult to impose the present on the past. It is easy to construct the past as an ideological mirror of ourselves. In this way the past itself becomes passive. More difficult is to give the past an active role. But the experience of the past can shed new light on the present, if it has an authority derived from the partial autonomy of the past. It is only by being objectively different that the past can confront the present and contribute to it.

This is not to argue that the past and present can be absolutely separated, or that the archaeological past can be objectively described as pure, free from contemporary interests. But it is to argue that past and present are constructed in relation to each other. They contribute to each other in objective ways, by which I mean that the present would be different if derived from a different past while the past would be different if constructed in a different present. Past and present contexts move dialectically in relation to each other.

So in the end I return to the position expressed in the preface to this book, and reject that voice of angst with which I was arguing and came to agree with in Chapter 10. The critique of my work within post-processual archaeology led me to see that I did not want to go all the way down the road of value-commitment and political motivation (contrast Chapter 7). Neither did I want to accept a deconstructionist approach and the open play of meaning (contrast Hodder 1989). In both cases it seemed to me that the ability of archaeology to contribute to social debate was weakened. I want to be value-committed and politically concerned in my archaeology, but I realise that to be an active member of society I have to remain an archaeologist. I might be listened to and have power which enables me to speak *as an archaeologist*, not as a politician or critical theorist or feminist. Much as I want to include political, critical or feminist dimensions in my work, it is my control of the archaeological data which gives me a right to speak and be heard. It is my position within a professional discipline with well-defined procedures and structures of power which contributes to me an authority. But control and authority are undermined if based solely on privilege, tradition and arbitrary judgements. Rather, control and authority must to some degree be based on archaeological data as objectively patterned and 'other'.

Thus, while the archaeological data have to be read differently in different contexts and as such they are like texts, it is not the case that any reading is as good as any other. I have come to view archaeology and archaeological data in a certain way as a result of a whole series of contingent factors. But my viewpoint is embedded in the reality of two contexts – past and present. To argue that 'anything goes' places me outside society and outside archaeology. I cannot shirk my responsibilities as an author and as an archaeologist. The past is important to people. It shapes people's lives. 'I' can only play a role in society by relating real past to real present, by being situated in both the gradual construction of myself and the gradual reconstruction of the past. What is needed then, is an approach in archaeology which combines a commitment to understanding the original meanings of the past with a commitment to the reflexive use of the past in the present. This apparent *double entendre* must be made real.

REFERENCES

Baker, F. and Thomas, J. (eds) (1990) *Writing the Past in the Present*, Lampeter: St David's University College.

Bapty, I. (1990) 'Nietzsche, Derrida and Foucault: re-excavating the meaning of archaeology', in I. Bapty and T. Yates (eds) *Archaeology after Structuralism*, London: Routledge.

Bapty, I. and Yates, T. (eds) (1990) *Archaeology after Structuralism*, London: Routledge.

Barrett, J. (1987) 'Contextual archaeology', *Antiquity* 61, 468–73.

Binford, L. and Sabloff, J. (1982) 'Paradigms, systematics and archaeology', *Journal of Anthropological Research* 38, 137–53.

Gero, J. and Conkey, M. (1991) *Engendering Archaeology*, Oxford: Basil Blackwell.

Hodder, I. (1986) *Reading the Past*, Cambridge: Cambridge University Press.

—— (ed.) (1989) *The Meanings of Things*, London: Unwin Hyman.

Leone, M., Potter, P. and Shackel, P. (1987) 'Toward a critical archaeology', *Current Anthropology* 28, 251–82.

Moran, P. and Hides, D. S. (1990) 'Writing, authority and the determination of the subject', In I. Bapty and T. Yates (eds) *Archaeology after Structuralism*, London: Routledge.

Olsen, B. (1990) 'Roland Barthes: from sign to text', in C. Tilley (ed.) *Reading Material Culture*, Oxford: Basil Blackwell.

Patrik, L. (1985) 'Is there an archaeological record?', in M. Schiffer (ed.) *Advances in Archaeological Method and Theory* 8, New York: Academic Press.

Rowlands, M. (1984) 'Objectivity and subjectivity in archaeology', in M. Spriggs (ed.) *Marxist Perspectives in Archaeology*, Cambridge: Cambridge University Press.

Shanks, M. and Tilley, C. (1987a) *Social Theory and Archaeology*, Cambridge: Polity Press.

—— (1987b) *Reconstructing Archaeology*, Cambridge: Cambridge University Press.

Thomas, J. (1990) 'Same, other, analogue: writing the past', in F. Baker and J. Thomas (eds) *Writing the Past in the Present*, Lampeter: St David's University College.

Tilley, C. (1990a) 'On modernity and archaeological discourse', in I. Bapty and T. Yates (eds) *Archaeology after Structuralism*, London: Routledge.

—— (ed.) (1990b) *Reading Material Culture*, Oxford: Basil Blackwell.

Watson, P. J. (1986) 'Archaeological interpretation, 1985', in D. Meltzer, D. Fowler and J. Sabloff (eds) *American Archaeology Past and Future*, Washington DC: Smithsonian Institution Press.

Yates, T. (1990a) 'Archaeology through the looking-glass', in I. Bapty and T. Yates (eds) *Archaeology after Structuralism*, London: Routledge.

—— (1990b) 'Jacques Derrida: "There is nothing outside of the text" ', in C. Tilley (ed.) *Reading Material Culture*, Oxford: Basil Blackwell.

12

TOWARDS A COHERENT
ARCHAEOLOGY

The ecological and evolutionary approaches, borrowed from the
biological sciences, were not designed to explain motivational and
symbolic systems.

(Dunnell 1982, 521)

Archaeology is a story we tell ourselves about ourselves through
meditation upon the archaeological record.

(Brumfiel 1987, 513, with apologies to Geertz)

The above quotes summarise the problem. On the one hand an objective, natural science position must be limited to the non-arbitrary and
universal and must therefore disregard so much of what makes us
human. On the other hand a commitment to culture, creativity, meaning and action apparently loses claims to scientific rigour so that all we
can do is tell 'stories' and become fiction writers.

In the preceding chapters I have described how I felt caught between
two poles. On the one hand, the processual reaction to post-processual
archaeology demanded more distanced objectivity. On the other hand,
the reaction within post-processual archaeology to my particular version
of it demanded more political commitment and openness to other
voices. In the end, I can see the need both for some claim for objectivity
and for a more socially embedded archaeology. It seems to me now that
for many archaeologists the processual/post-processual opposition has
had its day. Some practitioners on both sides of the debate have moved
to accommodate the other point of view, as was shown in Chapters 9
and 11.

There is a need to reject empiricism (the view that the data are self-
evident so that the analyst passively experiences data) and positivism
(the view that theories can be tested against objective data using independent instruments of measurement). Few archaeologists would now
argue that such objectivist positions could be sustained. Equally, few
would argue for relativism. By the latter I mean the view that ideas and
values do not have universal validity, but are valid only in relation to

169

particular social and historical conditions. There can, according to relativists, be no higher appeal than to a given conceptual scheme, language game, set of social practices, or historical epoch (Wylie 1989, 4, quoting Bernstein). Observation and theory cannot be separated.

There is a need to move beyond these stark contrasts between objectivism and relativism (ibid.). There is some truth to the relativist position which has the value of enhancing praxis and diversity. But a total commitment to relativism cannot be sustained by a discipline which seeks to retain a position of authority from which to speak and wield power. Disciplinary power and authority may come to be repressive and must be open to critique, but they are also enabling. The archaeologist is enabled to act in the world from a position of disciplinary authority. In Chapter 1 I argued that a discipline defines itself through theory (at all levels from observation and method to high-level abstractions – see Clarke 1973). Social praxis depends on the construction of a coherent theoretical framework. The challenge is to accommodate a coherent theoretical position with diversity and situated multivocality.

Archaeologists need to find some coherent way of dealing with the double hermeneutic. On the one hand there is the framework of meaning within which past participants in cultural systems acted. On the other hand there is the framework of meaning within which present-day archaeologists reconstruct the past. How can we plausibly overcome the opposition and contradiction between past and present, whereby the past is (objectively) separate from but yet is constructed in the (subjective) present?

My own path to at least a provisional resolution of these dilemmas came from three directions, all related to practice. *First*, I realised that I had overemphasised the arbitrary nature of material culture symbolism (Hodder 1989 and Chapter 14). In each historical context, new secondary, symbolic meanings can be given to objects. In an ultimate sense, these meanings are arbitrary, dependent on historical contexts. But the arbitrary meanings are influenced by material considerations which may have universal significance. Particular historical meanings are often built up from universal characteristics of materials and practices (Chapter 14). Economic practices undoubtedly constrain and channel social and conceptual forms. The use of a stone axe to cut down a tree constrains the shape of the axe and the range of meanings it can take on. The materiality of material culture allows some emphasis to be placed on universals and these universals provide clues or an initial key as to how to enter into another context. A link can be made between past and present contexts by material universals.

A similar point has been made (Chapters 2 and 3) in relation to the emphasis on symbols 'in action'. Concepts, however abstract, are used in social practices in order to have effects in the world. I came to realise, influenced by Ricoeur, that the emphasis on action meant that we needed to shift from language to text as a metaphor for material culture. One aspect of this shift is that material culture, like a text, can have multiple meanings depending on the context of the 'reading'. But another aspect of texts as opposed to language is that they are material, concrete, practical. Unlike the abstract meanings of words, texts are written to do something in the world. Written with pen and ink, for a specific purpose, they link abstract linguistic meanings and codes to material and social action. Similarly, material culture, as its name indicates, incorporates cultural beliefs and concepts in material actions. Material culture embraces both idea and practice which influence and constrain each other (see Chapter 14).

Concepts thus contribute to the patterning of material culture and its residues. However subjectively constructed, these material patterns objectively constrain what we can say about them. As in the example of Neolithic tombs which meant houses, internal meanings can be accessed by accommodating theory to specific material patterning. Undoubtedly an interpretive moment remains in the search for arguments which link together different aspects of the material data. The need for subjective, interpretive insight is essential for scientific progress in understanding other cultures. But the practical materiality of human action allows those theories which 'fit best' to be determined. Objective links between past and present contexts or hermeneutics can be made. These links may only be 'guardedly' objective (see Chapter 13) because they are constructed within a subjective framework of meaning, but they are also 'objective' in that they concern real material patterning existing independent of our constructions.

Second, it initially came as a shock to me that post-processual archaeology was having little impact on data acquisition. If it really is the case that data, method and theory are all linked within a hermetically sealed framework of meaning, then a change to post-processual theory should lead to a change to post-processual data collection. If data are observed within theory then new theories should produce new data. Archaeologists writing in different social and political contexts should produce different observations as well as different theories.

However, the effects of post-processual archaeology, feminist archaeology, even indigenous archaeologies, seemed to be mainly at theoretical and epistemological levels and in the area of writing archaeological texts (e.g. Chapter 18). It was mainly at the theoretical level that processual archaeology was shown to be wanting, and the main impact was the shift from functionalist theories to those concerned with ideology, power, text and so on. The practices of archaeology remained largely unchanged except in general aspects such as the treatment of data contextually, that is the comparison between different data sets (such as bones, seeds, pottery) *within* a site or region rather than the isolation of data for cross-cultural comparison. People have begun to be successful in using faunal data (e.g. Richards and Thomas 1984) and archaeo-botanical data (e.g. Hastorf 1991) to make sound inferences about symbolism and social practice. But on the whole, answers to questions such as how to sample a region or site, how to excavate a pit, ditch or posthole, how to construct a Harris matrix, how to source pottery and obsidian, how to reconstruct subsistence activities, were unaffected.

Thus certain aspects of processual and post-processual archaeology are complementary rather than opposed. The processual contribution to scientific method, sampling design, environmental reconstruction and the like appears to be able to coexist with the higher level of interpretation engendered by post-processual archaeology. Initially I was worried that method and theory should appear independent in this way. But it is undoubtedly the case that a post-processual archaeologist can reuse data collected for quite another (processual) purpose in order to come to post-processual conclusions. The successful reuse of very old archives, as in Barrett, Bradley and Green's (1991) reinterpretation of the nineteenth-century work of Pitt-Rivers, indicates the partial autonomy between higher-level theory and data acquisition. Although data are collected within a theoretical framework, as long as that framework is understood, the data can be reused within other frameworks. This ability to reuse old archives within new theories confronts both positivist and relativist positions which both, in different ways, argue that data are collected within and are dependent on theoretical questions. I came to see that the relative autonomy of theory and observation was important in the attempt to break out of a relativist position. In the causewayed enclosure excavations described in Chapter 15, new interpretations were reached using established excavation procedures. We were gradually able to accommodate our theories to the data which were sufficiently robust to support some theories in preference to others. Our theories and our data were certainly locked into a hermeneutic spiral – they were only *relatively* autonomous. But to some degree, social theories are separate from theories about recognition of ditches, layers, artifact densities and so on. There does seem to be a *gap* between different levels of theory which allows for some dialectical movement, for some lack of fit, for a creative tension. The problem with the relativist position is that it often retains an assumption of wholeness and coherence. It is assumed that there is one conceptual scheme through which the whole world is viewed. But in fact, there may be contradictory perspectives within any cultural or disciplinary whole. There may be considerable decoupling between different aspects of theory. I do not argue here for a necessarily absolute independence of general and observational theories. All aspects and levels of theory may be linked in complex ways. Nevertheless, some gap or movement between observation and theory seems plausible. Taken in conjunction with the first point made above, that some non-arbitrary relations of the material world can be identified, we can now argue that observational theories may be grounded in universal, objective relations and that observed data *can* confront theories.

As shown in Chapter 15, the hermeneutic circle does not, therefore, have to be vicious. Because of the relative autonomy of theory and observation, and because of the materiality of the archaeological record, interpretation does not simply form data into its own image. Rather, theory and data are formed in relation to each other. Instead of a vicious circle, we have a hermeneutic spiral (Chapters 13 and 15).

The *third* area of practice which showed me that the relationship between past and present was not entirely circular, was the writings of a number of historians. The work of Duby (1980), Le Goff (1988) and Ladurie (1980), in particular, demonstrated that 'thick' internal, contextual interpretation could at the same time refer to generalities which had a wider relevance. Thus, Le Goff's (1960) study of medieval concepts of time is relevant to understanding the construction of time found in capitalism. Duby's (1980) interpretation of the role of the concept of 'three orders' in medieval France leads to a general understanding of the dialectical relationship between structures, contingencies and events. Rather than getting bogged down in epistemological issues, these scholars were getting on with using historical data to contribute to general debate. And they were doing this without claiming absolute objectivity. They simply accepted that past and present moved in relation to each other. They used 'thick' description to make their accounts plausible and were unashamed of the authority that their scholarship gave them.

My own attempt to follow this line resulted in *The Domestication of Europe* (Hodder 1990), a summary of part of which is provided in Chapter 16. The aims here were first to undertake particular, detailed, 'thick' description which showed the possibility of making plausible interpretations of prehistoric symbolism. Second, the aim was to contribute to general understanding of the relationship between long-term structure and local meanings. Third, I wanted to explore the general relationship between object and subject, simultaneously showing my own interpretations to be transparent, dependent on contemporary concepts and words (hence the use of contrived terms like 'domus'), while yet my subjectivity was constructed interactively through experiencing the objective data.

Thus, I wanted to write a plausible account which retained sufficient authority to contribute to wider debates but which remained critically reflexive. In terms of a general debate, *The Domestication of Europe* argued that the adoption of agriculture could only be adequately understood by setting the economic and social changes within the long-term development of conceptual schemes. I argued that a particular concept of the

173

wild (the agrios) was set up by opposing it to a particular understanding of the home (the domus). The process of symbolic domestication of the agrios then became used as a metaphor for domesticating people and society. Especially by locating the process in the home, people were placed in the house, placed in the structures of society which the house represented. People were 'settled down'. But people were at the same time domesticated practically as they became caught in the longer-term dependencies of the delayed returns for labour. The dual practical and symbolic processes of domestication fed off each other, interactively.

The process of creating 'docile' bodies in settled villages does not have to be seen as an intentional plot hatched by dominant groups. Rather, I saw the process as one in which people interpreted events and consequences in terms of historically derived codes and within the necessary links between the domestic scale of production, storage, technology and environment. The whole process is in specific terms 'accidental' rather than 'driven'. It is dispersed in every aspect of society. The domus links idea, economy and social relations of dominance through the control of production, reproduction and exchange. It was seen by me as a discourse of material power, social value and prestige – a power–knowledge–truth network in Foucault's (1980) terms. I argued that this network was transformed and reinterpreted through time in relation to changing circumstances, but that it also channelled over the long term the way people reacted to those circumstances.

In my view, archaeology can contribute authoritatively to such debates about the transformation of societies over the long term but it can at the same time be critically reflexive and be open to alternative perspectives. In *The Domestication of Europe* I tried to show this in two ways. First, I drew attention to our dependence on language in thinking about the past. I used terms such as domus and agrios which are specific and constructed. I would have perhaps come to different conclusions if I had used oikos and played on its links to economy and ecology. Instead I played on the links between domestic and domesticate, dominate, dome, tame and dame. These links in our language are one way in which we think through language so that, to some degree, language channels our thought. Second, I showed how my ideas about the Neolithic in Europe had developed contingently as a result of a series of apparently haphazard meetings, events and opportunities. The work I had happened to read, the data I happened to come across, all this influenced the particular interpretation I came up with. This provisional and contingent nature of my writing, of all our writings, does not undermine the authority of what we write as long as we accept that part of the contingent process is the interaction with and experience of the data.

For me, the most important realisation in writing about the domestication of Europe was that 'Catal Huyuk and I, we bring each other into existence. It is on our joint interaction, each dependent on the other, that we take our separate forms' (Hodder 1990, 20). Of course, it is easy to argue that Catal Huyuk is constructed by archaeologists, and this is both the positivist and the relativist position – that we are somehow locked into the present and can only interpret sites such as Catal Huyuk in terms of our own theories derived from present interests. Such views lead to the pessimism about the archaeologists' abilities to find out what really happened in the past, as Watson (1986) has shown (see discussion on p. 148). It is altogether a different view to argue that Catal Huyuk constructs archaeologists. This may seem a fanciful claim, but I think it has some truth to it. We come to know ourselves through interaction with the world. What we think and feel is influenced by our experience, what we happen to have read, seen, heard, felt and so on. Few would deny such an obvious statement. The excavation of any site introduces us to new experiences. However much our interpretations of the site may vary, there remains for each of us a material experience that adds to our store of interactions with the world. We remove the earth which hides and protects, and there is a certain amount of unpredictability about what we will find there. We discover objects such as the Catal Huyuk figurine (Figure 23) and our experience of the world has been changed. Certainly, our interpretation of the figurine depends on a contemporary understanding, but that understanding has been influenced by its extension to new data, to new experience.

Thus we arrive at a more optimistic view about the relations between past and present and about the ability of archaeologists to contribute authoritatively to contemporary debate. As much as I have imposed an interpretation on the Neolithic of Europe and the Near East, my own understanding of the world, of its potentials and constraints, of a series of specific issues from the origins of agriculture to feminism (Chapter 17) has been transformed as a result of my interaction with the data. I construct the past but the past constructs me in a dialectical relationship. This dialectic is to some degree closed, a vicious circle, but it is also continually in movement as subject and object interact, constituting each other in a hermeneutic spiral.

CONCLUSION: THE RELATIONS BETWEEN PAST AND PRESENT

I have argued above that three areas of practice are essential to the development of a coherent archaeological theory. First, the secondary, symbolic meanings are not purely arbitrary and abstract. They are also related to practical and material considerations and to the 'objective' patterning of the material world. Second, there is a relative autonomy between theory and observation so that the practice of archaeological investigation can confront archaeological theories. Third, not only do the data confront the archaeologist, but they also contribute, interactively, to the archaeologist's understanding of the world. The practice of archaeology thus has the potential to contribute to the constitution of society.

One of the main problems which it seems to me has impeded the resolution of the objectivist/relativist opposition in archaeology is the simplistic opposition between past and present (and its various correlates such as statics and dynamics, dead and living). It is taken for granted that past and present exist and can be distinguished. On this basis, a subjective present is set up against the past. We test theories about the past in the present. The past is interpreted in terms of the present. We have reified a coherent, hermetically sealed present which faces a dead past which has to be brought alive through interpretation and yet which is objectively independent.

On the whole, archaeologists probably have a fairly clear idea about what they mean by the past – it is the distant past. But the present is usually not well defined. Does the present refer to today, this month, this year, this decade, this century? Does it refer to western capitalist societies only? Does it refer to a normative group of western views? When and where did the present begin?

The asking of such questions brings into view the notion that past and present are not absolute terms. The present can only be defined in relation to the past (for example, we might say that the present refers to the past two generations), and the past can only be defined reciprocally in relation to the present (for example, the past is everything before our grandparents). Indeed, the present and the past are not 'things' with objective, independent existence. Rather, they are categories imposed, according to interest, on the continual flow of time. What we mean by the present, is usually some definition of the recent past. We look backwards and forwards, breaking up the continual flow of time into narratives which include terms like past, present and future.

It follows, then, that we do not simply 'exist' as archaeologists in a present which can be opposed to a dead and gone past. The past constructs us in the present in that we are members of societies which have been structured in the past, economically, socially and ideologically. We think through language which is handed down to us across the generations. These various past structures construct us as individuals and as archaeologists. Some of these structures may retain some echoes from a distant past but most are recent and they all contribute to our consciousness. And yet there is some variability and uncertainty as to which aspects of the past we will experience. Different people experience and construct different pasts. We make sense of the world by making links beween different aspects of our knowledge. We construct stories from the recent and distant past in order to guide action. In this process of bricolage we continually mix and match from the past, adjusting abstractions to experience, forming our images of ourselves in our interaction with the world – and the only world we can know is the distant and the recent pasts of various forms.

The opposition then is not between the past and the present; it is not between a dead past and our static 'existence' in the present. We are continually reflecting on our experience, which is always 'past experience' even if only a few moments ago. We construct images of ourselves and of some abstracted 'present' from these interactions and experiences. We do not so much 'exist' in a static present as 'become' in a continual process, in the continual flow of time. Notions of past and present are part of our attempt to understand the world but they can themselves be transformed in different historical situations. The only opposition is not between static, real past and present, but between our experience, informed by the objective world, and our understanding of that experience at the conceptual level.

It may initially appear contradictory to argue that (a) we construct the past in the present, but that (b) the past has a certain autonomy in relation to the present and can affect the present. But the contradiction is overcome if we cease to reify past and present, and instead see them as processes. In the process of becoming, of constituting ourselves as social, we construct narratives which use data of both the distant past and the recent past (which may be termed the present). This relationship between different types of data may be metaphorical. We can only come into existence through the dialogue between abstract understanding and practical experience. The distant, as well as the recent past (the present) data, contribute to that experience. They thus contribute to our understanding of the self and the world.

Although we interpret the world in terms of our understanding of it, we nevertheless have to adjust our understanding in the light of experience. No movement would occur if the world was always exactly as we expected. But the guarded objectivity of the data and the relative autonomy of observation and theory for which I argued above, ensure that as we experience the world of the distant past we come up against new experiences.

A creative tension thus exists between two hermeneutics. In a past situation, a particular frame of meaning and materials provided a context in which 'texts' could be 'written'. In the 'writing' the context was itself changed. Despite this continual movement between text and context, and between experience and understanding, an historical flow of meaning constituted a hermeneutic. In a 'present' situation, there is another frame of meaning within which the archaeologist works. This time texts are literally written within a context which includes dimensions of power, authority, the rhetoric of writing and so on, and which includes the residues which have survived from the first hermeneutic.

The problem has been that archaeologists have simply opposed these two hermeneutics. This opposition has run into difficulties because the past has had to play a dual role: it is both objectively separate in the past, and yet it is incorporated into our interpretations in the present. But the past is not either subjective or objective. Rather, it is both at the same time: it objectively contributes to our subjectivities and it is subjectively constructed. In Ricoeur's (1984) terms, the past is other and the same. It is different from us, and this otherness provides a basis for reflection on and critique of the present. But it is also the same as us since we have to make sense of it in our terms.

Rather than saying, therefore, that prehistory both is and is not the past, it may be more helpful to summarise the complex dialectical view that I have put forward in this section by arguing that prehistoric interpretation is neither in the past nor the present. Rather it mediates between the two. Understanding or interpretation involves trying to accommodate or link an interpretation derived from the recent past (the 'present') with patterned residues produced meaningfully in the distant past (the 'past'). The aim is to align these interpretations and experiences. To interpret is therefore to make an analogy between past and present (distant and recent sources of experience and understanding).

Within the process of interpretation itself there is both observation and theoretical reconstruction, which are also in a relation of creative tension. Observation is linked both to data and to theory. In other words, our observations of the independently patterned material remains (the data) are theory-laden, but they nevertheless accommodate to the physical data. As with interpretation, observation is again perhaps best described as neither data nor theory: it mediates between the two.

Interpretation contributes to both past and present. It constructs past and present and mediates between them, but only in relation to their objective existence. The double-ended arrows in Figure 16 are meant to represent this creative tension between objective and subjective. This dialectical view seeks to avoid the pitfalls of objectivism or relativism. It allows a guarded objectivity and independence of the archaeological data. It allows for a relative autonomy between levels and types of theory. It allows theories to be tested against data. It recognises subjectivity. It allows that subjectivity to be critiqued by reference to the past. It allows multivocality. It allows at the same time authority to be claimed by archaeologists. It recognises the essential dependence and creative tension between theory and practice.

I have come, therefore, to what I see as a coherent position which

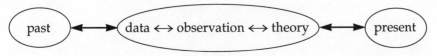

interpretation
Figure 16 Interpretation as a hermeneutic mediating between past and present hermeneutics

allows for objectivity and subjectivity, for authoritative science and social diversity. In reaching this position I have gone towards relativism, radical diversity and political commitment, and towards post-structuralism, but I have then withdrawn from some of the excesses of such viewpoints. Perhaps my own back and forth undermines my attempts to be authoritative. How can I argue for a coherent final position when the 'end-point' has been reached historically? Surely the supposed 'end' coherence will itself be transformed in time? I hope I have shown how such questions can be answered, how an authoritative discipline can be open to diversity, change and critique.

Any viewpoint that we take as members of society is constructed dialectically through experience. As archaeologists we argue that our specialist experience is objectively grounded, and it is on this basis that we claim an authority to act in the world from a particular standpoint. But we can use this specialist experience of the distant past to make analogies with the recent past and to contribute towards the future in different ways. As members of society, as well as specialists with different experiences of the archaeological data, archaeologists will hold different views and will construct the distant and recent pasts differently. This diversity can be challenging and the archaeological past thus becomes active. The diversity is not undermining as long as the analogies that are made between distant and recent pasts in order to construct a better future are grounded in objective material experience. Archaeologists tell stories about the past, and so about the present and future, but their stories differ from fiction by their basis in the material experience of 'other' worlds. Diversity can thus coexist with and gain strength from a scientific concern with evidence.

Our understanding of ourselves is derived from experiences in the world which can include experiences of the distant past. We tell stories about ourselves by meditating on the archaeological record, but those stories are influenced by the experience of that record. Archaeological record and contemporary society constitute each other.

REFERENCES

Barrett, J., Bradley, R. and Green, M. (1991) *Landscape, Monuments and Society*, Cambridge: Cambridge University Press.

Brumfiel, E. M. (1987) 'Comments on Earle and Preucel', *Current Anthropology* 28, 513–14.

Clarke, D. (1973) 'Archaeology: the loss of innocence', *Antiquity* 47, 6–18.

Duby, G. (1980) *The Three Orders*, Chicago: University of Chicago Press.

Dunnell, R. (1982) 'Americanist archaeological literature: 1981', *American Journal of Archaeology* 86, 509–29.

Foucault, M. (1980) *Power/Knowledge. Selected Interviews and Other Writings*, ed. C. Gordon, New York: Pantheon Books.

Hastorf, C. (1990) 'Gender, space and food in prehistory', in J. Gero and M. Conkey (eds) *Engendering Archaeology*, Oxford: Basil Blackwell.

Hodder, I. (1989) 'This is not an article about material culture as text', *Journal of Anthropological Archaeology* 8, 250–69.

—— (1990) *The Domestication of Europe*, Oxford: Basil Blackwell.

Ladurie, E. R. (1980) *Montaillou*, London: Penguin.

Le Goff, J. (1960) 'Au Moyen Age: temps de l'eglise et temps du marchand', *Annales* 15, 417–33.

—— (1988) *The Medieval Imagination*, Chicago: University of Chicago Press.

Richards, C. and Thomas, J. (1984) 'Ritual activity and structured deposition in Later Neolithic Wessex', in R. Bradley and J. Gardiner (eds) *Neolithic Studies*, Oxford: British Archaeological Reports British Series 133.

Ricoeur, P. (1984) *The Reality of the Historical Past*, Marquette: Marquette University Press.

Watson, P. J. (1986) 'Archaeological interpretation, 1985', in D. Meltzer, D. Fowler and J. Sabloff (eds) *American Archaeology Past and Present*, Washington DC: Smithsonian Institution Press.

Wylie, A. (1989) 'Archaeological cables and tacking', *Philosophy of the Social Sciences* 19, 1–18.

Part IV

PRACTISING ARCHAEOLOGY

13

INTERPRETIVE ARCHAEOLOGY
AND ITS ROLE[1]

What is interpretation and why does it seem an appropriate term to use in the archaeology of the 1990s? In this paper I hope to answer both these questions. While I have elsewhere discussed interpretation in terms of a contextual approach (Hodder 1986), I have not situated the latter in relation to wider traditions except the rather outdated views of Collingwood (1946). I intend in this paper to provide a wider definition of contextual archaeology within an interpretive framework.

This article will discuss hermeneutics as an important component in an interpretive or contextual archaeology. For many writers, hermeneutics is more than an epistemology for the human sciences in that it accounts for being. I recently came across a good example of the everyday working of hermeneutic principles while listening to the radio in the United States. I heard the phrase, or thought I did, 'it was necessary to indoor suffering'. Inspecting these 'data' I first thought the phrase was an example of the liberty that North Americans often take with the English language. After all, North Americans often make nouns and adjectives into verbs (as in 'to deplane'), so it seemed entirely possible that 'to indoor suffering' meant 'to take suffering indoors'. I did not see why it should be necessary to suffer indoors, but then I know that North Americans, especially if they live in California from where the programme came, are willing to try anything. So initially I understood the term as it sounded to me and assumed that the same word had the same meaning. I then corroborated and adjusted this meaning by placing it in the peculiar and particular rules of North American culture. This was the first stage of my hermeneutic interpretation.

Gradually, however, this process of internal evaluation made less and less sense as I continued to listen to the radio programme. My interpretation of the sound 'indoor' no longer made what was being said coherent. The programme was about suffering in general, not just about suffering indoors. Sentences such as 'to indoor the suffering I took a pain killer' made little sense. I could only make sense of these examples when I hit upon the idea of another component of my understanding of

183

the North American context: North Americans often pronounce words 'wrongly'. Coming back from this contextual knowledge to my own general knowledge about English words and their meanings I searched and found 'endure'. Now everything made coherent sense and the whole had been re-established. The hermeneutic circle had been closed.

Of course, all this happened in a few seconds. But the speed and trivial nature of the process cannot but emphasise the wide dependence of human communication and understanding on the procedures of hermeneutic interpretation. We evaluate many arguments not so much by testing universal, general knowledge against data using universal, independent instruments of measurement, but by interpreting general understanding or foreknowledge in relation to our understanding of particular contexts. We place the thing to be understood (in this case the sound 'indoor') more and more fully into its context, moving back and forth between 'their' and 'our' context until coherence is achieved. The emphasis is on part–whole relations. We try to fit the pieces into an interpretive whole at the same time as constructing the whole out of the pieces. We measure our success in this enmeshing of theory and data (our context and their context) in terms of how much of the data is accounted for by our hypothesis in comparison to other hypotheses. This working back and forth between theory and data, this revelling in context and texture, tends to be more concerned to understand the data in their own terms and to use internal, as well as external, criteria for judgement.

It has for some time been argued (Hodder 1986; Trigger 1989) that processual archaeology placed little emphasis on interpreting general knowledge in relation to internal understanding. But it is also appropriate to ask whether post-processual archaeology has sufficiently engaged in interpretation of the general in relation to the particular. I would claim that, so far, much post-processual archaeology has avoided an interpretive position, except superficially. On the whole, post-processual archaeology has concerned power, negotiation, text, intertext, structure, ideology, agency, and so on. Many of these concerns may move us in an interpretive direction but they remain general and theoretical interests that dominate our present thoughts. They represent the interests of a predominantly western, white, male discourse. There have been very few post-processual studies that have said 'I will put the theory in second place, treat it simply as baggage, and set off to tell a story about, for example, the development of Bronze Age society in Bavaria'. On the whole post-processual archaeologists, including the author of this article, have been more concerned with showing the validity of our universal theoretical apparatus. The data have been only examples manipulated to demonstrate, often inadequately, some theoretical point. There has been insufficient interpretation.

The tendency to develop a universal theoretical discourse and impose it on the past is common to both processual and post-processual archaeology. In both cases there is insufficient sensitivity to the independent difference of past contexts and to contextual meanings. This insensitivity derives from two different directions. Processual archaeology put many of its eggs in the basket of methods. A universal method was supposed to allow us to read off dynamics from statics and so there was little attempt to construct interpretive procedures which were sensitive to internal meanings. Conversely, to a large extent, post-processual archaeology has been weak on method (Watson 1986). Indeed, it might be claimed that so much emphasis has been placed on theoretical discussion and theoretical criteria that the method of post-processual archaeology is theory. The rigours of theoretical criteria have replaced those of method but have equally detracted from the interpretation of specific, internal historical meanings.

The scarcity of interest in internal meanings in both processual and post-processual archaeology also relates to an inadequate concern with the context of archaeologists. The lack of reflexivity in processual archaeology is widely accepted but the claim in relation to post-processual archaeology is perhaps surprising. My suggestion derives from the observation made above that in practice, post-processual archaeological writings have largely concerned theory rather than method. It was mainly at the theoretical level that processual archaeology was shown wanting. The practical result of a purely theoretical debate tends to be posturing. Theoretical debate involves defining terms, defining boundaries, and setting up oppositions. Theoretical meaning is always referential (to other theories) and tends to be confrontational by nature. Argument is over the top of, rather than through the data that become relevant only as examples. The argument is entirely about the present, not about the past. It manipulates the data for presentist concerns, and while post-processual archaeology has successfully opened up the area of critique, it has insufficiently scrutinised its own preconceptions.

I would argue that as a result, as radical as post-processual archaeology would claim to be, it merely re-establishes older structures of archaeological research. It tends towards doing the same thing in a different way. Perhaps a good example of continuity in structures of power within academic discourse despite claims for radical change in the content of ideas, is the fact that Grahame Clark, David Clarke, Ian Hodder, Christopher Tilley and Michael Shanks, covering a range of different theoretical positions through time, were or are all associated with Peterhouse – one small, reactionary, exclusive college in Cambridge.

Much of what post-processual archaeology has argued for has not been evaluated critically and the effects of its actions have not been reflexively probed. For example, the new theories and the new ways of writing them often serve to make archaeological texts more obscure and difficult for anyone but the highly trained theorist to decipher. How can alternative groups have access to a past that is locked up both intellectually and institutionally? Subordinate groups who wish to be involved in archaeological interpretation need to be provided with the means and mechanisms for interacting with the archaeological past in different ways. This is not a matter of popularising the past, but of transforming the relations of production of archaeological knowledge into more democratic structures.

One danger of this view, as has been argued by Renfrew (1989) for example, is that if we accept that the past is partly constructed in the present (in the dialectic between past and present, object and subject), and that we must listen to and incorporate other voices and historical meanings constructed by, for example, women and ethnic minorities, where can we draw the lines around legitimate archaeological research? Should we also welcome the voices of creationists, looters, metal detector users and other 'fringe' archaeologists within a tower of babbling? On what grounds is it possible to claim a legitimacy and primacy for the different but universal projects of, for example, processual or post-processual archaeology?

One alternative to hermeneutic approaches within the humanities and social sciences emanates from writers, precursors and champions of post-modern and post-structuralist thought who raise similar questions about the boundaries of legitimate research by seeking multivocality, fragmentation and dispersal. These writers, including Nietzsche, Foucault (Tilley 1990b), Kristeva, Barthes (Olsen 1990), and Derrida (Yates 1990) suspend meaning within chains of signifiers, and emphasise the openness of interpretations within our dependence on language. Post-structuralist work is having an increasing influence in archaeology (Tilley 1990a; Bapty and Yates 1990; see also Hodder 1989b) and is important because it opens up a central issue. What is the boundary between an open multivocality where any interpretation is as good as another and legitimate dialogue between 'scientific' and American Indian, black, feminist, etc. interests?

In my view, the non-hermeneutic, non-interpretive strands in post-processual archaeology and in all post-modern social science, serve further to re-establish positions of dominance which are threatened by the same openness to alternative, non-scientific perspectives as is feared by processual archaeologists (e.g. Renfrew 1989). The influence of post-structuralism (Hodder 1989b; Bapty and Yates 1990; Tilley 1990a) is towards multivocality and the dispersal of meaning. Truth and knowledge are claimed as contingent and multiple, and relativism is to some extent entertained. At first sight, this development toward a non-hermeneutic, post-structuralist position seems benign. It opens up the past to other voices and deconstructs the universality of truth claims. But the feminist critique of post-modernism (e.g. Mascia-Lees *et al.* 1989) is particularly revealing here. Dominant theorists and specialists have, since the excited certainties of the 1960s, increasingly lost the monopoly to define archaeological truths as alternative positions have been argued by women, ethnic minorities, and by all the different perspectives in archaeological theory, never mind all the fringe archaeologies. As identified by Mascia-Lees *et al.* (1989; see also Eagleton 1983), the post-structuralist response to this loss of authority is subtle. The notion that truth and knowledge are contingent and multiple undermines the claims of subordinate groups. It *disempowers them* by alienating them from the reality they experience. Irony and relativism appear as intellectual possibilities for dominating groups at the point where the hegemony and universality of their views is being challenged (Mascia-Lees *et al.* 1989). In effect, a new, more subtle universal claim to truth is produced out of the critique of truth. The post-structuralist emphasis on multivocality, metaphor, and fragmentation may be constructed to capture the complex and contradictory nature of social life. But in fact what is provided is a resolution of conflict into a pleasing whole in which the author is scarcely present. He or she is also fragmented, distanced, uncommitted, disengaged, powerful but always absent and therefore not answerable to criticism.

The post-modern theoretical discourse, then, subtly disempowers critique and establishes a new distanced authority. Its radical political claims are undermined by the insecurity and multivocality of knowledge claims. Post-structuralist archaeology becomes a movement without a cause. As a result of its links with post-structuralism and post-modernism (Hodder 1989b), post-processual archaeology has not always been concerned with opening dialogue with 'other groups'. There has been little incorporation of alternative claims on the past in a multi-ethnic Britain or United States. There has been little dialogue with feminist archaeology in, for example, the writing of Shanks and Tilley (1987a, 1987b), despite the fact that it can be claimed plausibly that the growth of post-processual archaeology depended on the growth of feminism and feminist archaeology. But this 'other voice' has often been appropriated and dominated within post-processual archaeology (M. Conkey, pers. comm. 1990).

Rather than embracing post-structuralism, post-processual archaeology should grasp an interpretive position in order to avoid the above problems and to break from established relations of dominance in the production of the archaeological past. In this initial discussion I have begun to identify three essential aspects of an interpretive approach in archaeology. (1) A guarded objectivity of the past needs to be retained so that subordinate groups can use the archaeological past to empower their knowledge claims in the present and to differentiate their claims from fringe, ungrounded archaeologies. By 'guarded' objectivity I mean that the 'data' are formed within a dialectical relation. In the example I gave of the radio programme, I heard, *or thought I did*, the phrase 'to indoor suffering'. The sound I picked up from the radio only became sound data through my interpretation of voice from crackling background and through my (incorrect) recognition of certain words. My interpretation was based on objective sound waves but it also penetrated into their definition as data. The data are dialectically produced. (2) An internal, hermeneutic component needs to be retained in interpretation. We need to be sensitive to the other. The attempt to understand the past in terms of the experiences of social actors allows the past to be released from abstract specialist theory into the realms of everyday human understanding and simultaneously provides a basis for the critique of universal propositions in the present. It allows for a relevant human story to be told. There is a need to move away from theory and get on with interpreting data, by which I mean move away from an assumption of the primacy of theory towards relating theory to data as part of a learning process. (3) A reflexive consideration of the production of archaeological knowledge will lead to a critical engagement with the voicing of other interests, by identifying the causes for which the past is constructed, and by locating the mechanisms which make it exclusive.

The search, then, within post-processual archaeology is for an adequate integration of these three aims with clearly defined methodological procedures. There is a need to give science a context in archaeology as methodology, not as a final goal or as the only relevant body of theory. I have already argued that this scientific component of archaeological work is necessary to avoid ungrounded undermining of knowledge claims by interested groups and in order to avoid a subsuming of the past within a homogenised theoretical present. But how are we to integrate such scientific concerns for a guardedly objective past within a non-positivist archaeology? How are we to accept the commitment to process which is broader than ecological and adaptive relations and which incorporates human action? In my view, answers to these questions can be gained from developments in the debate surrounding hermeneutic studies.

HERMENEUTIC PROCEDURES

Beyond the trivial example given at the beginning of this paper, what does a hermeneutic, contextual approach involve and how might the inferential methods be employed in archaeology? Does the approach allow us to get at internal meanings while maintaining a guarded commitment to objectivity and independence and while remaining reflexive?

It may be helpful to outline the main ideas and problems of a hermeneutic archaeology by discussing briefly the history and development of hermeneutic ideas since the founding work of Friedrich Schleiermacher and Wilhelm Dilthey (Ormiston and Schrift 1990). Their starting point was the principle that understanding and knowledge depend on the dialectical relation between part and whole – the hermeneutic circle. Dilthey extended Schleiermacher's concern with the intentions of the author in producing texts to include a wider hermeneutic circle such as historical background, social customs, cultural and political institutions and so on. Martin Heidegger (1958) dealt with some of the problems with this approach. In particular, he emphasised that our understanding of the past 'other' is dependent on prejudice and tradition. In other words, the past hermeneutic we are trying to interpret is dependent on, and may be enclosed by, the hermeneutic circles within which we work as archaeologists and members of society. Shanks and Tilley (1987a) identify four hermeneutic circles within which the contemporary archaeologist works when trying to understand past material culture 'texts'. Although Heidegger claimed that the enclosing hermeneutic circles are not vicious, in that they do not involve hermetically sealed 'circular arguments', it is difficult to see how, within his version of hermeneutic procedures, it is possible to do more than interpret the past in our own terms. The same criticisms have been made of contextual archaeology (Binford 1987).

Although I have argued (Hodder 1991a) that Hans-Georg Gadamer (1975) tried to deal effectively with these problems of circularity of argument, it can nevertheless be claimed that he retained a subjectivist position. Indeed, this is the criticism of Emilio Betti (1955, translated 1984), who argued for a hermeneutic methodology that would safeguard the objective standards of interpretation. Betti's approach is of interest to the current debate in archaeology in view of the call that is made frequently, particularly by North American archaeologists, for post-processual archaeologists to define their methods (e.g. Watson 1986; Earle and Preucel 1987). Betti's methodological guide involved the following principles: (a) the autonomy of the object – the idea that a past context should be judged in its own terms; (b) the notion of coherence (see also Collingwood 1946) or the principle of totality – the idea of part–whole relations and the notion that the 'best' hypothesis is the one that makes sense of most of the data; (c) nevertheless, the past 'other' has to be appropriated and translated in the present so that (d) the aim of the analyst should be to control prejudice while bringing his or her subjectivity into harmony with the data.

The latter parts of this proposal remain ambiguous so that Gadamer was able to respond by questioning the validity of the subjective/objective opposition and showing that understanding is not a matter of a subject confronting an alien object (Ormiston and Schrift 1990). Rather it is a dialectical process of question and answer. Thus the past object and the present subject constitute each other in the hermeneutic process of interpretation. Thus, in my analysis of Neolithic Catal Huyuk I interpreted Catal Huyuk in my own terms, but in the experience of trying to understand the 'other' of Catal Huyuk 'my own terms' changed (Hodder 1990). For example, my assumptions about the roles of women were contradicted by the evidence for the roles of men. In my experience of interpreting the Neolithic data I found I was using different assumptions for men and women even when, at different points in time, the evidence for each gender was similar. As a result I changed my views on the nature of female powers (Hodder 1991b and Chapter 17). I had in the end both changed my own position and changed the past so that a new hermeneutic circle was produced that made more complete sense of both past and present. In the act of interpretation, Catal Huyuk and I brought each other into existence. My subjectivity is partly constructed by the interpretive experience of the 'other'.

Nevertheless it can be argued, following Jurgen Habermas (1990), that Gadamer did not sufficently critique the tradition within which preconceptions and prejudices about the data are formed. The tradition needs to be subject to the critique of ideology and needs to be examined as distorted communication within certain historical conditions. It is Ricoeur (1971; 1990; Moore 1990; Thompson 1981) who has dealt most effectively with the linking of hermeneutics and Marxist critical theory. In archaeology, the relevance of various forms of critical theory has increasingly been brought into post-processual discussion (e.g. Leone 1982; Leone et al. 1987; Shanks and Tilley 1987a). Ricoeur points out that the Marxist critique of ideology is itself founded on a hermeneutic (see also Hodder 1986, 168) in the sense that any critical reflection makes claims for a privileged understanding and makes claims for universality which appear dogmatic. In other words, the Marxist critique is locked into its own hermeneutic circle. Indeed, Ricoeur sees hermeneutics and the critique of ideology as necessarily complementary.

According to Ricoeur, not only are critical approaches dependent on hermeneutic circles, but hermeneutics retains within itself the basis of critique and a way out of the circularity of interpretation. In this, in my view, he emphasises the partially objective nature of other contexts as suggested by Betti. Ricoeur argues that rather than only emphasising prejudice in the process of going to the past with questions, we can place emphasis on the return from the past with answers. He shows that any 'text' (written or material culture) is distanced from its 'author'. It is the product of meaningfully organised activity, and it is itself patterned by those activities. This patterned organisation, distant from its original meanings, has an independence that can therefore confront our interpretations. In attempting to understand the past 'other' it is possible to suggest hypotheses (about past cultural rules and meanings) that make more or less coherent sense of the objectively patterned remains by moving back and forth between whole and part. The answers we return with can be unexpected. As a result no horizon (viewpoint or perspective) is universal because the tension between self and other is not surmountable. Only by placing myself in relation to the independent (objectively organised and different) other can I confront myself and my society with its taken-for-granteds. There is a need for the 'creative renewal of cultural heritage' (Ricoeur 1990, 332) as the basis for the critique of contemporary ideologies.

The moment of critique in the hermeneutic process is the interaction with data to produce 'possible worlds' (Bruner 1986) or stories which open up possibilities beyond the conventional. Always the distance of the 'text' defines and critiques my subjectivities and opens my closed 'false consciousness'. Material culture as excavated by archaeologists is different from our assumptions because organised according to at least partly other cultural rules (from social organisation to refuse deposition). But past material culture also confronts our interpretations and assumptions in so far as it is not only meaningfully but also pragmatically organised (Hodder 1989a). In other words, *we are not just interpreting interpretations*, but dealing with objects which had practical effects in a non-cultural world – an ecological world organised by exchanges of matter and energy. These universal, necessary relations confront the tendency of our interpretations to 'run free' as has been shown, for example, in Binford's (1983) reappraisal of hypotheses of early hominid behaviour through a consideration of the universal nature of scavenging animals and their 'signatures'.

So we need to retain from positivist and processual archaeology a guarded 'objectivity' of the material 'other' that provides the basis of critique through the reality of difference. The supposed viciousness or closure of the hermeneutic circle resides in the view that in 'fitting theory to data' in the search for coherence we enclose the data entirely within our prejudices. But the organised material remains have an independence that can confront our taken-for-granteds. The notion that the data are partly objective is an old one in archaeology, and it was the basis for processual and positivist archaeology. But the trouble with positivist and processual archaeologists was that they did not incorporate hermeneutic and critical insights. From a hermeneutic point of view, the failure of the processual archaeology of the 1970s and early 1980s was that it too often took a cavalier, externally based approach where the data were simply examples for the testing of universal schemes, with too little attention paid to context and to understanding the data in their own terms (Hodder 1986; Trigger 1989, 348–57). The possibility that radically different processes might be encountered was thus difficult to entertain. From the point of view of critique, the failure of processual archaeology was its blindness to its own ideologies (e.g. Trigger 1980; Conkey and Spector 1984; Patterson 1986).

Both processual and hermeneutic approaches accept that every assertion can only be understood in relation to a question. But in hermeneutic archaeology, prejudice and tradition are not opposed to reason without supposition. Rather they are components of understanding linked to the historical nature of being human. We need a perspective to understand the world. Archaeology poses meaningful questions, does meaningful research, and gets meaningful results only in terms of a perspective or a set of questions. Processual and hermeneutic approaches of course differ in their approach to the validation of hypotheses, emphasising external and internal criteria of judgement respectively, but both have suffered from the same blindness to the conditions which make their different perspectives possible. Both fail to explore the way in which the asking of questions and the expectation of certain answers are situated in historical processes. There is thus a need to retain the Marxist emphasis on critical reflection. We can only understand the past in its own terms if we understand our own context in the dialectic between past and present. The past can only inform the present through the dual endeavours of understanding present and past as different but dependent. Objectivity may help us to define the past as different, and hermeneutics may help us to understand what it meant through the part–whole, question-and-answer method, but it is critical reflection which shows most fully what it means to us.

So far I have identified three directions within archaeology that are also found throughout the social sciences. These correspond to the spheres of interest identified by Habermas (1971; see Preucel 1991). The first is technical or instrumental interest and corresponds with what most North American archaeologists identify as the 'science' of processual, ecological, evolutionary, behavioural, and positivist archaeology. The second concerns the historical or hermeneutic sciences dealing with communication, understanding, meaning and action (cf. Patrik 1985). The third concerns emancipation, critical social science and self-reflection (e.g. Leone et al. 1987).

These three directions each have roles to play in archaeology, but modified in relation to the others. Thus processual archaeology needs to be subsumed within a relation to critique and hermeneutics, and post-processual archaeology needs to react to the charge of methodological naïvité. An integrated but diversified approach needs to incorporate three perspectives. (1) The past is objectively organised in contexts which differ from our own. It is in the experience of this objective and independent difference that we can distinguish between competing hypotheses to see which fits best. (2) However, if the present is not simply to be imposed on the past, we need not to impose external criteria but to accommodate our external knowledge to internal relations. We need to understand the past partly in its own terms by using the criterion of coherence in part–whole relations. This internal understanding includes symbolism, meaning, the conceptual, history, action as opposed to behaviour, people as well as systems. This is not a cognitive archaeology (Renfrew 1989) because the latter does not deal with the central question of meaning, and it does not involve getting into people's minds. Rather, the hermeneutic approach involves getting at the public and social structures of meaning through which people make sense of the world. It is recognised that these secondary, conceptual realms of meaning are historical and arbitrary, but it is argued that they can nevertheless be interpreted, using the part–whole hermeneutic approach, because the secondary, abstract meanings were used in social action and thus produced repeated patterned effects in material culture and the organisation of spatial and temporal relations. Returning to point (1), these objective patternings allow us to distinguish between hypotheses about which secondary conceptual meanings were operative in producing the archaeological remains. (3) The third component of interpretive archaeology is the self-reflexive aspect of new ethnographic and some emerging archaeological writing (Clifford and Marcus 1986; Hodder 1989c; Tilley 1989; and Chapter 18). This perspective involves being aware that writing has an audience to which it needs to be critically responsible, and a rhetoric that acts to persuade. It involves introducing the 'I' into archaeological accounts, dialogue between co-workers or between researchers and indigenous 'owners' of the past, and it involves telling the story of the contingent context of work in which hypotheses were formulated.

We might gloss these three points by saying that interpretive archaeology is about constructing narratives, or telling stories. Of course, all archaeology has always told stories about evolution, diffusion, maximisation, adaptation, survival, and so on. But in these stories the rhetoric of the story line was not acknowledged or criticised as contributing to the construction of the message or hidden agenda. The stories were often not told at the human scale, and were not inclusive of the viewpoints of the actors. The accounts were validated through external science rather than internal meaning, and they lacked the narrator, who was mysteriously absent. In all these ways, the stories were not interpretations.

INTERPRETIVE ARCHAEOLOGY AND THE CULTURAL HERITAGE

In many ways, the calls for an interpretive archaeology mirror contemporary concerns for heritage and the environment. It is no accident that interpretive or heritage 'centres' rather than museums are increasingly appearing on the landscape in both Britain and North America as interpretive approaches are increasingly discussed within the discipline. These new centres are often more concerned with telling a story and may contain few artifacts. They often involve a narrator, whether it be a recorded voice at the Yorvik Centre, York, England or cardboard cut-out Asterix and Obelix figures in the reconstructed Iron Age huts in the Bois de Boulogne, Paris, France. Increasingly emphasis is placed on showing sequences of activities, and involving the public in experiencing the past.

In order to understand these relations and the need for an active interpretive archaeology within environmental and heritage management, it may be helpful to return to the traditional goals of anthropology. The latter may be described as the salvage of distinct forms of life from the processes of global westernisation, the recognition of the non-western as an element of the human just as crucial as the western, and scepticism concerning western claims to knowledge and understanding.

These traditional anthropological concerns have been reasserted in post-modern anthropology (e.g. Clifford and Marcus 1986), and they imply that anthropology has a counter-cultural potential. It can be argued that the current increases in student enrolment and job openings in sociocultural anthropology in the United States relate to a switch from the 'me' generation to one more concerned with green issues (Roy Rappaport, pers. comm. 1990).

The rise in the centrality of global environmental issues has a double effect on anthropology. On the one hand, many of these global effects are ecological and involve a world of universal measurements, energetics, causes, and effects. On the other hand, the realisation that we are destroying each other on a global scale leads to a greater concern with other cultures. In order to arrest the environmental impact of oil spillage, pipe lines, the use of fossil fuels among the growing populations of the developing world, and rain forest depletion, we are forced to understand the needs and practices of other cultures and to enter into dialogue with them. The cost of destruction of societies by the agents of development cannot be simply *counted* numerically. It is not only a question of numbers and of survival, but also of values and morality. In such a context, the call is for a qualitative anthropology that can inform on and assist dialogue with other cultures that we might destroy or that might destroy us.

Archaeology readily fits in here, as several of the One World Archaeology volumes (Unwin Hyman) have shown (e.g. Gathercole and Lowenthal 1989; Layton 1989a, 1989b). A concern for the archaeology of a region is a concern for the environment of that region, and not just a physical environment but a *peopled* environment, given cultural values and meanings. Peoples around the world use archaeology to help maintain their pasts in the face of the universalising and dominating processes of westernisation and western science. The physical archaeological remains help people to maintain, reform, or even form a new identity or culture in the face of multinational encroachment, outside powers, or centralised governments. Related arguments concern the use of the past by ethnic minorities, women, and other groups to define and reform their social positions within national boundaries in relation to the dominant culture.

The past that is used by subordinate voices in this way is not just a resource, and here is the link to the need for an interpretive archaeology. Subordinate groups do not necessarily want to fit their archaeologies into universal schemes in western academic institutions. Rather, subordinate groups may wish to explore, perhaps archaeologically, the meaning that their monuments have for them. The past is not a resource that can simply be quantified, tabulated, or otherwise manipulated at arm's length within our theoretical frameworks. Rather than that terrible term 'Cultural Resource Management', what is needed is a qualitative archaeology, sensitive to context and meaning, open not to multivocality for its own sake, but to dialogue that leads to change. Many peoples do not want a past defined as a scientific resource by us, but a past that is a story to be interpreted. In these ways the public debates about the contemporary role of archaeology and the dissemination of archaeological knowledge run in parallel with the call for an interpretive archaeology.

In North America the confrontation between desires to tell different stories, as in the reburial debate, has a particular form. In Britain archaeology plays a role in a different context of great public interest and nationalist concerns for, for example, an 'English Heritage'. But even here, in this cocoon that denies the multiethnic nature of 'our' past, archaeology may be playing a counter-cultural, interpretive role. The heritage boom that we have witnessed in Britain over recent years (Merriman 1989) has included a massive increase in numbers of so-called museums. In fact, as already noted, these often contain few objects and are more devoted to interpreting the landscape or the past, telling a story about a local area, giving it a meaning to local inhabitants and visitors. In England, archaeologists increasingly are employed by environmental consultants and planning consultants. Developers need to take account of local desires and senses of place if planning authority is to be achieved. Archaeology is literally the price that often has to be paid for development. In some cases developers are keen to provide means not only for archaeology to be conducted, but also for the results to be displayed permanently. Thus the past is being used to give a sense of

local identity and place in the face of universalising large-scale development and destruction of the environment. The heritage or interpretive
centres tell a story that links people into communities that are increasingly being threatened and fragmented.

Clearly there is a danger that I present a romanticised view. Archaeology
in Britain is being manipulated by big business to make money, to buy
development and to excuse its activities. Many of the interpretations are
commercialised, fragmented, and unconcerned with local or any social
issues (Shanks and Tilley 1987a). Nevertheless, in the negotiation that
occurs between developers, planning authorities and local inhabitants, the
archaeology can play an active role. The past can sometimes be used by
people to tell a story about themselves in the face of external pressures. In
my own involvement with excavating and displaying information from
prehistoric sites near Cambridge, I was impressed by the attempts of a local
village community to retain access to its own past. I also had to confront the
fact that the community did not want an abstract past defined by me.
Rather, the local people wanted me to engage with them in working out a set
of stories, told at the human level, which they could enter. In a regional
Fenland context of community fragmentation, high residential mobility and
destruction of traditional farming employment, the archaeological remains
helped in practice to form a local community.

CONCLUSION

This experience of mine is just a small example of the way the archaeological past is being used by social groups, including ethnic minorities,
women, non-western peoples to find a voice. My claim is that an
interpretive approach in archaeology is more able to articulate this voice
than are processual or post-structuralist archaeologies. This is because,
to answer directly the first question posed at the beginning of this paper,
interpretation is translation. It involves the archaeologist acting as interpreter between past and present, between different perspectives on
the past, and between the specific and the general. Interpretation therefore involves listening and understanding, accommodation between
different voices rather than solely the application of universal instruments of measurement. This response leads directly to the answer to my
second question posed at the beginning. The role of interpretive archaeology is to facilitate the involvement of the past in a multicultural
present. This function is integral to the three aspects of the definition of
interpretive archaeology which I have given in this paper.

1   The partially objective, grounded and material nature of the past
    allows subordinate groups to empower themselves through the
    evidential aspect of archaeology. For example, it is possible to show

unambiguously that indigenous communities inhabited South Africa before the arrival of white settlers. Equally, the objective component of archaeological data means that the analyst can be confronted with the otherness of the past. Since argument is through, rather than over the data, we have to shift our positions in the experience of the data. The data and I bring each other into existence dialectically. The past then allows the possibility for a sense of other which is increasingly being eroded in an expanding, homogenised western ethic.

2   Interpretive approaches at least try to understand the other in its own terms in that they look for internal rather than external criteria of plausibility in order to support their arguments. They thus encourage other groups to develop their own senses of past. In addition, interpretive approaches incorporate the conceptual, the way people made sense of the world. They therefore bring the past to the human scale rather than locking it up in distant, abstract science or theory. To interpret is therefore to act because the interpretation releases the past into public debate. It forces us to translate the past into a story we can understand. Interpretation forces us to *say something*, and therefore to engage with others that would tell different stories. It forces us to unlock the abstract ivory-tower theory and show what it means in practice, in relation to the data.

3   Interpretive approaches encourage self-reflexivity and dialogue. The past is always 'owned' by someone in some sense. But ownership is always an interpretation. Archaeologists need to retain the authority to be able to say that a particular interpretation does not fit the data (point (1) above), but they also need to be open to dialogue and conflicts with vested interests other than their own and to understand the social implications of the knowledge they construct. And they need to realise that subordinate groups can be provided with the mechanisms (the material and educational possibilities) for engaging with the past in their own ways. A critical position recognises that the telling of stories grounded in the data depends on the relations of production of archaeological knowledge.

As indigenous, different interpretations of ownership increasingly develop, there is a real concern, both in the United States and in other parts of the world, about whether archaeology as it has been defined scientifically will be able to continue to exist (Kintigh 1990; Lovis 1990). Archaeology must change if it is to exist in the contemporary multicultural world. The issue is not just one of getting American Indians to change or of teaching them 'our' archaeology. Rather, it is one of involving them as we change ourselves and our concepts of science. There is a need to break the mould in archaeology, discussing not from within a closed science, but opening up that science to dialogue, narrative, rhetorical analysis and meaning. These are the topics now being debated in sociocultural anthropology. But there is also a need to build interpretations of the archaeological past informed by these issues. We cannot continue to cling to a narrow science.

Interpretive archaeology can be an active, doing archaeology. We need to see post-processual archaeologists launching into coherent and sustained interpretations of the past, involving themselves in whatever contemporary issues those interpretations raise. In my case the relevant interpretations may involve the nature of Neolithic burial near Cambridge, or the nature and origins of the concept of prehistoric Europe after the events of 1989 and as the unification of 1992 approaches. In the United States the relevant debates may concern interpretations of slave quarters on a South Carolina plantation or the interpretation of American Indian remains. There is a direct link between these calls for interpretations in archaeology and reburial issues, land claims, public archaeology, the presentation of the past and so on. Post-processual archaeology should not involve going into an ivory tower of abstract theory, and slamming the door. The way post-processual, in fact all archaeology, will endure is by not remaining indoors.

NOTE

1 Copyright Society for American Archaeology (1991).

REFERENCES

Bapty, I. and Yates, T. (1990) *Archaeology after Structuralism*, London: Routledge.
Binford, L. (1983) *In Pursuit of the Past*, London: Thames and Hudson.
—— (1987) 'Data, relativism and archaeological science', *Man* 22, 391–404.
Betti, E. (1984) 'The epistemological problem of understanding as an aspect of the general problem of knowing', in G. Shapiro and A. Sica (eds) *Hermeneutics: Questions and Prospects*, Amherst: University of Massachusetts Press.
Bruner, J. (1986) *Actual Minds, Possible Worlds*, Cambridge, Massachusetts: Harvard University Press.
Clifford, J. and Marcus, G. (1986) *Writing Culture*, Berkeley (CA): University of California Press.
Collingwood, R. (1946) *The Idea of History*, Oxford: Oxford University Press.
Conkey, M. and Spector, J. (1984) 'Archaeology and the study of gender', in M. Schiffer (ed.) *Advances in Archaeological Theory and Method 7*, New York: Academic Press.
Eagleton, T. (1983) *Literary Theory*, Oxford: Basil Blackwell.
Earle, T. and Preucel, R. (1987) 'Processual archaeology and the radical critique', *Current Anthropology* 28, 501–38.
Gadamer, H.-G. (1975) *Truth and Method*, New York: Seabury.
Gathercole, P. and Lowenthal, D. (1989) *The Politics of the Past*, London: Unwin Hyman.
Habermas, J. (1971) *Knowledge and Human Interests*, Boston: Beacon Press.
—— (1990) 'The hermeneutic claim to universality', in G. L. Ormiston and A.

D. Schrift (eds) *The Hermeneutic Tradition*, Albany: State University of New York Press.

Heidegger, M. (1958) *The Question of Being*, New Haven: University Press.

Hodder, I. (1986) *Reading the Past*, Cambridge: Cambridge University Press.

—— (1989a) 'This is not an article about material culture as text', *Journal of Anthropological Archaeology* 8, 250–69.

—— (1989b) *The Meanings of Things*, London: Unwin Hyman.

—— (1989c) 'Writing archaeology: site reports in context', *Antiquity* 63, 268–74.

—— (1990) *The Domestication of Europe*, Oxford: Basil Blackwell.

—— (1991a) 'The postprocessual debate', in R. Preucel (ed.) *Processual and Postprocessual Archaeologies*, Carbondale: Southern Illinois University.

—— (1991b) 'Gender representation and social reality', in *Proceedings of the 1989 Chacmool Conference*, Calgary: University of Calgary Press.

Kintigh, K. W. (1990) 'A perspective on reburial and repatriation', *Bulletin of the Society for American Archaeology* 8(2), 6–7.

Layton, R. (1989a) *Conflict in the Archaeology of Living Traditions*, London: Unwin Hyman.

—— (1989b) *Who Needs the Past? Indigenous Values and Archaeology*, London: Unwin Hyman.

Leone, M. (1982) 'Some opinions about recovering mind', *American Antiquity* 47, 742–60.

Leone, M., Potter Jr, P. and Shackel, P. (1987) 'Toward a critical archaeology', *Current Anthropology* 28, 283–302.

Lovis, W. A. (1990) 'How far will it go?: A look at S. 1980 and other repatriation legislation', *Bulletin of the Society for American Archaeology* 8(2), 8–10.

Mascia-Lees, F., Sharpe, P. and Cohen, C. B. (1989) 'The postmodernist turn in anthropology', *Signs* 15, 7–33.

Merriman, N. (1989) 'Museum visiting as a cultural phenomenon', in P. Vergo (ed.) *The New Museology*, London: Reaktion Books.

Moore, H. (1990) 'Paul Ricoeur: action, meaning and text', in C. Tilley (ed.) *Reading Material Culture*, Oxford: Basil Blackwell.

Olsen, B. (1990) 'Roland Barthes: from sign to text', in C. Tilley (ed.) *Reading Material Culture*, Oxford: Basil Blackwell.

Ormiston, G. L. and Schrift, A. D. (1990) *The Hermeneutic Tradition*, Albany: State University of New York Press.

Patrik, L. E. (1985) 'Is there an archaeological record?', in M. Schiffer (ed.) *Advances in Archaeological Theory and Method* 8, New York: Academic Press.

Patterson, T. (1986) 'The last sixty years: toward a social history of Americanist archaeology in the United States', *American Anthropologist* 88, 7–26.

Preucel, R. (1991) *Processual and Postprocessual Archaeologies*, Carbondale: Southern Illinois University.

Renfrew, C. (1989) 'Comments on archaeology into the 1990s', *Norwegian Archaeological Review* 22, 33–41.

Ricoeur, P. (1971) 'The model of the text: meaningful action considered as text', *Social Research* 38, 529–62.

—— (1990) 'Hermeneutics and the critique of ideology', in G. L. Ormiston and A. D. Schrift (eds) *The Hermeneutic Tradition*, Albany: State University of New York Press.

Shanks, M. and Tilley, C. (1987a) *Re-constructing Archaeology*, Cambridge: Cambridge University Press.

—— (1987b) *Social Theory and Archaeology*, Cambridge: Polity Press.

Thompson, J. (1981) *Critical Hermeneutics*, Cambridge: Cambridge University Press.

Tilley, C. (1989) 'Discourse and power: the genre of the Cambridge inaugural lecture', in D. Miller, M. Rowlands and C. Tilley (eds) *Domination, Power and Resistance*, London: Unwin Hyman.

—— (1990a) *Reading Material Culture*, Oxford: Basil Blackwell.

—— (1990b) 'Michel Foucault: towards an archaeology of archaeology', in C. Tilley (ed.) *Reading Material Culture*, Oxford: Basil Blackwell.

Trigger, B. (1980) 'Archaeology and the image of the American Indian', *American Antiquity* 45, 662–76.

—— (1989) *A History of Archaeological Thought*, Cambridge: Cambridge University Press.

Watson, P. J. (1986) 'Archaeological interpretation, 1985', in D. Meltzer, D. Fowler and J. Sabloff (eds) *American Archaeology Past and Future*, Washington DC: Smithsonian Institution Press.

Yates, T. (1990) 'Jacques Derrida: "There is nothing outside the text" ', in C. Tilley (ed.) *Reading Material Culture*, Oxford: Basil Blackwell.

14

MATERIAL PRACTICE, SYMBOLISM AND IDEOLOGY

Given the long tradition which considers the symbolic in terms of signs in a language (Hodder 1989), the challenge of a symbolic archaeology is to explore the relationship between material culture and language. To what extent is a pot or an axe symbolic in the way that the words 'pot' or 'axe' carry meaning? Are the material culture meanings, like the linguistic meanings, arbitrary, organised by, for example, paradigmatic and syntagmatic relationships?

If there is indeed a close relationship between linguistic and material culture signs, then we might expect a correspondence of the following sort.

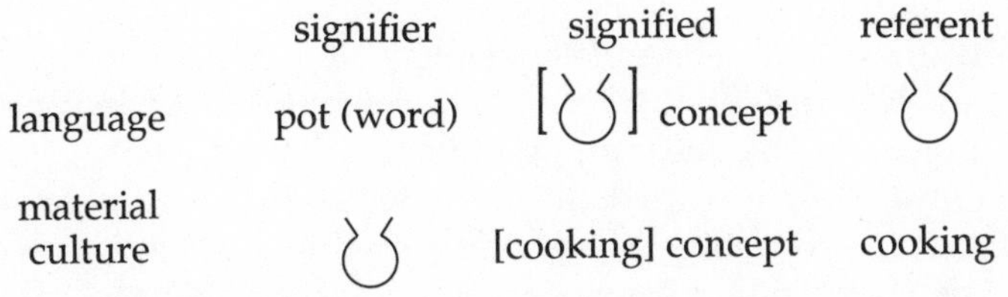

	signifier	signified	referent
language	pot (word)	[∪] concept	∪
material culture	∪	[cooking] concept	cooking

Figure 17 The relationships between signifiers, signifieds and referents in language and material culture

It is on the basis of such a correspondence that a structuralist and post-structuralist archaeology has been built (Hodder 1986; Tilley 1990). However, in some ways the language and material culture examples are different. In particular, the arbitrariness of the signifier–signified relationship in the linguistic case is not equivalent to the relationship between material culture signifier and signified. In the latter case, the pot in its materiality and use participates in the construction of the signified (the concept cooking). The material culture references are motivated and non-arbitrary.

We can perhaps summarise this difference by saying that in language a word is rarely both sign and referent. Language is largely referential in that words refer to abstractions or objects, although we do refer to words themselves when discussing grammar or the interpretation of specific terms. Onomatopoeia certainly involves words partaking in their referents but such cases are relatively rare. It is normally the case, on the other hand, that material culture is both sign and referent. It can be referred to as an object at the same time as having sign functions. It is an object with functional, material and technological constraints and characteristics. Hardness, porosity, friability and so on exist and cannot be seen as entirely independent of the sign properties. The objective, non-arbitrary characteristics of the signifier impinge upon and contribute to its reference potential.

A second difference between language and material culture symbolism concerns the different emphases on reference. In Figure 17, the word 'pot' looks forward to some referent. The signifier expects a signified. The primary function of language is communication. Many material symbols such as road sign arrows or gestures have a similar communication function. But it is always the case with material culture that the material symbol appears to have a greater independence from any referent. The material symbol can be 'read' and often the readings are obvious, but they nevertheless involve moving beyond the primary qualities of the object or gesture. Thus the material pot does not expect or need a symbolic interpretation in terms of cooking. The symbolic abstraction of 'cooking' may well be part of the use of pots in the practice of cooking, but the abstracted association of pots and cooking does not necessarily have any referential qualities. The transformation of the material and abstract association into a reference is an interpretation which supplements the meaning of the pot.

There are of course many other differences between linguistic and material culture meanings. For example, the distinctions made by Ricoeur (1971) and others between speech and writing are relevant to material culture. Unlike speech, writing and material culture often endure long after their production. Material culture meanings are therefore often interpreted away from the 'author' or maker who therefore has little control over how the object is given significance. Meaning is distanced from the author. Another difference between language and material culture is that the latter is often 'read' through bodily movement, practice and use. In other words, we know that someone has got the meaning of an object 'right' not because that person can give the correct definition, but because he or she uses it 'correctly'. Many more differences could be listed, but for the moment I wish to concentrate on what seem to be the two fundamental differences described above: material culture meanings are less arbitrary and less referential than language.

Tarlow (1990) has suggested that, in view of the differences between material culture and language, material symbols should not be seen as organised by abstract and arbitrary chains of signifiers but by chains of loaded or motivated relationships. In other words, the secondary meanings of objects are linked by metaphorical relationships to the practical nature and uses of those objects. Tarlow notes that like metaphor, material culture symbolism involves the abstraction of certain properties. The metaphoric abstractions are built upon certain aspects of a thing in order to provide a secondary meaning which is less a reference than an evocation to be interpreted. For example, some linguistic metaphors involve synecdoche which is the substitution of a part for a whole as in the use of the word 'hand' to describe a worker. A material culture instance might be the use of a lock of hair to represent a whole person. Metonymy is the substitution of an attribute, effect or association for a thing as in the use of the word 'crown' or a real crown for monarchy. For our purposes, the subtle and rather difficult differences between these terms are less important than the general point that metaphor involves various forms of symbolic substitution of associated features. Thus the secondary symbolic meanings of material culture are related to various associations in the world of experience. For example, in certain cultural contexts ash may come to mean fire, hearth, home and woman through abstraction from real material practices so that the symbolic meanings are non-arbitrary.

A similar point can be arrived at by taking another tack. So far I have been equating an object such as a pot with a word such as 'pot'. Perhaps a better analogy for a pot is a sentence. Certainly the pot is the result of a long sequence of activities or production 'statements' and this sequence is continued in the use and discard of the pot. This sequence is organised and structured in parallel with the grammatical organisation of a sentence. Sentences provide a more appropriate parallel than words because sentences, like material objects, are more clearly worked out in relation to specific real-world contexts. They are concerned with saying something in an active social context (Ricoeur 1971). The purposeful and motivated nature of sentences contrasts with the more abstract nature of word meanings. The *chaines operatoires* of material production are, like sentences, embedded in a real-world context and their meanings are yet more closely related to that context.

In general, then, material culture signifieds and referent are less arbitrary than words in speech. Of course, all manner of different meanings are given cross-culturally to right, left, the different parts of the body, blood, nature and so on. There is an ultimate arbitrariness organised only by historical convention. And yet this arbitrariness is embedded within certain material factors in the biological and physical worlds through technology and use. The abstract symbolic meanings of the material world are related to that world by relationships of association, analogy, substitution, metaphor and so on.

I have also wanted to go further and argue that much material culture does not 'mean'. Wallpaper is a good example. It may provide an appropriate setting, evoke the 'right' atmosphere, but it does not have a specific meaning in the same way that words or sentences do. Material culture meanings are different from linguistic meanings. The wallpaper evokes various associations. It might substitute for a grand room of state in the front room of a terraced house, or it may be a metaphor for peaceful country scenes in an urban environment. The wallpaper may work effectively and convey the desired messages even though that message might only be translated into a verbal account with some difficulty. Thus not only are material culture and linguistic meanings organised differently, but also the former seem to work without referring directly to anything specific. The wallpaper might simply 'feel' right at the non-discursive level. Similarly ash may have the 'meaning' of fire, hearth and home but this meaning results from association rather than from reference. Thus it is perhaps better to say that the ash does not mean fire, hearth and home but is associated with and can evoke those things.

The differences between language and material culture underlie the failure of archaeologists and ethnoarchaeologists to gain sensible answers to questions such as 'What does this pot mean?' or 'Why are you engraving that pot with that design?' Answers to such questions are often constructed, forced and unhappy, unlike the simpler question 'What does that word or that sentence mean?' The material meanings cannot be reduced to linguistic meanings. They are of a different nature.

Of course, material culture often has referential functions but I have been arguing that these are more organised in grounded contexts than are the floating chains of linguistic signification. As a further example, people with severe psychiatric disorders which involve an inability to relate to other people are sometimes treated by standing them in a circle and getting them to throw a ball between them. The thrown ball does not *represent* a relationship between thrower and catcher, it creates or *is* a relationship. The basic starting point of a ball linking two individuals can then be used as a metaphor for a social relationship. Grounded in the experience of throwing and catching the ball, the metaphor is based on the material likenesses between exchanging a ball and the give and take of social relationships. At a yet more abstract level one could begin to categorise different types of exchange. The patient thus moves from the practice of throwing a ball to various metaphoric associations (understanding of which does not necessarily involve speech) and finally to the use of an abstract referential discussion using arbitrary signs of speech. The material act comes to refer and represent. Thus it comes to have language-like qualities, and yet its referential functions are built up from non-arbitrary associations rather than from abstract sets of differences.

We can summarise the differences between language and material culture by referring to Bloch's (1991) conclusions derived from a wedding of cognitive science and anthropology. Bloch argues that practical knowledge is fundamentally different from linguistic knowledge in the way that it is organised in the mind. Practical knowledge is 'chunked' into highly contextualised information about how to 'get on' in specific domains of action. Much cultural knowledge is non-linear and purpose-dedicated, formed through the practice of closely related activities (ibid., 192). In contrast, linguistic knowledge is linear and sentential.

KNOW-HOW AND KNOWLEDGE

Material culture both *represents* and *is*, and this duality has implications for the ideological use of material culture as we will see below. For the moment I want to try to gain a better understanding of the different nature of material culture meanings. In particular I want to look at how the symbolic meanings interact with the material meanings. A number of French students of technology have developed a complex set of ideas about the sequences of actions (*chaines operatoires*) which result in a material object (e.g. Pelegrin 1990; Pigeot 1990). They make distinctions between three types of knowledge. The first is *connaissance* or general knowledge and it includes categories, relationships, primary and secondary meanings about objects and their uses. The separation of a symbolic or theoretical knowledge about objects from practical knowledge is equivalent to a long tradition in western philosophy. Aristotle distinguished the theoretical thinking of philosophers who ask why questions from the practical thinking of artisans who want to get things done. In archaeology, this idea was already discussed in the nineteenth century with the work of Pitt-Rivers who distinguished the intellectual mind which was able to reason, from the unconscious automaton mind which allowed one to walk or ride a bicycle. These distinctions have certain similarities with that between Giddens' (1979) discursive and practical consciousness.

I have already implied that it would be more appropriate to distinguish within this first category discursive and non-discursive knowledge about general categories. Thus, for example, actors might recognise at a non-discursive level that certain activities had a higher social value than others. The oppositions culture/nature or left/right might be absorbed and acted upon at a non-verbal level. This form of general knowledge can be separated from that verbalised in an abstract system of linguistic signs. So, *connaissance* can be both discursive (explicit and linguistic) and non-discursive (implicit and non-verbal). But in general this first type of knowledge can be distinguished from *savoir-faire* or know-how. According to Pelegrin, the second type of knowledge about material objects is ideational or comparative know-how. It involves the ability to evaluate a stone tool during its manufacture and recognise that it is like other tools in a category, or it implies the ability to recognise that one type of pot would be good for cooking but another type would not. It involves 'feel', 'eye', 'aesthetic'. On the one hand, this knowledge derives from the material world in that it involves comparisons of weight, texture, sharpness and so on and incorporates recognition of the properties of materials. On the other hand, this type of knowledge is an 'embodiment' of the general cultural values and classifications. The object 'looks right' or 'feels right' because it fits into a general category.

The third type of knowledge is motor or generative know-how or *savoir-faire*. Included here, for example, are the motor skills involved in removing a blade from a flint core – the sequences of hand movements, the forces of blow and the angles at which the hammer and core are held. In a more modern context this type of knowledge involves, for example, the sense of balance and other skills which are used in riding a bicycle or the adjustments of body position needed in order to keep upright while windsurfing. We can be told how to do all these things, but usually the verbal knowledge is insufficient for us to be able to do them. We normally need practical experience and training.

The above tripartite scheme was developed in the context of the production of material objects such as stone tools. But it does seem more widely relevant and to be applicable to use and discard. For example, the use and discard of a pot is organised by (1) general verbal and non-verbal knowledge about categories and associations of pots, (2) ideational know-how about, for example, the feel and weight of pottery that might be used for different types of cooking or which might most easily break, and (3) motor know-how about how best to carry heavy pots and how to handle them without breakage. Production, use and discard are all organised by the three levels of knowledge. In all cases, the three levels interpenetrate. Thus the general cultural knowledge affects what are considered to be effective motor skills (for example, whether to carry a pot on the head or in a sling on the back). At the same time, the motor know-how constrains the types of general knowledge that can be constructed. What most contemporary researchers in the area of technology do seem to agree on is the need for an interactive or integrative approach which embeds operational and technological procedures not only in the physical world, but also in the social and symbolic world. Thus, once again, the partly non-arbitrary and non-referential components of all material culture meaning are exposed.

Despite important work by Bourdieu (1977) in his attempt to build a 'theory of practice', it seems that we still have very little idea of how know-how or practical knowledge works and how it relates to the more general and abstract levels of meaning. Archaeologists may find it useful to forge links with psychologists working on motor skills and everyday cognition (e.g. Rogoff and Lave 1984). On the one hand, clinical psychologists have demonstrated a certain independence of symbolic and motor skills. In evolutionary terms, the generalisation of abstract terms (as in language) would seem to be dependent on such a split. Bloch (1991, 183) has pointed out that studies of expertise show that 'in order to become an expert at a familiar task or a set of tasks a person needs to organise his or her knowledge in a way which is not language-like'. On the other hand, cross-cultural work on everyday practical cognition has found particular mental representations and cognitive skills involved in culture-specific practices such as navigation, weaving and tailoring. For example, features of tailors' performance on a pure arithmetic paper-and-pencil task could be linked to the quantitative operations they used every day in sewing trousers for a living (Rogoff and Lave 1984, 13). Such linkages underline the emphasis I have been placing on the non-arbitrary structuring of all types of knowledge including the most abstract, even if the organisation of knowledge is different at the different levels.

IDEOLOGY

Clearly more work is needed in order to build a theory of practice. However, for the moment I wish to move towards exploring the ideological implications of the partly non-arbitrary and partly non-referential nature of material culture. The ideological potential for material objects unfolds as follows. I have argued that in an ultimate sense the meanings of material symbols are arbitrary. There is always a choice about the abstract meanings and metaphors. Blood, for example, has qualities which constrain its symbolic meaning but a range of specific meanings (from danger and death to the source of life) can be given. The ultimate arbitrariness is, however, inseparable from a non-arbitrariness which derives from the links of the material symbol to a material practice. The ideological implications of this duality are that the meanings of objects, while imposed by convention, appear based on necessity. The non-arbitrary component of material culture meanings naturalises the ideological message.

Similarly, I have argued that although material culture does have a referential function or can be given that function, its meanings are often associative, evocative and non-referential. Often, material culture does not appear to 'mean' at all. This self-evident quality thus hides or masks the references that are being made. The ideological messages are hidden behind the supposed non-communicative nature of material culture. The duality of reference and non-reference suggests that material culture, in its pragmatic innocence, should play a powerful ideological role. Our difficulty in recognising this role is the basis of its success.

As a hypothetical example, it might have been argued in the past that in contrast to other stone tools, hunting tools needed to be more carefully flaked and fluted. This more careful preparation may have been seen as necessary (as it is seen today – Torrence 1986) because there is no time to compensate for a failed tool during the hunt. The more elaborate tool with greater investment of skill might also allow the projectile to be thrown better, to penetrate better and to be more easily recognisable during recovery. Such arguments present 'natural' and 'necessary' justifications for focusing time, energy, skill and aesthetic senses on hunting tools rather than on scrapers, digging and gathering implements. The careful flaking of the projectile point does not seem arbitrary and it does not refer in a direct way to prestige. Nevertheless, the pragmatic knowledge has the effect of locating prestige in the domain of hunting and giving a secondary role to other activities.

I define ideology as the use of symbols in relation to interest. It is that component of symbol systems most closely involved in the negotiation of power from varying points of interest within society. As is clear from the edited volumes by Miller and Tilley (1984), Miller, Rowlands and Tilley (1989) and McGuire and Paynter (1991), most archaeologists would now accept the inadequacies of the thesis that societies are dominated by one ideology which represents the interests of the dominant group and which dupes all members of society. There is rather recognition that subordinate groups are able to penetrate dominant ideologies and engage in resistance and social action in relation to different interests and ideologies. There is thus not one ideology but many, and there are many different types of power and prestige that are negotiated in relation to each other.

If the ideological symbols are linguistic, or if they have the dominantly linguistic properties of arbitrariness and reference, then the ideology is always in danger of exposing its own provisional character in relation to the practices of daily life. The definition of power is insecure since it is linked to relative values constructed by an arbitrary language. Power is based on mere words, labels, classifications, opinions and arguments.

But ideologies often seem far from fickle. They seem to have great duration and to be embedded deeply rather than superficially. We have tended to take the 'naturalisation' and 'embedding' of ideologies for granted. But how does the naturalisation occur? Even if we take a line that argues that the ideology arises directly from the infrastructure, how does it arise?

Such questions are easier to answer in relation to material symbols if it is recognised that the symbolic meanings are built upon, by association and metaphor, the material world. Thus if systems of prestige (as in the case of hunting points) are constructed in relation to necessary functional and technological relations, then the ideologies which they underpin have a non-arbitrary, natural logic. The ideology is thus less transparent and less open to critique. It becomes necessary.

Roland Barthes (1977) shows how a photograph or film is a potent ideological mechanism since it appears so 'real' that the ideological message is effectively masked. We do not see that the camera lies or that the photograph is not just a direct copy of reality but tells a story in its composition, lighting, etc. Even more so, then, the lived world of experience hides its own arbitrariness behind an apparently necessary functional logic.

Of course, I do not deny that ideology is an abstraction or conceptualisation. And I do not deny that there is always a tension between theory (ideology) and practice which generates change. But I do argue that the motor for ideological change frequently occurs at the practical level, not because I espouse a materialism, but because it is mainly at the level of practical consciousness that people understand ideologies. Ideologies are experienced in the lived world. The verbal abstractions and conceptualisations that we make are often manipulations and legitimations of a practical know-how which incorporates a necessary logic and hides a conventional cultural scheme.

Ideologies, at least those using material symbols, are deeply embedded in a practical knowledge. As another example, we might start from the obvious point that for spears to be effective they must be long and straight. We might also add the less obvious view that for them to be thrown with adequate force young men need to do the throwing. Bourdieu (1977) shows how, in a particular cultural context, the notion of straightness can be linked (by metaphor) to valued notions of 'talking straight', 'being straight', as opposed to being bent over, submissive. Thus men might be told to 'stand up straight' and in this simple statement a whole cosmology, a whole political philosophy concerning the relations between men and women is imposed. The metaphor that men are straight like their spears is based on a necessary technological knowledge (that spears have to be long and straight) which we all recognise but do not articulate.

Reverting to psychology, other instances can be provided of the way ideologies are engrained within a bodily understanding of the world. For example, in relation to funerary practices Bloch (1982, 227) argued that ideologies 'take over certain pre-cultural biological and psychological phenomena . . . so that they appear homogeneous with legitimate authority'. In another example, recent research at the Applied Psychology Unit at Cambridge has suggested that spider phobia may well be an inherited disposition, linked to their fast unpredictable movements. Let us assume that it is indeed the case that many or most of us have such an innate disposition to fear spiders. It is certainly possible to surmount such a fear and cure oneself of the phobia. But any innate tendency towards fearing spiders can be used as a metaphor in cultural rules. For example, in Anglo-American society, nursery rhymes play on this fear as when 'Miss Muffet' is frightened away by a spider, and witches are associated with spiders at Halloween. Our society attaches cultural values to a whole range of creepy crawly things, including spiders. These cultural values incorporate abstract oppositions such as culture/nature, and they also involve social categories and evaluations. But the social and cultural meanings are experienced in terms of a bodily knowledge. An arbitrary categorisation is given a necessary basis and a self-evident air. As we rush screaming from a room in which a spider has appeared we do not stop to think 'my fear is culturally manipulated'. We do not stop to think whether our 'instinctive' reaction to spiders underpins a social evaluation of young women like 'Miss Muffet'!

Ideologies are thus not created in abstract in order to legitimate a particular set of social realities. Rather they are made possible by being embedded within those realities. Ideologies are made possible at the level of the physical and biological world to which they are related by arguments of necessity, efficacy, substitution, association and metaphor. We experience ideologies as much as we think them. So I may feel a certain discomfort at removing a spider from my living room but this seems to be a deep, spontaneous bodily fear. I do not realise that my culture has worked upon any disposition I may have had towards spiders so that my attitudes to spiders have an ideological implication.

In so far as dominant groups in society wish to promote certain ideologies in their own interests, they will need to control training and enculturation of practical activities. If successful ideologies are largely experienced at the level of practical, non-discursive consciousness then it becomes necessary to control the details of bodily movements and behaviour as the cultural rules are internalised through repetition and constraint. Children are taught to hold the knife in the right hand, to stand up straight, not to be 'silly' about spiders, and so on. In these ways a political philosophy is imbued. Children can become a battleground for competing interests, and control of their enculturation becomes of central importance. It is often argued that women have power in small-scale societies partly through practical control in the domestic context even if they have few public rights (Moore 1986). In the terms I am using in this paper, an individual's ability to make verbal interpretations and conceptualisations of practical knowledge may be limited within a particular society. But since I have argued that ideologies are largely understood at the non-discursive practical level, then control over the enculturation of practical knowledge does indeed provide some degree of power. If that control is at least partly in the hands of women, then they do gain a *de facto* power.

CONCLUSION

Bourdieu (1977, 91) talks of 'the mind born of the world of objects'. I have tried in this paper to argue for the importance of this insight. The recent attraction in archaeological theory towards post-structuralism has led archaeologists perilously close to disregarding the most important aspect of their data – their materiality. We do not simply dig up texts, either literally or figuratively. We do not only dig up interpretations of interpretations. Material culture does indeed have a linguistic, abstract, referential component. It is partly organised into structured sets of differences by historical conventions. But we cannot limit the study of material culture signs to a linguistic type of analysis (cf. Bloch 1991). Rather we need to understand the way in which the biological and physical world is embedded within social and cultural meanings, and we need to explore the tensions between the arbitrary and non-arbitrary, and between the referential and non-referential aspects of material culture.

As yet we still understand very little about the organisation of practical know-how. As noted above some progress has been made with lithic technologies but we are still far from understanding how the making of a stone tool or ceramic pot can be both mechanism and metaphor for disciplining the human body into a cultural mould. We are still far from understanding how knowledge about striking blades and flakes from flint nodules is organised, learnt and adapted. And we are far from understanding how, for example, the shift from knapping flint flakes to blades might be related, in particular social and cultural contexts, to a new bodily discipline and a new political philosophy. Both as archaeologists and ethnoarchaeologists we need to have the confidence to delve into the practical world of technological operations in order to build theories about the embodiment of meanings and thus about the relationship between material practice and conceptual structure.

But at least now the problem becomes manageable. While the meaning of flakes and blades was seen as entirely arbitrary, organised only by sets of similarities and differences like language, the interpretation of meaning depended on having a rich network of similarities and differences surviving in the archaeological record. As a result, most successful symbolic interpretation has been in later periods and in historical periods where written accounts are preserved. But in earlier periods, the lack of rich 'texts' (both material culture and written) made interpretation difficult. There simply was not enough to relate, for example, blades and flakes to. But now we see that the symbolic meanings of blades and flakes will be integrated into the different technological processes of blade and flake production. Even in early periods archaeologists often have good evidence of productive processes and it is on this basis that interpretation can be built. The only limitation here is our lack of theoretical knowledge about the way in which *savoir-faire*, know-how, everyday practical knowledge is organised and related to higher levels of abstract symbolic thought.

REFERENCES

Barthes, R. (1977) *Image – Music – Text*, London: Fontana.

Bloch, M. (1982) 'Death, women and power', in M. Bloch and J. Parry (eds) *Death and the Regeneration of Life*, Cambridge: Cambridge University Press.

—— (1991) 'Language, anthropology and cognitive science', *Man* 26, 183–98.

Bourdieu, P. (1977) *Outline of a Theory of Practice*, Cambridge: Cambridge University Press.

Giddens, A. (1979) *Central Problems in Social Theory*, London: Macmillan.

Hodder, I. (1986) *Reading the Past*, Cambridge: Cambridge University Press.

—— (1989) 'This is not an article about material culture as text', *Journal of Anthropological Archaeology* 8, 250–69.

McGuire, R. and Paynter, R. (1991) *The Archaeology of Inequality*, Oxford: Basil Blackwell.

Miller, D., Rowlands, M. and Tilley, C. (eds) (1989) *Domination and Resistance*, London: Unwin Hyman.

Miller, D. and Tilley, C. (eds) (1984) *Ideology, Power and Prehistory*, Cambridge: Cambridge University Press.

Moore, H. (1986) *Space, Text and Gender*, Cambridge: Cambridge University Press.

Pelegrin, J. (1990) 'Prehistoric lithic technology: some aspects of research', *Archaeological Review from Cambridge* 9:1, 116–25.

Pigeot, N. (1990) 'Technical and social actors: flintknapping specialists at Magdalenian Etiolles', *Archaeological Review from Cambridge* 9:1, 126–41.

Ricoeur, P. (1971) 'The model of the text: meaningful action considered as text', *Social Research* 38, 529–62.

Rogoff, B. and Lave, J. (eds) (1984) *Everyday Cognition: its Development in Social Context*, Cambridge, Massachusetts: Harvard University Press.

Tarlow, S. (1990) 'Metaphors and Neolithic–Bronze Age burial mounds', Unpublished M.Phil. dissertation, University of Cambridge.

Tilley, C. (ed.) (1990) *Reading Material Culture*, Oxford: Basil Blackwell.

Torrence, R. (1986) *Production and Exchange of Stone Tools*, Cambridge: Cambridge University Press.

15

THE HADDENHAM
CAUSEWAYED ENCLOSURE –
A HERMENEUTIC CIRCLE[1]

Through recent decades academic archaeologists have been exhorted to conduct their research and excavations according to hypothesis-testing procedures. It has been argued that we should construct our general theories, deduce testable propositions and prove or disprove them against the sampled data.

In fact, the application of this 'scientific method' often ran into difficulties. The data have a tendency to lead to unexpected questions, problems and issues. Thus archaeologists claiming to follow hypothesis-testing procedures found themselves having to create a fiction. In practice, their work and theoretical conclusions partly developed from the data which they had discovered. In other words, they already knew the data when they decided upon an interpretation. But in presenting their work they rewrote the script, placing the theory first and claiming to have tested it against data which they discovered, as in an experiment under laboratory conditions.

Archaeological interpretation always seems to involve a circularity. We start out with a site, or a region or a theory or a problem – or some mixture of these. Already our data and theory are related in that we have background knowledge about the site or region and about the interpretations that have been made of similar data. We may have some pet theories that we want to try out. Undoubtedly, the data that we collect are 'prefigured'. We expect certain things and our interpretations are lying in wait for them, already formed. We pounce and may feel satisfied, confirmed. Or we may find that the data do not really conform to our expectations. In this case we adjust our theories, but always in relation to more general theories which we have espoused or take for granted.

What I have just described is a simplified version of the hermeneutic circle (see Chapters 12 and 13). In my view, hermeneutics provides a far better description of what archaeologists actually do than any positivist hypothesis-testing procedure. What we try and do as archaeologists is to work back and forth between theory and data, showing that some theories account for more of the data than others, and adjusting our theories according to the data. Rather than emphasising generalisations and external comparisons we try and situate our general theory in relation to as much of the data as possible. In other words we try and contextualise our theories and data. The notion of a hermeneutic is closely linked to that of context. We try to give meaning to a particular piece of data by embedding it more and more fully in its surrounding data. When a theory makes all the data 'fit', then we say that the data 'make sense'.

The main problem with the hermeneutic circle is that it is potentially vicious in that arguments overtly or covertly assume what they are trying to prove. We do not approach the data with blank minds. Our context frames our definition of the archaeological context. It could be argued that we work in a closed circle which encompasses past and present. We 'read' the data by translating them into our own terms.

On the other hand, it can be argued that the hermeneutic circle is more properly described as a spiral in that we never return to exactly the same spot as we move between theory and data. According to this view the experience of data forces us to adjust our interpretations. There is some degree of partial independence between past and present contexts. We learn as we read.

Certainly in approaching the Haddenham causewayed enclosure (excavated between 1981 and 1987) I and my co-workers came with a vast baggage of theoretical knowledge. We knew first of all that it *was* a 'causewayed enclosure'. The typical arrangement of ditches and partially observable inner palisade on the air photographs allowed us to classify the monument and begin its interpretation. As the paradox of hermeneutics claims (Scruton 1982), 'no interpretation is possible until interpretation has begun'.

What, then, were the main pieces of baggage that we brought with us once we knew we were dealing with a causewayed enclosure? By far the largest piece, and also the most dangerous, was labelled ritual. The literature on causewayed enclosures encourages us to assume that while some or all of the enclosures had some occupation, stock management or defensive functions, they were also foci for burial and other rituals involving feasting and 'special' activities. Deposits of largely complete pots or animal joints which in Iron Age ditches would be interpreted as 'dumping' suddenly take on a quite different significance in the ditches of Neolithic causewayed enclosures. Here they become 'placed' and 'structured' deposits with ritual significance.

We also came with another large piece of baggage labelled social evolution. It has become generally accepted that, following the work of Renfrew (1973), we are in the Neolithic of Britain dealing with a low level of political development characterised by lineages which may have been emerging into chiefdoms. While the causewayed enclosure heralds this higher level of development, long barrows represent lineages.

Within this general notion of a segmented, relatively decentralised society much of the Neolithic data has been interpreted as representing small-group organisation. For example, both the mounds of long barrows and the ditches of barrows and enclosures have been claimed (e.g. Bradley 1984) to be built in sections, perhaps by 'work gangs'. So, one of our expectations at Haddenham was that we would find variability amongst the ditches and evidence that individual ditches had been dug in smaller segments. The way we initially approached the ditches, for example by digging so as to leave a longitudinal section in 1982, was designed to pick up pitting along the ditch lengths. This may have been a good example of hypothesis-testing but the procedure was gradually abandoned as we realised that it was obscuring our understanding of the full range of activities in the ditches.

More specifically, on the air photograph we saw, or thought we did, evidence of the varied, decentralised nature of the society which produced the causewayed enclosure. In some parts of the circuit an inner palisade was clearly visible. In other sections there was either no palisade or a palisade set well back from the ditches. For most of the enclosure a single ditch could be seen. But in the northwest zone two parallel ditches occurred as in the multiple circuits found at other enclosures in England (e.g. Windmill Hill). The 1981 excavations were thus located over the double ditches so as to check one aspect of this internal difference.

I have explained the main baggage that we brought with us as we approached the first season of excavation at the enclosure. Of course, there was much else, both general and specific, but I have defined the main themes. So that we did not simply take the themes of ritual, social evolution and so on for granted, we needed to remain sensitive to the particular contextual data. This involved digging the enclosure ditch by ditch and gradually building up an argument which accommodated both data and theory. One ditch on its own would tell us little unless we were happy with fitting it immediately into our general schemes. But we can increase our understanding of the individual ditch through its similarities and contrasts with other ditches in the 'whole' which makes up the enclosure. In other words, we can gradually place each ditch into the context formed by all the ditches. The resultant 'whole' is not a given but is an interpretation built up from the parts. In relation to each ditch we construct an interpretation which we then use for other ditches. These ditches force us to change the interpretation and so we have to reinterpret the first ditch, and so on in an endless circle or spiral. Moving back and forth we work within the hermeneutic circle.

It so happens that we did indeed excavate the causewayed enclosure in a circle. In those years in which we excavated at the enclosure (1981, 1982, 1984, 1987) we gradually moved round the circuit in a clockwise manner (Figure 18). Right at the end of the 1987 season we returned to

215

the 1981 excavation and reconsidered our earlier interpretations. We had thus come full circle, both spatially and in our circle. Or perhaps we had come to the same point on the ground but to a different place on the hermeneutic spiral. Had we avoided the viciousness of the hermeneutic circle? An answer to this question must await the account of our circular journey.

THE ENCLOSURE DITCHES

The 1981 season

As we removed the peat layer overlying a buried prehistoric soil, we immediately saw one of the two concentric enclosure ditches which had appeared on the air photograph at this point. It snaked across the northern part of the excavated area. The ditch itself (F01) was clearly filled with peat deposits and it had a gravel upcast bank on either side but the southern bank was more substantial. This made sense because this larger bank was on the inner side of the enclosure. The hermeneutic circle was beginning to be pieced together. Other evidence too made

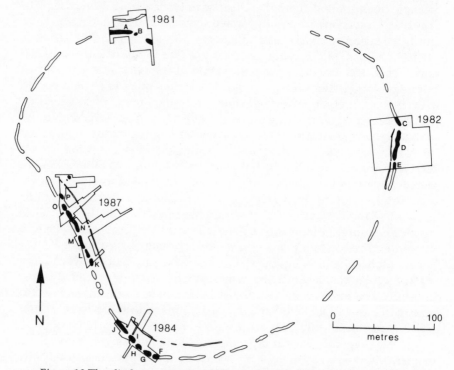

Figure 18 The ditch sections (A to P) excavated in different years at the Haddenham causewayed enclosure

sense. In the deepest part of the ditch there was a quantity of water-logged wood, and above this a concentration of large animal bones. Skull, mandible, pelvis and scapula were the main body parts represented and there was very little pottery or flint associated. Surely this was clear evidence of a ritual 'placed' deposit.

We had no bone specialist on site, but one of the bones was a horse mandible. This was disturbing because domesticated horse is thought to have been introduced into Britain only at the end of the Neolithic. Could this be a late Neolithic enclosure? Several eminent Neolithic specialists visited the site during this period and pronounced their verdict. Yes, they could see that the ditch had shallower portions which represented the causeways. The deeper pit with wood and bone represented the butt end of a ditch. The data fit well with other causewayed enclosures where concentrations of finds have been claimed at the butt ends of ditches. Yes, the small undiagnostic sherd was probably late Neolithic, fitting in with all the flint artifacts found in the ditch fills. How wonderful to have such good preservation in a causewayed enclosure.

But where was the other ditch? We simply could not see it. This was especially surprising because we examined the prehistoric soil below the peat in the rest of the uncovered area very carefully. Perhaps we had incorrectly rectified the air photographs or incorrectly surveyed the position of the ditches in the field. We checked and double-checked. Nothing seemed wrong. In frustration we decided to get the machine back to dig a deep slot trench at the western edge of the site, to the south of the ditch F01. Again, nothing.

Why could we not see the other, inner ditch? A clue emerged towards the end of the excavation. At the northern edge of the site, after we had taken off several spits of prehistoric soil, a hearth (F05) suddenly emerged. This must originally have been cut from the top of the prehistoric soil and yet it was no longer visible on the surface. Other evidence began to point to a heavily leached and discoloured prehistoric soil. Acidity tests showed that pH levels increased from 4 to 6 with increasing depth through the prehistoric soil, largely due to leaching during peat formation and water coverage.

Something clearly was not right. The hermeneutic circle which we had constructed looked substantially cracked. Why was the F01 ditch clearly visible on the surface of the prehistoric soil, filled with peaty soil, while other prehistoric features had been heavily leached during their coverage by the peat? The features and the F01 ditch must be of substantially different dates. In any case, as we excavated it became clear that the 'causeways' in the F01 ditch simply did not exist, even though we desperately wanted to see them. The ditch seemed to be continuous. So where was the other and perhaps main causewayed enclosure ditch? I kept sending the most experienced members of the team over to wade in the water at the bottom of the slot we had dug by machine on the western edge of the site to clean the sections. But they kept returning saying there was no ditch there.

On the penultimate day of the scheduled excavation, in sheer frustration, I went over myself to the machine section. There *was* a slight

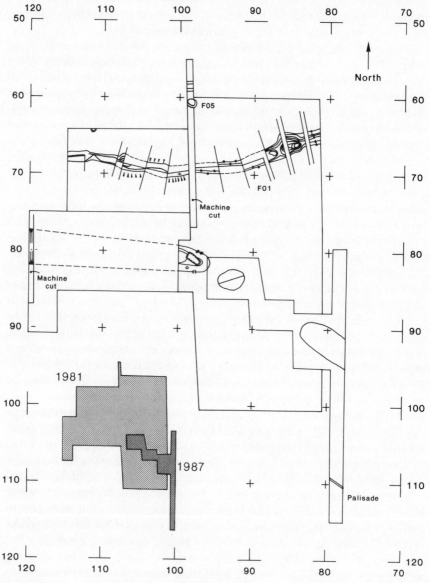

Figure 19 The 1981 and 1987 areas of excavation at the Haddenham causewayed enclosure

thickening of the peat layers. And there a slumping of the prehistoric soil. Then finally I saw what was, in comparison to ditch F01, an enormous ditch. It was difficult to see because filled with gravel and lenses of clays and silts as in the surrounding Pleistocene gravels. And it was so much bigger than our train of thought, which had understood the shallow F01 ditch to be the causewayed enclosure, had led us to expect. But this much more substantial ditch was much more what was expected on the basis of other causewayed enclosures.

Suddenly everything made sense and a new hermeneutic circle could be formed. The large ditch was the main causewayed ditch (later called ditch segment A), on the same alignment as a large 'pit' later called ditch segment B. These causewayed ditch segments could not easily be seen in the surface of the prehistoric soil because of the leaching process. Ditch F01 must have been cut through the prehistoric soil at a much later date. Indeed, we were later to obtain a C14 date from this ditch indicating that it was late Iron Age. The horse was thus explained. Shame-faced we reinterpreted the deposit of wood and large bones as butchering residue without ritual component.

The causewayed enclosure at this point did not after all have a double ditch. We quickly recorded what we could of the 'real' 'inner' ditches (A and B, see Figure 18) although we were never able, in the short time remaining to us, to understand them properly. We could, however, conclude that the 1981 causewayed ditches consisted of two (A and B) and possibly three (if A was itself causewayed) segments of a single line of ditches. The primary fills of sand and gravels had been recut along both edges of ditch A. A later recut was associated, at the butt end of ditch A, with evidence for later activities including burning, possible post-holes, further recuts and deposits of carbonised cereals. There was no evidence for such activities in the clean upper fills of ditch B and no evidence of activities in the large causeway to the east of ditch B. There was no evidence of a bank to the south of the ditch, nor of a palisade.

The 1981 excavations provide a good example of how the hermeneutic circle is constructed. We started with certain assumptions which affected our initial understanding of the data but we gradually modified theory and data until they harmonised. Thus we had expected Neolithic ritual and found it in butchering residues in an Iron Age ditch. We had wanted variability and had found double ditches in this part of the enclosure. But the need for internal coherence in our arguments gradually forced us to correct our interpretations. We noticed bits and pieces which did not fit. These included later prehistoric horse bones in what should have been middle Neolithic ditches and the lack of convincing causeways in the F01 ditch. It did not make sense that the F01 ditch was easily visible while other features turned up underneath the prehistoric soil surface. Finally an alternative was found which made sense of the

219

data. There was only one causewayed enclosure ditch containing later recuts and covered by a leached soil. The F01 ditch was Iron Age in date. The hermeneutic circle had proved not to be vicious. We had been able critically to compare contexts (past and present) and move in a spiral.

Our revised hypothesis still allowed for variability since we had not found a palisade trench as was visible on the air photographs in other parts of the enclosure. And we had found an enormous causeway to the east of ditch B. Variability was still a possibility but segmented digging of the ditches would have to be explored by complete excavation of ditch segments now that we knew what they looked like and how difficult they were to see. Our revised hypothesis also left room for ritual. Although we had not found 'placed' deposits, the fills of the Neolithic ditches had produced very few artifacts. This may partly have been a matter of less good preservation in the upper layers but as far as the flint is concerned it implies that there were few flints in the surrounding soil when the ditches filled up. Low densities could simply indicate a low intensity of occupation but they did not rule out ritual activities.

As a result of the initial mistakes described above, we left the 1981 excavations without having understood the causewayed ditch very well. We did not understand the strange double recut leaving a central mound within ditch A, and the numerous later recuttings. We would clearly need to excavate other parts of the camp in order to put these initial findings in context, to identify those parts of the initial evidence which were salient, and to evaluate the still general expectations about variability and ritual.

The 1982 season

In an attempt to answer these questions and to close the circle of our interpretations we moved clockwise in 1982 to the eastern side of the enclosure. Actually, at no point during the four seasons of excavation did we realise that we were digging in a circular manner. The choice of excavation was always based on local and contingent factors. For example, in 1982 we had managed to make good relations with the different landowner in this part of the enclosure and his fields were under a cereal crop that would allow us five weeks of excavation in September and October. We also thought that there may be a major entranceway at this point in the ditch circuit. An argument was beginning to develop amongst ourselves. Was the enclosure built in a variable, segmented way or was it planned as an overall design implying greater centralisation of decision-making? To what extent was the enclosure a hermeneutic circle in the past? What was the relation between part and whole? The presence of a major entranceway would provide some insight into these questions.

In 1982 three lengths of ditch were discovered, labelled C to E from north to south. They allowed us to begin to fill out the hermeneutic circle with repeated solid data. Ditches C, D and E all seemed similar to each other in general outline and sequence, with primary and secondary phases of fill and activity, and with burning associated with the secondary activities. Perhaps these phases recalled the primary and secondary recutting in ditch A. The evidence was as yet too scanty to allow generalisation but the possibility was emerging that all the ditches had gone through similar phases of use.

On the other hand, the differences from A were marked. The 1982 ditches did not appear to contain recuts. The variability was indeed quite marked. The palisade accompanied ditches D and E but not C. Ditch C was on a different alignment. Evidence of bone concentrations and burning was found at different places along the ditches (for example, in the terminal of C but in the centre of D) and was absent from E. There was no evidence of a major entranceway between ditches C and D, although it remained possible that C, without its palisade, was not part of the circuit at all, but acted to channel movement into the interior of the enclosure. The other side of an entranceway may have been found by excavating farther to the north. This hypothesis seems unlikely given the similarity of this ditch to those to the south and given the lack of special activities associated with the northern butt end of ditch D. The air photographs rather suggest that the circuit changed its course abruptly at this point as it did in the northwest corner (Figure 18). The lack of entranceway undermines the notion of a unified plan and concentrates our attention once again on the variation and segmentation of activities around the enclosure. Indeed it was possible that the two deeper butt ends of ditch D somehow indicated segmented activities but we had no evidence of this as yet.

The densities of artifacts and activities in the ditches were low and there was little to suggest ritual deposits. All the evidence could be contained within a hypothesis of mundane dumping and burning. Overall, the evidence seemed relatively simple. Was this because relatively little had happened in this part of the site or was it because we had missed the evidence? After all, 1981 had shown us the difficulties resulting from inexperience of the site. We had made progress in 1982, but had we really discovered all we might have? To make matters worse, the weather had been extremely dry during the September excavation and on the well-drained gravels the stratigraphy had been difficult to see. Conversely, in the final week, when we were digging the lower levels of the ditches, the weather was remarkably wet and so too were these deposits. In addition to these climatic problems, perhaps we had still to learn how to see recuts. The 'data' are part of the hermeneutic circle. We saw what we had the experience to see. We would need to excavate other sections of ditch in order to evaluate the existence of recuts.

The 1984 season

So we set off around the hermeneutic circle. The next time that we could excavate on the causewayed enclosure ditches was in the late summer of 1984. The specific location of the excavations was again partly contingent, depending on the harvesting and planting regime of the farmer of this part of the land. But we also chose a spot where, on the air photograph, the palisade seemed to be set much farther back from the ditches than in 1982. Was this an example of variability around the enclosure, and in what other ways were the ditches here different from those in other parts of the enclosure?

We excavated five ditches (F to J) of the enclosure circuit in 1984. In the first ditch (F) we seemed to see at least one deeper butt end. This evidence recalled the two deeper ends of ditch D. Were we beginning to see a repeated pattern? And what did it mean? The immediate problem was that the evidence could be interpreted in opposing ways. The uneven shape of the base of the ditch (F) could simply be the result of the way in which the ditch was dug as one event and by one group. The unevenness would then simply be the result of informality in the digging process. Alternatively the ditch could initially have been dug as two events, either by two 'gangs' at the same moment in time or by one group producing recuts at different moments. It began to be necessary to construct event and sequence hypotheses.

The issue extended to the fills of the ditches. It was rarely possible to distinguish recuts from sequential layers with any certainty. Ditch F could be seen according to the sequence view as having undergone four recutting events after the initial ditch had been dug. More parsimonious, the event view saw only one recutting when ditches F and G were joined at a late stage.

Despite this possibly greater complexity of some ditches, some patterns seemed to hold, such as a major division into two phases of activity in the primary and secondary fills and a distinction in artifact patterning between the central and end portions of the ditches.

Both ditches G and H were relatively simple, according to both event and sequence viewpoints. Ditch G had one or two recuts while even sequence thinkers only claimed three recuts for ditch H. Both ditches had a low density of finds.

Ditch I (Figure 20) was remarkable in its complexity and it was the first ditch for which it was possible to argue for a ritual interpretation. It is not at all obvious why some things seem ritual to archaeologists. The initial impression is that the term is used for the odd and the not understood. This emphasis on oddness is often the starting point too for ethno-

222

graphic interest in ritual (Sperber 1974). Certainly ditch I was odd in various ways. At its base it contained a central ridge or mound which was an odd thing to leave in the centre of a ditch. The ridge was at a different angle to the smaller humps which were found in the base of other ditches. But oddness is clearly not an adequate basis for defining ritual. Universal definitions of ritual need to be tempered by contextual definitions. The latter involve contrasting different types of deposit. Ditch I seemed special in that it contained not only very complex recutting in comparison to the other ditches, but also human bones and a polished axe. This assemblage, associated with the axial mound in the ditch and thus intentionally 'placed', suggested formalised behaviour related to burial. It was difficult to argue that the deposits were purely the result of refuse discard from domestic or feasting activities.

Also relevant to the ritual interpretation of the ditch are the parallels which can be drawn between the overall sequences of activities in the ditch and in an adjacent long barrow (Hodder and Shand 1988). First the two linear halves of ditch I were dug so that the central axis remained, as the long barrow was built respecting a central axis. Ditch I was then filled but recut leaving a mound in the centre of the ditch. Deposits were then placed at the southern or southeastern end of the mound, filling ditch I at this point. As a result a ditch with a U-shaped plan had been produced within ditch I, for all the world like the U-plan ditch around the long barrow. Human bones were associated with both the ditch and the long barrow. A broken axe was placed on top of the mound in ditch I.

The U-plan ditch in I filled up but was recut two times at the northern end in order to redefine the axial mound. Burnt material was deposited in these recuts as it was in the fill which covered over the mound. The final fill of the ditch contained redeposited soil. These penultimate acts of burnt material which in effect 'close off' the use of the ditch and its central mound recall the use of burning towards the end of the activity at the long barrow.

There are of course differences between ditch I and the long barrow, particularly in the way in which artifacts were deposited and in their orientation. It may not be too fanciful to suggest, however, that the human bone deposit at the southeastern end of the ditch mound parallels the human bone deposit at the northeastern end of the long barrow mound. In both cases the opening in the U-plan ditch is associated with the human bone deposits. In both cases the mound is higher with a steeper 'front' at the eastern end.

Moving across what appeared to be a narrow but was earlier a wide causeway, we came to a long section of ditch (J). Ditch J continued the evidence of a long sequence of activities found in ditch I. Not only were these two ditches distinctive in the amount of activity which occurred in them, but also the sequences of activity had an overall similarity. Soon after the gap between them had been narrowed, the focus of activities in

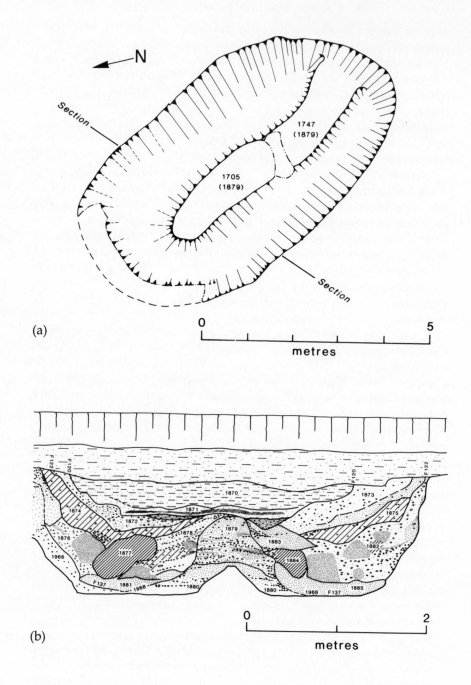

Figure 20 Ditch I, Haddenham causewayed enclosure. (a) Plan, (b) cross-section

each of the ditches shifted to the butt ends on either side of the causeway. Clearly in the latter part of the period of the use of the ditches the entranceway had come to take on a special significance. This entrance-related activity was not evident earlier on.

Summary of 1984 season

We began to think that we had missed a lot of evidence in earlier years on the enclosure ditches. Our greater familiarity with the difficult and leached soils allowed us in 1984 to find more evidence of recutting. And our relaxation of the policy of maintaining longitudinal sections allowed us to understand the ditches more as wholes. As a result we had to develop event and sequence viewpoints which were argued out on a daily basis on the site. Was the irregularity in the cutting of the ditches the result of different 'work gangs' or sequences of different events? Should the layers of fill be interpreted as recuts? The resolution of these problems was not always clear, but at least we were now raising the questions.

The notion of variability was now certainly a central issue. On the one hand, the variation in the activities in the ditches was marked. Ditches I and J were much more complex than those adjacent to the south (F, G, H). Also, there was variation through time in that ditches F and G were joined into one at a late stage, and the early large gap between I and J was later narrowed. On the other hand, the gap between ditches I and J could be interpreted as a major entranceway into the enclosure. In this case, the complex deposits in ditches I and J related to activities associated with entering the enclosure as a whole. The evidence from the palisade (p. 234) showed that the I–J gap had been an entrance which was later blocked by closing the palisade at this point. The existence of one or a few entrances would imply an overall plan to the site and therefore draw attention to the whole rather than to segmentation and variability. Indeed some aspects of the layout of the enclosure could be argued to support the notion of an overall plan with major entranceways (Evans 1988).

Despite the variability through time as the relationships between ditches changed, there was also evidence for continuity of use in the way in which some ditches were used. Ditches I and J with complex series of early activities also had complex secondary fills. The axial mound in ditch I was retained by being remodelled or recut later on.

The 1987 season

In the years between 1984 and 1987 we argued over the issue of whether there was an overall plan to the enclosure. On the one hand it seemed possible to point to all the variability we had found and to the apparently random variation in length of ditch as one moved around the circuit. The palisade was either absent (1981 season) close to the ditches (1982 season) or distant from them (1984 season). On the other hand, we had also begun to discover regularities in the way the ditches were dug and used over time, particularly in terms of distinctions between primary and secondary fills. Perhaps we should excavate a part of the circuit where an entrance seemed most likely on the air photographs.

The search for major entrances was combined with a decision to excavate as large a section of the perimeter as was possible within the season's constraints. Six ditch segments (K to P) were excavated over a considerable area (Figure 18). The aim was to obtain a further idea of the variability between ditches within a localised part of the perimeter. If another extensive length of ditches was uncovered, what type of variability might be found? We were unwittingly moving around the enclosure in a clockwise direction, but in our thinking we were trying to close the hermeneutic circle and make overall sense of the data in terms of unity, variability, sequence and ritual.

By the end of the 1987 season we felt that the circle was beginning to close in the sense that we were finding the same things over and over again. We had cracked the code, found the structure. In particular, the sequences of events in the ditches were similar – even the evidence that we had collected early on could be 'reread' to fit into the same pattern. Normally we had found multiple phases of early pitting at opposed ends of the ditch, associated with careful cleaning out of earlier fills. The bottom of the ditch was then allowed to fill up quickly with sands, gravels, clays and marl. During this period items such as skull, antler, pot and polished axe were deposited in the ditch, often on the central axis. The end of this phase of initial filling of the ditch was usually associated with evidence of charcoal and burning. Recuts also occurred in the secondary, slower fills and there was often evidence of marking the butt ends of the ditches with late pits and post-holes.

Another pattern which was clarified in the 1987 season was that although concentrations of finds and recutting were found to move towards the butt ends in the secondary fills (e.g. ditches L, N, O) as had been found in 1984, such activities were also concentrated in the butt ends in primary fills (e.g. K, L, M, N, O).

Perhaps a greater regularity would occur in relation to entrances. After all, we had excavated in this spot in order to find a major entrance. Had we found one? The answer to this question must partly await the discussion of the palisade, but the only obvious 'pairing' of ditches as had been found in 1984 with I and J occurred between N and O which had the smallest of causeways between them. Clearly this was not a major entrance. We had expected the entrance between M and N. Certainly there was a large causeway here (although no larger than that between O and P), and certainly the southern end of N, nearer the 'entrance', contained much evidence of recutting and finds deposition. But the northern 'entrance' end of M did not contain high densities of artifacts and there was more evidence of recutting at its southern end. Human bone was found in the northern butt end but it was difficult to argue on this basis for a major entranceway at this point.

If the variation between ditches could not be related to major entranceways, what other factors might be considered? The variation was after all very marked. Some ditches such as K and P were relatively simple while others such as L, M, N, O were extremely complex in that they had many recuts and deposits of artifacts. In fact, at least in the case of P there seemed to be a correlation between little evidence of recutting and few artifacts. This recalled the similar evidence from G and H. In addition, all these 'simple' ditches were relatively small. An idea began to emerge. Perhaps the more complex ditches were larger or were nearer larger ditches than the simple ditches. This was a matter that would have to be followed thoughout the whole enclosure (see below, p. 230).

Perhaps the most important result of the 1987 season was the vindication of the sequence view – beyond even the wildest dreams of the sequence thinkers themselves. What we were digging was not so much a thing as a process. A certain bipolarity was evident, with repeated evidence of a division of the ditches into two ends. But within this balance seemingly anything could happen. Ditches were continually being recut and realigned, joined up to adjacent ditches or 'paired' with them, divided into shorter ditches and then combined again. It was difficult to see any method in this complexity apart from the duality of ends and the sequential structure outlined above. Once again this was a matter that would have to be examined throughout the enclosure.

We had completed the circle. We had built up a general understanding of how the ditches were organised. But archaeology is not simply a matter of amassing objective data in a linear sequence. Rather, we tend to go back, or 'round', to the data we first collected and reinterpret them in the light of our most recent interpretations. And so all our 'data' have a provisional character. We are continually circling back on them to give them new meaning, trying to find an interpretation that makes sense of the whole in terms of the parts and the parts in terms of the whole. So it is necessary to go on round the enclosure again to reconsider our early tentative data. Could we now make sense of our early mistakes?

The circle is not a vicious one. Although we were back where we had started, with the 1981 ditches A and B, we had moved on. The circle was really a spiral. We may not have progressed but we had certainly changed our position. We had proved ourselves not to be hermetically sealed within our own assumptions.

The 1981 season – again

Towards the end of the 1987 season we began to think that we must have missed some important evidence concerning the 1981 palisade. We had initially tended to assume considerable variability around the enclosure, and so had accepted that the palisade did not exist in the northern part of the enclosure, as it did not seem to exist inside ditch C. However, we had now found the palisade everywhere else except ditch C and we also now knew that the palisade was sometimes set well back from the ditches. In 1981 we had not excavated to the base of the prehistoric soil in the area farthest from ditches A and B. Perhaps we had missed the palisade there. In addition, we had not found a ditch to the east of ditch B. Was the causeway there really so big or was it possible that the ditches did not continue around the whole enclosure?

In order to settle these questions we used a machine in 1987 to uncover the 1981 trenches. The information obtained is shown in Figure 19. We had been correct in our identification of the small ditch B and there was a substantial causeway to its east without features. But we had just missed the beginning of a further ditch to the east. In addition, our trenches had not extended far enough to the south to pick up the palisade.

It was also possible to reconsider other aspects of the 1981 data. For example, we could now try to make sense of the fills of ditch A. The upstanding central block of 'pale orange-grey sand' in the ditch probably represented a deposit of what we later came to call marl – a natural deposit as in ditch J. Less likely, it could have represented a central ridge or mound as in ditch I. The lens of 'pale grey' above the marl may well have been evidence of burning just beneath or at the base of a secondary recut.

Other evidence too began to make sense. The late features found in the butt end of ditch A were similar to those found elsewhere (e.g. ditch O). In fact a pit containing grain in Ditch A suggested that these later activities may have been more 'occupational' than the earlier activities. This possibility would mean that we would have to go around the whole circle again looking for support or denial of this shift from ritual to occupation by reconsidering the evidence.

Even ditch B began to fit into a pattern. We had found very little in the ditch. It was a small ditch and we did not see any evidence of recutting. Even though we could have missed such evidence, ditch B was a possible example of the correlation between ditch size, complexity and finds density.

The 1982 season – again

Clearly we could go on round the circle *ad infinitum*, gradually reinterpreting our reinterpretations. After a bit we would reach a certain stability until either our data or our ideas changed. I do intend to change the data by moving to another aspect of the whole circle that makes up the enclosure – the palisade. However, before summarising the evidence we have gained from the ditches it is necessary briefly to reconsider the 1982 season.

The main problem we were left with here was whether we had in 1982 missed substantial evidence of recutting because of our inexperience. The data are not independent of our expectations. If we had not excavated in 1984 and 1987 we would have said the 1982 data did not indicate recutting. We could not see recuts in the trench sections. But, having been round the hermeneutic circle, we realised that we had almost certainly not seen data that would have allowed a different interpretation.

The only ditch which had been excavated along its entire length in 1982 was ditch D. Reconsideration of the plan of this has showed realignments. The ditch had a narrower and shallower central section and two deeper ends. These aspects of the evidence recalled ditches excavated in later years not only in terms of bipolarity, but also in terms of changes through time in the layout of the ditch (cf. particularly ditches M and N). It was difficult to reconstruct the sequence of activities in D in any detail, but almost certainly some recutting had occurred.

Summary of the ditches

In writing a summary of the results of the excavations of the ditches, the aim is not to reach a point at which we can say 'that's it'. There is no finality, for a number of reasons. First, we would have reached different conclusions if we had excavated more of the enclosure ditches. Second, we will need to consider other data such as the palisade and the finds. In a sense, then, we will be able to keep going round the circle of our interpretations, gradually transforming them as we adjust to new data. Third, even without new data, interpretations will change in the future as our ideas and theories change – as we learn to see with new eyes we will come back to the data and look at them from a new angle.

The most obvious points about the ditches have already been made in the summary of the 1987 evidence. There was clear evidence of structure in the ditches, both in terms of the sequence of activities and in terms of a spatial bipolarity. Other structure, such as an overall emphasis on the southern ends of the ditches, a move through time towards activities at the terminals, and a shift through time from ritual to occupational use, was evident only ambiguously.

Indeed, the second most obvious point was the evidence of variability. Of course, this had been one of our expectations before we began digging and there must always be some suspicion when we claim that we found what we were looking for. The variability was not so much in the relation between the ditches and the palisade which was found everywhere, except at ditch C. Rather the variability concerned ditch length, causeway length and sequences of recutting and other activities.

It is not my intent to 'explain' this 'variability', in the true fashion of processual archaeology, by drawing upon universal correlates. Rather, I will attempt to look for internal correlates with the help of Figure 21 and to enmesh these within an interpretation which will form part of a circle, later to be linked to other aspects of the data in attempting to construct a whole.

It was immediately clear from a consideration of the evidence that some ditches were more elaborate than others in that they had more recuts, more placed deposits, more finds, more evidence of burning and human bone. Also clear was that these more elaborate ditches tended to occur together. Thus in 1984 ditches G and H formed a pair of simple ditches (perhaps linked with F) in contrast to the more elaborate pair I and J. In 1987, the sequence started and ended with the simple ditches K and P, whereas in between were found increasingly and then decreasingly complex ditches (L, M, N, O).

The clusters of more elaborate ditches might have been thought to relate to the position of major entrances into the enclosure. The difficulty here, in interpreting the evidence, is that our excavation strategy had been guided by the idea of entrances. We had not, therefore, excavated in areas without what looked like major entrances, except in 1981 when the evidence was in any case difficult to interpret. As is always the case, our excavation strategy had to some extent ensured that we found what we were looking for. Nevertheless, in terms of the evidence available to us, the entrance hypothesis seemed at least incomplete since there were pairings of complex ditches which were not entrances and other wide causeways without elaborate ditches. The evidence would not fit together by taking this line of attack.

The group of elaborate ditches in 1987 seemed larger than could be explained by reference to any putative entrance. Four ditches (L, M, N, O) were involved here. An alternative 'whole' which might begin to make sense of the data was that the more elaborate ditches concentrated around longer ditches. The lengths of ditches in the 1987 season gradually increased and then decreased from K to P. In the middle of the elaborate ditches was ditch N, 25 m long. Similarly in 1984, one of the elaborate pair of ditches (I and J) was very long (J being 19 m). Indeed, we had not excavated any long ditch which was simple. In 1982 we had excavated ditch D which was 29.2 m long and our reinterpretation of this ditch suggested that it too must have been relatively elaborate with placed deposits and sequential digging or recutting.

The link between ditch length and complexity is shown in Figure 21.

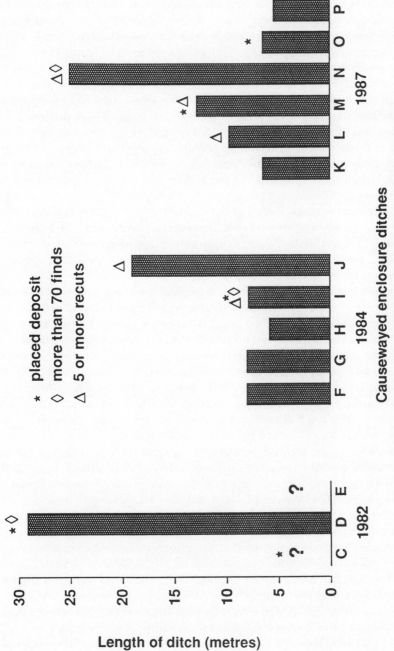

Figure 21 Lengths of the Haddenham enclosure ditch segments in relation to nature of deposits, numbers of finds and recuts

Here it is clear that long ditches were both more elaborate themselves and were surrounded by more elaborate ditches. How might we interpret this pattern, which is itself an interpretation? We need to start by establishing what type of social unit was represented by the ditches. It is difficult to argue that they simply represent work units which came together merely to dig the ditch. The process involved more than digging a hole in the ground. The hole was carefully cleaned out and remodelled and deposits including human bones were sometimes placed in it. This use of the ditch through time showed clear evidence of continuity. Complex primary deposits were often followed by complex secondary fills and vice versa. The specific uses of the ditches also showed continuities. For example the central mound was reformed in ditch I. These various continuities through a range of different activities imply that more than a work 'gang' was involved. Rather, the ditches related to units which had a longer, and therefore a social and structural existence.

Let us assume, therefore, that the size of the ditch, the way it was dug and maintained, and the depositional practices within it, were partly a matter of social display. Larger or more successful groups were able to mobilise more labour. Perhaps the digging, care and use of the ditches helped to define social status.

The ditches were not, however, independent of each other. Adjacent ditches were often similar, they often seemed 'paired' across causeways and sometimes they were physically joined or brought closer through time. Let us further assume, therefore, that the groups which excavated and used adjacent ditches were more closely 'related' in some way than those which used distant ditches. Those groups or work units which constructed and used ditches near the larger ditches may have formed a larger grouping that benefited from the greater success of the larger ditch unit. The ditch cluster as a whole was able to gain access to more labour through time to tend to cleaning and recutting of the ditches, was more able to gain access to prestigious goods (such as polished axes), and was more able to conduct depositional and burial rituals. Peripheral or smaller groups were less able to become involved in these activities.

The competitive nature of ditch-digging and use activities is seen clearly through time. As already noted, the enclosure was less a thing than a process. Ditches were continually being subdivided or joined. Emphasis changed from ditch centres to terminals or from one terminal to its opposite. Within the overall unity or 'whole' of the enclosure there was tension at various scales. At one scale, we could see from the air photographs that some ditches were larger than others, and this variability was confirmed in the excavations of the ditches. At another scale, the common structure of the ditches was continually being transformed. If a link is made between the ditches and social units, the ditch evidence seems to be telling us that social alliances were continually being realigned and renegotiated.

To some degree we have done little more than define 'elite' and 'non-elite' groups – but in relation to ditches rather than to burials or houses. However, we have made three further important claims. First, the social structure has been argued to be organised but competitive and continually negotiated and changing. Second, we have begun to define the basis for the definition of social groupings. While access to polished axes and other exchange goods and involvement in burial rituals may have formed components of social position, the component most directly observable to us at the enclosure was control over labour. The most elaborate ditches were those associated most closely with ditches in which most earth had been moved both initially and in the later recutting. Third, we have implicitly begun to make assumptions about the ideas which lay behind the competitive display and the control of labour. These ideas involved defining and perhaps defending the enclosure as a whole. The contribution of the segmented labour activities was to the formation of a larger entity. But that larger entity was formed in a specific way – the movement of large amounts of soil and digging into the ground. Deposits seem to have been especially placed in the ditches as they were filling up (as deposits were placed on the facade of the long burial mound as it was being built up). Somehow or other, in ways which remain to be explored, the digging of and deposition within the ground defined not only the larger enclosure group, but also the way in which that group expressed competitive endeavours.

So far we have tried to encapsulate the evidence from the ditches into an interpretation by accommodating part to whole and by showing that alternative interpretations (for example, that variation can be explained solely by the positions of entrances) provide a less good fit. However, our preferred interpretation will need to take into account further evidence. The more we can accommodate our theory and data through arguments of coherence and correspondence, the more plausible does our account become. In the full report of the site we will move 'round' all the data metaphorically. For the moment, we can continue to move round the data literally by following the palisade around the enclosure in the different years of excavation.

THE PALISADE

Unlike causewayed enclosure ditches which have been the subject of much debate concerning their supposedly ritual nature, fewer causewayed enclosure palisades have been excavated. We therefore approached the palisade, or what we assumed from the air photographs to be a palisade, with very different expectations. Our initial assumptions were that this feature would be simple, without ritual. Our major difficulty was expected to be one of dating. How could we discover whether the ditches and palisade were contemporary? From the air photographs it was clear that the gaps in the palisade sometimes corresponded to the causeways between the ditches. They had to be at least partly contemporary, but were they entirely so?

We did not expect that the answer to this question would necessarily be simple. As already noted, we assumed initially that there would be great variability around the enclosure and we expected the palisade to be part of this. It did not unduly worry us, therefore, when we did not discover the palisade in 1981. As the 1987 re-excavations of the 1981 area showed we had not taken our trenches far enough into the interior of the enclosure to pick up the palisade which at this point was well within (c. 13.5 m within) the ditches.

The trench for the palisade, as discovered in 1982, was very deep and regular. The average depth was 0.75 m (below base of the prehistoric soil). Almost no finds were found in the 1982 palisade trench fills, implying little occupational use of the soils before and during construction. The gaps in the palisade closely followed those in the ditches, suggesting at least partial contemporaneity. No evidence was found in the fills of the palisade trench of a collapsed interior bank.

Moving clockwise around the 1984 palisade circle was parallel to moving round the 1984 ditches. As one moved from south to north the ditches had become more complex (I and J) with more recutting. Similarly, as one moved northwards along the palisade it became deeper, with clearer evidence of gravel packing and with clearer evidence of recutting. This evidence, therefore, supported the impression gained in 1982 that the palisade and ditches were closely contemporary. There was also a certain sequential similarity in that the post impressions found in the 1984 palisade seemed to have been associated with burning, recalling the late posts and burning in several of the ditches.

On the other hand, evidence from 1984 suggested that the link between the palisade and the ditches was less strong than in the 1982 area. In the first place, the palisade was set well back from the ditches. In the second place, the gaps or breaks in the palisade did not appear to correspond with the causeways between the ditches.

This second point involved several uncertainties. Superficially, all the 1984 palisade, except the small southern segment, could have been seen as one continuous stretch. The evidence from the post impressions certainly suggested that for much of its length the palisade had ended up as a continuous fence. Thus anyone entering the enclosure through the 1984 causeways would at some point in time have been met by a continuous fence allowing no entry except perhaps through doorways for which no evidence was found.

However, part of the 1984 palisade was added later and may have filled in an earlier gap corresponding to the earlier causeway between ditches I and J. Other segments of the palisade appeared to be constructional, but it was also possible that they too represented later closing of gaps in the palisade.

The combined evidence from the 1982 and 1984 palisade indicated that the palisade and ditches were at least partially contemporary. But it was now beginning to look as if the palisade was associated with a late use of the enclosure. After all, there would have been little point in allowing multiple entrances into the enclosure through the ditches if a solid palisade existed at the same time. The 1984 ditches had provided evidence of gradual restriction of access through time. For example, ditches F and G had been joined at a late date in their use and the gap between I and J had been narrowed. The palisade as a whole, or at least the filling in of any gaps in it, may also have played a part in this process of closure.

There was little evidence in the fills of the palisade for a substantial bank behind it. In any case, the soil from the ditches would have been unlikely to have been placed behind a palisade at such a distance from them. A tight functional link between ditches and palisade was therefore not warranted in our arguments.

The evidence from the 1987 excavations again showed that the palisade had probably been constructed in segments. But in 1987, distinct entrances were more frequent than in 1984. Two of the three entrances corresponded only inexactly to the causeways. The other palisade gap occurred to the north of the excavated ditches but could have corresponded to a causeway north of ditch P. The imprecise link between palisade gaps and causeways may have been related to the considerable distance between the palisade and ditch circuits at this point.

The finds densities from the 1987 palisade trench were very low in contrast to 1984. There were also other differences between the two areas. In particular, while the 1984 palisade had by the end of its life severely restricted access into the enclosure, the 1987 palisade retained more entrances, one of which was elaborated by an inturn. The variation between the excavated palisades was beginning to be clearly marked and needs now to be explored over the enclosure as a whole.

The palisade – conclusion

We had first found the palisade in 1982. Here the palisade was set close to the ditches. In the same way our interpretations began by being closely linked to those of the ditches. For example, the close spatial linkages suggested a similar date for both circuits and a similar function. In addition, the segmentation of the palisade seemed to mirror that in ditch D.

But as we moved round the enclosure, our interpretations of the two types of circuit began to diverge as indeed did the palisade and ditches themselves. By the time we had returned to the 1981 excavation and re-excavated it in 1987 in order to locate the palisade, we had amassed evidence for considerable differences between palisade and ditches. The palisade at this point was a full 13.5 m within the ditches, whereas it had started at a distance of 1.5 m in 1982. In between, in 1984 and 1987 the distance varied from 7.6 m to 12.0 m. Interpretations and circuits had diverged in tandem. The hermeneutic circle was indeed spiral-like.

The difference in interpretation partly concerned function and social role. On the one hand, both palisade and ditches had evidence of segmented construction. Both palisade and ditches had evidence of recutting. Despite these similarities, it was undoubtedly the case that the palisade had less evidence of recutting than the complex ditches. As we moved round the palisade circuit we realised that the palisade did not have the 'placed' deposits or complex recuttings we thought we were able to identify in the ditches. The segmented palisade may have represented social competition and display but there was less evidence of a long series of activities. And there was nothing we could call 'ritual'.

Another difference in interpretation concerned date. As we moved round the enclosure the palisade became farther removed from the ditches. In addition, the detailed correspondence between palisade gaps and ditch causeways became increasingly inexact. Already in 1982 we had noted that the alignments of ditch D and the palisade were different. But in 1984 and 1987 it was not always clear that specific gaps in the palisade could be equated with gaps between the ditches.

It was impossible to deny all association, however. The link between gaps and causeways in 1982 had been precise, and in 1984 we noted increasing complexity of both ditches and palisade towards the north end of the excavated area. It was also not to be denied that we had found an inturned entrance in the palisade at approximately the place where we had seen an entrance through the ditches on the air photographs (between ditches M and N).

How were we to reach a compromise between the similarities and differences between the palisade and ditches? The 1984 evidence offered the most elegant solution. Here the closure of the palisade by F126 related to the late narrowing of the causeway between I and J. The general nature of the palisade in the 1984 area was to close off the enclosure and this was a tendency also noted in the late joining of ditches F and G. An overlapping but late date for the palisade was also suggested by the evidence of burning of the palisade, perhaps associated with the late burnt post-holes and other features towards the top of many of the ditches (e.g. see p. 226). The palisade may therefore have been a relatively late feature, concerned less with ritual functions and more with restricting access to the enclosure.

But as with the ditches it would be wrong to assume an overall unity of purpose for the palisade. In general terms, the different excavated portions of the palisade were very similar. The trench was always similar in form and the fills were comparable. However, there was also considerable variation around the enclosure, not only in relation to the distance between palisade and ditches. For example, the size, depth and spacing of post impressions varied.

The overall evidence supports the notion that the palisade, like the ditches, was involved in various scales of social display and competition by related but different groups. That these groups were not just work gangs is suggested by the link between ditches and palisade in 1984, where the northern more elaborate ditches were parallel with the more complex palisade sections. It was not just the construction of the palisade and ditches which were involved but their use. Through time, then, groups built portions of the palisade as part of their endeavour to contribute to the enclosure as a whole. The palisade could be used to realign relationships between groups – sometimes restricting movement to and from the interior of the enclosure, sometimes drawing attention to certain inturned entrances.

THE INTERIOR

We found little pottery in the prehistoric soil within the enclosure, and little bone, probably largely because of the poor survival in highly acidic conditions (p. 217). Our main evidence for Neolithic and Bronze Age activity thus derived from flint distributions. The typological dating for this material suggested that it was mainly of middle and late Neolithic date.

Sampling of the prehistoric soil within and outside the enclosure by digging 1 m pits on a 50 m grid had produced flint densities varying from one to fifty pieces per m² but with an overall concentration in the south-central part of the enclosure. We collected flint artifacts systematically from the prehistoric soil in the areas excavated within the perimeter of the enclosure.

As we went round the evidence, from category to category, the hermeneutic spiral of our interpretations began to be filled out. Repeated patterning emerged that confirmed but added to our developing ideas. The evidence from features and artifacts in the prehistoric soil in the interior showed that the variation around the ditches and palisade corresponded to variation in the density of worked flint and features within the enclosure. Thus the complex ditches I and J were associated not only with a more complex palisade, but also with a higher density of artifacts and features in the adjacent prehistoric soil. The 1981 and 1982 areas in particular were less complex in all respects.

237

Indeed it seemed necessary to return to an earlier point in our hermeneutic spiral. We had wanted to reinterpret the evidence from 1981 and
1982 to suggest that we had missed complex recutting in the ditches.
However, we now began to feel that we had perhaps been right in the
first place. The low densities of finds in the soil surrounding the 1981
and 1982 ditches implied that the ditches themselves might have been
simpler there, as we had at first thought. In any case, a sectoral idea
seemed to be feasible.

CONCLUSION

I do not have space here to discuss in detail the various find categories
(animal bone, carbonised cereals, pottery, worked flint) to see how they fit
into and change the interpretation. The continuation of the spiral 'round'
these different data sets will be discussed in the full report on the site
(Hodder and Evans, forthcoming). I have tried to give some indication of a
hermeneutic exercise which relates parts to a contextual interpreted whole,
but yet which avoids an entirely circular, hermetically sealed argument.
Interpretation does not return to its starting point on the hermeneutic circle.
Our interpretations *are* prefigured and they do begin and end with generalities which must transcend the particular context being considered. But the
assumptions and theories are also transformed in the practice of dealing
with the patterned remains. What I have done is unremarkable since it is
what archaeologists always do, but the procedure does not fit a strict
hypothesis-testing view of science. The procedure emphasises general
interpretation which is sensitive to context rather than the insensitive
imposition of external criteria and measurement.

I have tried, in my writing, to give some sense of the contingent,
haphazard process which constitutes practical archaeological research.
Of course, we need to go to the data with questions and sample the data
in terms of those questions. Certainly, the data only make sense in terms
of the questions we ask. They have no universal, self-evident meaning.
But in practice, our interaction with the often thickly and richly patterned remains is influenced not only by their unexpected patterning,
but also by a host of specific 'in the field' experiences and arguments. It
cannot be scientific to ignore this real world context of our research. It
cannot be adequate to dress all this practical experience up in terms of
some well-controlled, idealised laboratory experiment. We need to write
about the fullness of the hermeneutic experience.

In the case of the Haddenham enclosure, we started with certain
hypotheses about ritual and the nature of social organisation in the
Neolithic. These hypotheses have indeed been confirmed in that part of
the activities observed do seem to be ritual in nature, at least in the sense
that special, odd, formalised behaviour associated with burial is found

238

in some of the ditches. However, a full account of the ritual nature of the enclosure must await a comparison with other Neolithic sites in the area in order to reach a contextual definition of ritual. It has also been possible to read the enclosure data in terms of competitive relations between small-scale groups or sectors, thus confirming a relatively decentralised account of Neolithic society in Britain. But, in this case, our interpretations do seem to have moved on in response to a detailed reading of the evidence. Rather than seeing the enclosure as a 'thing' which represents stable social relations, I have described it as a process in which relations between groups in the different sectors of the enclosure were continually and actively being renegotiated and realigned. Indeed, the wholeness of the enclosure seemed in doubt, its hermeneutic continually under threat.

Finally, it is endlessly possible to follow new spirals, to realise new spinoffs. For example, the medium for social display at the causewayed enclosure is ditch-digging, earth-moving, artifact deposition and burial. Such emphases are exactly those claimed for the long barrow (Hodder and Evans forthcoming). There are many other similarities between the two

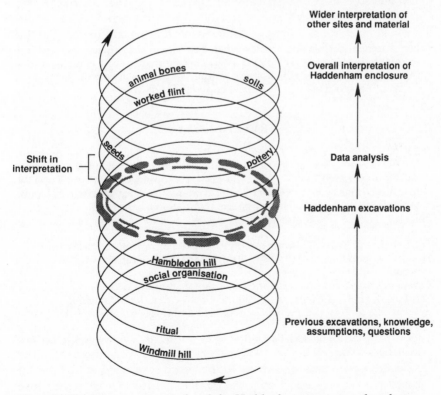

Figure 22 The hermeneutic spiral and the Haddenham causewayed enclosure

239

monuments, such as the layout of ditch I (see above, p. 223) and the overall move to closure and burning. The two monuments can be interpreted as part of a related context of meaning.

A wider interpretive whole can also be constructed by considering other evidence from Neolithic Britain. For example, the evidence of closure of the causewayed site through time recalls the suggestions made by Thomas (1988) in relation to the gradual restriction of access through time in the Severn-Cotswold burial mounds.

Another spiral would be to return to the deposit of animal bones in the Iron Age ditch. This was initially interpreted as a placed 'ritual' deposit because of its assumed Neolithic date. In the Iron Age, bone deposits are normally given more mundane readings. But, as J. D. Hill (1989) has effectively shown, it is possible to spiral back from the Neolithic and embrace the Iron Age in a 'Neolithic' hermeneutic in which animal and other deposits in ditches are indeed given a ritual meaning. The hermeneutic spirals in which we all work are endlessly interlacing and it is in this movement that any tendency towards closure of the circle can be countered.

NOTE

1 For another hermeneutic spiral that has been constructed around the Haddenham enclosure, see Evans 1988. This alternative view is referred to in this chapter as one in which major entrances exist. A debate between these different perspectives will be published in a full report on the site.

REFERENCES

Bradley, R. (1984) *The Social Foundations of Prehistoric Britain*, London: Longman.

Evans, C. (1988) 'Excavations at Haddenham, Cambs: a "planned" enclosure and its regional affinities', in C. Burgess, P. Topping, C. Mordant and M. Maddison (eds) *Enclosures and Defences in the Neolithic of Western Europe*, Oxford: British Archaeological Reports International Series 403.

Hill, J. D. (1989) 'Re–thinking the Iron Age', *Scottish Archaeological Review* 6, 16–24.

Hodder, I. and Evans, C. (forthcoming) *Haddenham Excavations: the Neolithic*.

Hodder, I. and Shand, P. (1988) 'The Haddenham long barrow: an interim report', *Antiquity* 62, 349–53.

Renfrew, C. (1973) *Before Civilisation*, London: Jonathan Cape.

Scruton, R. (1982) *A Dictionary of Political Thought*, London: Macmillan.

Sperber, D. (1974) *Rethinking Symbolism*, Cambridge: Cambridge University Press.

Thomas, J. (1988) 'The social significance of Cotswold–Severn burial practices', *Man* 23, 540–59.

16

THE DOMESTICATION OF EUROPE

The Neolithic revolution or the origins of agriculture has tended to be studied in archaeology in terms of a universal economic and practical reason. The major factors causing the change from a hunter-gatherer-fisher way of life to settled villages with domesticated plants and animals have been seen to be climatic change, population increase and resource availability.

This dominant view ignores and makes invisible something very visible if only our practical, economically oriented and disinterested logic could see it: a massive explosion of evidence concerned with the symbolic and apparently irrational. The appearance of all this symbolism in association with the origins of agriculture has tended to be ignored (but see Cauvin and Cauvin 1982) because it appears irrational. For example, human skulls with the faces modelled in clay are found in houses in the Near East, bulls' heads are placed in or on houses in the Near East and in southeast Europe, the beaks of vultures are set into protuberances on house walls at Catal Huyuk in Turkey where also are found models of women sitting on leopards, and complex ovens and hearths surrounded by elaborately decorated pottery are found in houses in southeast Europe, as are boulders with human heads carved to look like fish. What could all this and much more 'irrational' symbolism mean? And why should it appear with such a flourish contemporary with the adoption of agriculture in the Near East and southeast Europe, the two areas to be considered in this paper?

In trying to understand this symbolism and make it coherent within a different non-western rationality, I hope to approach the lived human experience of the adoption of agriculture in the areas considered. I want to approach the social meanings given to the processes involved. I hope to show that by including this hitherto ignored evidence we reach a different understanding of the origins of agriculture.

I will argue that much of the symbolism concerned the house and an opposition that was created between the idea of the house or home (domus) and the wild (agrios). The English language makes a link between domesticate and domestic and I will argue that these two concepts were linked in the past: a practical reason of economic domestication and a cultural logic involving the domus and the domestic. I will show how the house was used to create the domestic versus the wild. Certainly, the house probably always fulfilled this role. Palaeolithic caves or elaborate houses on the Russian steppes presumably defined home against outside in some sense. But with the origins of agriculture the opposition was used and emphasised by, for example, bringing the wild into the house and transforming it. This bringing in and opposing was done both economically (by domesticating some plants and animals), and symbolically (by, for example, placing representations of wild animals in house walls or by surrounding the cooking and presentation of food in elaborate decoration). The economic transformation was linked to a symbolic transformation.

In my view, the dual transformation occurred for two groups of reasons. (a) Through the late Pleistocene and early Holocene in Europe and the Near East hunter-gatherer groups often increased in size and sedentism. I see this process as one of social competition and dominance in the way described by Bender (1978). As she notes, social competition led to a need to increase production and therefore to the intensification of production which often involved specialisation on certain resources (such as gazelle or fish).

As Woodburn (1980) has shown, simple hunter-gatherers have immediate return for their labour input: the game is immediately shared with few long-term social commitments being implied. But the more sedentary, intensive hunter-gatherers who invest in nets and traps and forest clearance have a delayed return for their labour. The problem becomes one of holding the group together in the period between investment and return, guarding and controlling the distribution of stored foods and so on. Many of these developments occurred in the late Pleistocene and early Holocene.

One answer to this problem of how to hold the group together is simply that people got caught in a practical logic. They became trapped in the delayed returns which ensured the benefits of increased production. These benefits included social dominance, better access to goods, feasts and prestige. Those groups which had tighter social structures and could produce more gained greater prestige and dominance in relation to other groups. Ultimately, this process of submitting to constraints in order to benefit from greater productive success led, perhaps in the wider context of climatic change, to the adoption of yet more intensive resources – domesticated plants and animals.

There were negative aspects to the practical logic of intensification and increased production. The delayed-return system necessitated dependence on others and on wider social and economic structures. All individuals submitted to greater constraint and a loss of personal authority. In other words, *people* were being tamed and domesticated. They were brought into larger settlements and submitted to the structures of the delayed-return systems.

So one reason for the origins of agriculture was that economic domestication allowed greater social domination over larger groups. This domination was partly achieved through the benefits of increased production, and partly because people became trapped and disciplined within longer-term structures and dependencies.

If we limit ourselves to this type of explanation for the background to and the adoption of agriculture, the central problem becomes the following. Why should people allow themselves to be ensnared within the economic and social structures of delayed hunter-gatherer systems, agriculture and village life? Why should they accept the argument that greater social constraint would lead to greater productivity? Why should they want to achieve greater productive success? How was this argued? How was it seen and experienced from the inside? These people did not have some notion of universal rationality leading to capitalism, science and progress – that came twelve millennia later on! They could not justify the change in the name of progress and enlightenment, concepts of our own era. So what rationalities did they use? Why did it make sense to them?

To answer these questions I need to turn to my second group of reasons (b) for the origins of agriculture. According to this second view the process of domestication was not only a mechanism, but also a metaphor. Domestication involved creating the wild as 'other', and establishing the domestic, the house as the structured, the stable, the long term. As wild plants and animals were brought in and domesticated acording to a practical logic, so symbols of the wild were created and tamed symbolically. The symbols of the wild were controlled within a cultural metaphor within the house. The dangers of the wild were exaggerated and opposed to the haven of the house, home and hearth where women often played a central metaphorical role. People accepted the new social and economic constraints of agriculture because the constraints were given positive values in opposition to the wild, the dangerous, the unstructured. Success against the dangers of infertility and death was ensured by the reproductive fertility of society in house and hearth, by the idea of domus. The house provided both structure and continuity. This continuity was emphasised by, for example, repeated replastering and repainting of house interior walls and floors, and by building new houses above old. Most important, ancestors and the bones of relatives or past inhabitants of houses were placed beneath the floors, linking the present with the past through the house. The house actively constructed society in its fabric. It created the stability of long-term structures.

So people came to believe that the only way to ensure production, security, and social dominance over other groups was through being members of stable structures. People submitted themselves to longer-term social relationships and ritual structures, they became 'docile' bodies, domesticated people. This transition was constructed and made sense of in terms of the metaphor of the house. The house came to stand for the idea of being tamed in the same way that the domestic mode of production ensnared people practically within longer-term domestic dependencies.

As people became tamed within the stable domus (the idea and practices of the house), wider communities and dependencies could be built. These larger-scale or closer communities may have had greater productive potential and thus may have been able to compete successfully with smaller units. But they also implied greater within-group restraint and perhaps within-group domination. Once again the material expression of the domus provided a focus for group formation, both practically and metaphorically. The joint construction of settlement boundary fences or ditches, and the laying out of villages provided the stable framework for longer-term communities. Both within the house and within the village people became trapped within a dual cultural and practical reason.

THE NEOLITHIC IN SOUTHEAST EUROPE AND THE NEAR EAST

In order to demonstrate my case I want to show that in southeast Europe (for some other parts of Europe and for greater detail in southeast Europe see Hodder 1990) village formation and economic intensification through the Neolithic were indeed associated with an elaboration of the symbolism of the domus as opposed to and incorporating the agrios. The greater social constraints of village life and the greater productivity of agriculture occurred alongside a symbolic domestication. I will briefly introduce the European discussion in the Near East and Anatolia. Overall I wish to show the integrated way in which domestic symbolism, village formation and economic intensification changed.

To strengthen my case I will include briefly the later Neolithic in southeast Europe and show how a change occurred there to a new metaphor based more on the agrios.

In the Natufian culture in the Levant (10,300–8,500 bc), prior to changes in wild forms of plants and animals, there was intensive grinding of wild plant foods and concentration on certain animals (e.g. gazelle). This is an example of a delayed-return hunter-gatherer economy and it was associated with the greater constraints expressed in the appearance of more settled villages. Within these villages there was storage and some degree of social differentiation seen in houses and burials. Alongside this evidence of greater economic and social constraint and productivity, houses already show some complexity. They had well-prepared floors and fixed features. Burial sometimes occurred beneath the floors of the house indicating perhaps both that the house provided the locus for continuity with the ancestors and that the dangers of individual death to the long-term structures of society were contained or controlled by the domus.

As domesticated plants and animals were increasingly adopted in the Levant in Pre-Pottery Neolithic A and B, so village formation and domestic symbolism became more evident. But the close link between the activities surrounding the adoption of agriculture and domestic symbolism is also seen elsewhere. For example, in northern Iraq at the site of Qermez, right at the beginning of the aceramic Neolithic at the end of the ninth millennium bc, there were already some complex houses with plastered floors, ridges, pillars, stone settings and skulls (Watkins 1990; for other similar evidence see, for example, Kozlowski 1990 and Schirmer 1990).

In Catal Huyuk and Hacilar in Turkey in the seventh and sixth millennia bc the process reached a developed climax (Mellaart 1967). Catal Huyuk was a substantial village, with a fully agricultural economy. Some, but not all, houses were elaborated and thus differentiated. Not all sites in the area were this large and elaborate. How was this intensification, domination and aggregation argued? The reasons were perhaps partly socially and economically practical in ways that I have already argued. But the symbolism too is striking and points to a very non-western way of looking at things.

For example, the skulls of vultures, foxes and weasels and the tusks of boars were enclosed within clay protuberances on or in the house walls. Leopards and hunting scenes were depicted on the walls. And these were the interior walls of certain houses, not the external walls or the walls around courtyards. So it is as if various symbols of dangers in the wild were brought into the house in order to be incorporated within a domestic symbolism. But the domestic organisation of the symbolism was repeated in the different houses in the village according to societal-wide rules. For example, the symbolic elaboration tended to occur at the opposite end of the house to the hearth and oven. This repeated pattern in the absence of large public buildings suggests that a public order was based on a domestic symbolism. The general constraint and village structure were created out of the idea of controlling the productivity and danger of the wild within the house. The presence of wild dangers in the house provided the potential and the stimulus for domestic production. In the same way, the domestic productivity of the household unit and the village depended on the domestication of plants and animals – that is on the practical use and separation of the wild.

In this symbolic context, the woman acted as an important metaphor. At Catal Huyuk she was sometimes shown in the figurine material sitting on leopards or otherwise caring for them. The woman was in an imposing position, sitting upright with hands resting on the heads of the leopards (Figure 23). This dominant, 'lording' over nature and the wild again emphasised the control of the wild by human hand. These and many other female figurines are found in and around the houses and the metaphor of the woman was a central part of the idea of domus.

Another important aspect of the evidence at Catal Huyuk is the burial beneath the floors of houses, the finds of human skulls on the house floors (perhaps after abandonment of the house) and the depictions on the house walls of vultures associated with headless human corpses. This foregrounding of human death in the domestic context paralleled

Figure 23 Clay figurine from Catal Huyuk

the emphasis on death in the wild (as seen in the beaks, skulls and jaws of carnivores). Both the wild and the death symbolism occurred in the same inner part of the house, away from the hearth and oven, and both used the vulture image. The death symbolism could again be taken to emphasise the role of the house in controlling dangers – this time the dangers of human death, such as the loss through death of productive potential and of positions in the social structure. At the same time the burial of ancestors beneath the house floors emphasised the house as the focus of continuity across generations, the guardian of longer-term social structures.

It has to be remembered that not all houses at Catal Huyuk have evidence for elaborate symbolism. Mellaart (1967) suggests that there is some relationship between the elaborate symbolism and the burials. The variation between houses could simply be due to differences in position in life cycle of the members of the domestic unit. But it could also be due to the varying success of domestic units in gaining prestige and wealth through the dual symbolic and economic processes of controlling the wild. Many of the houses were replastered and repainted many times. In these acts of renewal, certain domestic units were more successful in emphasising the dangers and use of the wild through which social and economic structures could be built over the long term.

Similar evidence is found in southeast Europe, although here we can follow the changes that occurred through time more fully. At the site of Lepenski Vir, on the Danube, a hunter-gatherer-fisher community already lived in an ordered village at the end of the sixth millennium bc (Srejovic 1972). The abundant fish resources at this point on the Danube as well as wild resources in the forests allowed a certain degree of structure and sedentism. The houses were again elaborate, with burials beneath the house floors. The hearths in particular were well made and surrounded by settings of stones and in one case by a human jaw. The hearth, probably used in part to prepare food, was surrounded by death: in this way life and death were linked and continuity with the past was stressed. Around and behind the hearth were various carved boulders, some of which had humanoid faces with a possible fish-like appearance.

The full Neolithic way of life was only gradually adopted in southeast Europe during the sixth to fourth millennia bc. In some areas at least, early Neolithic subsistence strategies continued to depend on wild resources to a considerable degree and sites were only partly sedentary (Kaiser and Voytek 1982). But through time settlements became larger, more sedentary, more planned in layout, more often bounded, and more dependent on fully domesticated plants and animals. As this process occurred, so the domestic symbolism became more elaborate. By the fourth millennium bc there is more evidence of internally divided houses containing richly decorated ceramics and more figurines associated with the houses.

There was much regional and temporal variation in the expression of domestic symbolism in this period in southeast Europe. However, some overall patterns can be identified which allow a symbolic complex, termed the domus, to be reconstructed (Figure 24). Central to the domus complex were houses, hearths and ovens, pottery and women. These items were partly associated spatially. For example, pots and figurines were often found concentrated in and around houses and around ovens. In some cases, female figurines were actually fixed to the bases of ovens. Some male figurines do occur but they are heavily outnumbered by female representations. The items of the domus were also associated temporally in that, for example, domestic and ceramic symbolic elaboration often seem to increase and decrease in tandem as do the numbers of female figurines. There are other ways too in which the various attributes of the domus were linked. For example, pots were sometimes

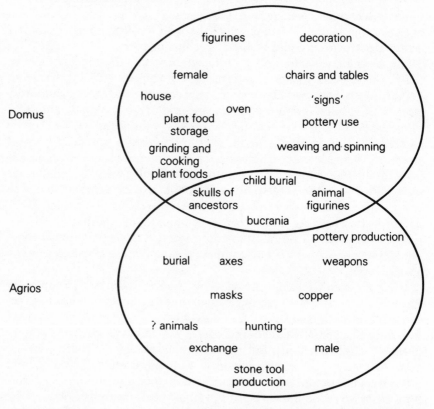

Figure 24 The domus (upper circle) and agrios (lower circle) in southeast Europe

248

made in the form of women, or women were shown holding or presenting pots. In addition, houses, women, ovens and pots all occurred as
miniatures. Sets of small ceramic models of these items, as well as
'tables' and chairs, are found. And similar types of spiral-meander
decoration are found on pots, female figurines, house models and on
surviving pieces of wall plaster. Overall, then, spatial and temporal
associations as well as models and decoration allow the various components of the domus to be linked.

Some bucrania (large modelled bulls' heads) and axe deposits did
occur in the houses, but overall the domus symbolism seems to be about
preparing and presenting food and drink in the domestic context, often
in association with women. I do not argue that women filled such roles
in reality, only that they filled such roles metaphorically. The symbolism
of the domus emphasised production in contrast to another set of
attributes which were largely absent from the house and from the
decoration and miniatures so far described.

This other set of features (Figure 24), termed the agrios, is initially
defined largely by its absence from the domus associations and by its
lack of visibility in the archaeological record. The latter is partly the
result of sampling bias in an area in which excavation has concentrated
on visible settlements rather than on cemeteries. But the lesser visibility
is of itself interesting. For example, while some burial of children (and
perhaps women) occurred early on in the settlements, cemeteries gradually increased in importance through the period into the fourth millennium bc. In some areas such as Hungary (Sherratt 1982) cemeteries
increased in visibility and importance as the house elaboration declined.
This temporal inversion of domus and agrios is emphasised by the
different types of artifact found in the cemeteries, such as at Varna. The
rich burials were often of men, and they were characterised by axes,
metal items, symbols of authority, items derived from long-distance
exchange. Female figurines are rarely found. Cemeteries provided a
focus for a different set of attributes which became more important over
time as the centrality of the domus decreased. By the third millennium
bc, many of the salient features of the domus had significantly declined.

Both at Hacilar in Turkey and in the Neolithic sequence in the Levant
adult burial was gradually removed from the house. We have seen the
same shift from Lepenski Vir to the Neolithic sites in southeast Europe.
This uncoupling of the domus and the ancestors expressed the growing
emphasis on community-wide structures rather than on domestic production alone. At the beginning of the Neolithic the house was used in
order to create long-term structures in relation to the ancestors. But
through time, as agricultural intensification and public works such as
the bounding of settled villages increased, so long-term structures at the
community scale became even more relevant. Indeed, although built out

of the activities and constraints within the domestic unit, the community-wide structures would also have become contradicted by an overemphasis on that smaller unit and its ancestral distinctiveness. The ancestors were thus removed from the house. They increasingly became common ancestors in common cemeteries outside the domus. Human death and the ancestors thus became more clearly separated from the domus, even if linked initially to its communal principles. The role of the domus as reproducer of life was retained in the burial of children in the house. In this way the separation of spheres was clarified.

As the communities of domestic producers increased their common involvement in more intensive agriculture and in the defence of their common interests in the fourth millennium bc, the symbolic role of warring and fighting increased in visibility. Items ranging from battle axes to defensive ditch circuits around villages became more common. The economic changes moving into the third millennium bc have been well outlined by Sherratt (1981) in terms of a Secondary Products Revolution. More of the landscape was domesticated, as the use of the plough and of secondary animal products such as wool allowed exploitation of new environments. The exchange of products between diverse regions stimulated the importance of types of power based on the control of exchange and of prestige goods. Indeed, new types of power were emerging outside the domestic context, based on warring and exchange.

The early Neolithic logic of increased domestic and community production had led inexorably to shifts in economic system later in the Neolithic and to an undermining of the centrality of the domus as new types of power emerged. The latter were expressed in a new symbolic idiom which had grown up historically in opposition to the domus and which I have termed the agrios. The domesticating of the wild had gradually produced the need for an opposing system based on warring and exchange. The latter was incorporated and given significance in relation to agrios principles which now emphasised individual prestige, male metaphors, the wild, hunting and drinking, and which had their main archaeological context in burial (Hodder 1990). This shift in and to the agrios is not the main focus of this paper, but it does contextualise the importance of the domus in the earlier Neolithic associated with the initial intensification of production and adoption of agriculture.

CONCLUSION

It should be emphasised that I do not see the domus/agrios opposition as universal and equivalent to culture/nature or private/public. Indeed, one of the main reasons for inventing specialist terms such as domus and agrios was to avoid such universal implications. In my view there are historical links between the adoption of agriculture in the Near East and southeast Europe, and the domus was defined in a particular and changing way within that historical context. In central Europe, on the other hand, the adoption of agriculture was couched in terms of a rather different domus based less on the metaphor of the woman, for example, and more on monumental construction and the control of spatial boundaries (Hodder 1990). In northern Europe, a more disaggregated settlement system meant that the idea of the stable long-term domus could not be represented effectively by the house and so the idea of the domus was transferred to tombs (ibid.). The domus was given different local meanings.

Certainly, knowledge of general oppositional structures has influenced my particular interpretation, but I have tried to interpret or translate the general terms into a specific and local context. I have argued that a set of specific abstractions (particular forms of domus and agrios) can be supported by their ability to make sense of the data. Thus, for example, if large numbers of female figurines or house models were to be found in cemeteries in southeast Europe, my interpretation of a separation between domus and agrios in that area would become untenable. My whole theory would collapse if in southeast Europe and the Near East it could be shown that domestic symbolism involving incorporation or opposition to the wild did not increase with sedentism and the adoption of more intensive subsistence strategies. According to hermeneutic principles, no interpretation is possible until interpretation has begun. The generalities allow interpretation to begin, but they have immediately to be reinterpreted in relation to the specific evidence and made to correspond with ('tested against') that evidence.

In summary, my interpretation runs something like this. In the period leading up to and during the adoption of agriculture, the main problem was one of domesticating people within longer-term social and economic structures. The practical desire for increased production was offset by the greater constraints of a delayed-return system, the protection of stored products and so on. So those within society who wished for greater production needed to make the constraints understandable, palatable and even desirable. In order to understand the adoption of agriculture we are thus forced into the realm of meaning.

I argue that the longer-term structures and stable way of life were constructed by creating a sense of home. The founding idea of the domus was to create the idea of home and to fix people at home. The most startling example of this concerns representations of women. At one level the placing of female figurines around hearths and the fixing of female figurines to ovens celebrated the metaphor of woman as producer, reproducer and giver of life. But at another level the physical fixing of woman to oven metaphorically fixed woman to the house and domus. But people were fixed to the domus in other ways too. At least in the early stages, the ancestors were buried beneath the floors of the houses, constructing links with the past and fixing people to their relatives in the house over generations. The stability of the house was not only expressed in its elaborate building and its links to the past, but also by foregrounding, incorporating or opposing in various ways the productivity and dangers of the wild, the agrios.

In these ways the domus became the means for thinking about disciplining people within longer-term social structures. During this period the notion of the agrios had to be invented as a prerequisite for the domestication of plants and animals. Cauvin and Cauvin (1982) have argued that cattle were domesticated symbolically at Mureybet before they were domesticated economically. In fact the cultural-symbolic and economic processes were probably dialectically related, feeding off each other. Thus the practical logic of increased production depended on setting up the idea of home as opposed to wild, or more specifically, domus as opposed to agrios. People accepted and wanted the constraints of economic domestication because the stable structures of house and home were believed to ensure continuity and survival against various perceived dangers.

2 Through time, in the middle and later Neolithic, wider community structures became more important at the expense of domestic production and new types of power based on warring and exchange became more central. As a result the emphasis on the domus ultimately declined and there is less archaeological evidence for symbolic elaboration in domestic contexts in the later fourth and third millennia bc. Rather we find cemeteries with rich male burials and other characteristics of what became the agrios.

REFERENCES

Bender, B. (1978) 'Gatherer-hunter to farmer: a social perspective', *World Archaeology* 10, 204–22.

Cauvin, J. and Cauvin, M.-C. (1982) 'Origines de l'agriculture au Levant', in T. Cuyler Young, P. Smith, and P. Mortensen (eds) *The Hilly Flanks*, Chicago: Oriental Institute.

Hodder, I. (1990) *The Domestication of Europe*, Oxford: Basil Blackwell.

Kaiser, T. and Voytek, B. (1982) 'Sedentism and economic change in the Balkan Neolithic', *Journal of Anthropological Archaeology* 2, 323–53.

Kozlowski, S. (1990) *Nemrik 9*, Warszawskiego: Wydawnictwa Uniwersytetu.

Mellaart, J. (1967) *Catal Huyuk*, London: Thames & Hudson.

Schirmer, W. (1990) 'Some aspects of building at the "aceramic-neolithic" settlement of Cayonu Tepesi', *World Archaeology* 21, 363–87.

Sherratt, A. (1981) 'Plough and pastoralism', in I. Hodder, G. Isaac and N. Hammond (eds) *Pattern of the Past*, Cambridge: Cambridge University Press.

—— (1982) 'Mobile resources: settlement and exchange in early agricultural Europe', in C. Renfrew and S. Shennan (eds) *Ranking, Resource and Exchange*, Cambridge: Cambridge University Press.

Srejovic, D. (1972) *Europe's First Monumental Sculpture: New Discoveries at Lepenski Vir*, London: Thames & Hudson.

Watkins, T. (1990) 'The origins of house and home?', *World Archaeology* 21, 336–47.

Woodburn, J. (1980) 'Hunters and gatherers today and reconstruction of the past', in E. Gellner (ed.) *Soviet and Western Anthropology*, London: Duckworth.

17

GENDER REPRESENTATION AND SOCIAL REALITY

I wish to share with the reader some problems I have met in dealing with gender in European prehistory not so much because I have come to clear conclusions, but because I think my experience demonstrates that interpretation of gender in prehistory leads to a re-evaluation of other apparently unrelated issues such as meaning, representation, power and general archaeological theory.

The data concern the Neolithic of southeast Europe and the Near East (for a full account see Hodder 1990). In these areas the early and middle Neolithic periods are associated with a high visibility of women and female-related artifacts. For example, in southeast Europe between the fifth and early third millennia bc female figurines are common whereas males are rarely represented. In the same area female representations are linked to houses, pottery and hearths and ovens. These links are produced by spatial associations (the female figurines occur in houses but rarely in cemeteries and female figurines are attached to ovens), by the use of similar decoration (on pots, figurines and houses) and by association in a 'set' of miniatures (women, houses, ovens and pots are all modelled in clay). The archaeological record is dominated by settlements, houses, pottery and female representations whereas male-associated artifacts are less easy to see. More precisely, the complex of female-associated traits is particularly associated with the adoption and intensification of agriculture. As domestication intensifies and settled villages are formed, so the elaboration of domestic symbolism, the numbers of female figurines and the subdivision and decoration of houses also increase.

However in the later Neolithic, culminating in the later third millennium bc in southeast and central Europe, a transformation occurs so that the female-associated items become less visible and are replaced by dominant representations of men. Female figurines become less common and in some areas settlements and houses become less substantial and complex. On the other hand, burials in cemeteries and barrows become more common and they are often dominated by rich burials of

254

men containing battle or display axes, hunting weaponry, exchange and prestige items of metal. This shift is in general terms associated with economic changes which involve a greater use of secondary animal products, a wider use of the landscape and a greater importance of cattle and exchange. The transformation is often seen as a move from kin and lineage systems to more complex systems in which exchange played a greater role.

In trying to give meaning to these patterns I accepted that the data only allowed me to discuss shifts in representational systems. The data did not warrant detailed discussion of the actual roles of men and women. While women were associated symbolically with houses, hearths and pottery, it remained possible that men played a dominant role in houses, in cooking and in making and using pottery. Similarly the symbolic association between men and hunting does not mean that in practice women did not hunt.

Nevertheless I initially thought that I could read the representational systems so as to gain insight into the social reality behind them. I thought I could talk about the relative social importance of men and women in Neolithic societies. In these terms there seemed to be two different conclusions one could draw from the data.

First, I could argue that in the earlier Neolithic women did have real power as expressed by the dominance of female representations. Such a view could be supported by a number of other lines of evidence. For example, it has often been noted that in many hunter-gatherer societies women play a dominant role in gathering activities. It is therefore reasonable to suppose that they played a dominant role in the domestication of plants and that in early agricultural societies in Europe women held power through their contribution to intensified production. Certainly feminists such as Barstow (1978) have argued that the elaborate symbolism at Catal Huyuk, in which female representations play such a central role, indicates a real power for Neolithic women.

I could also adopt the arguments of Weiner (1978) that in kin-based societies group membership is defined through procreation and in some such societies kin identity is defined through 'womanness' which is a timeless, transcendent power beyond the mundane efforts of men to build renown during their lifetimes (see also Meeker, Barlow and Lipset 1986). European earlier Neolithic societies are usually assumed to be kin-based, especially in areas where burial is in communal tombs. It seems reasonable to argue that kinship and reproduction defined social roles at this time and that women therefore played central roles expressed through the female symbolism. In the later Neolithic relations based on warring and long-distance exchange became more important, so the visibility of female symbolism declined.

Second, taking a quite different view, I could argue that the elaborate female symbolism in the earlier Neolithic expressed the objectification and subordination of women. Perhaps female figurines occurred plentifully in houses because that is where women were being encouraged to stay. Perhaps women were associated with leopards in the figurines from Catal Huyuk in Turkey (Hodder 1987) because women were seen as dangerous. Perhaps women rather than men were shown as objects because they, unlike men, had become objects of ownership and male desire.

It would not be difficult to argue that the power of women decreased in the early Neolithic with the adoption and intensification of agriculture. Authors such as Draper (1975) have shown that women in hunter-gatherer societies have a great deal of autonomy and influence which they tend to lose in settled agricultural villages. From Engels to more contemporary Marxist writers like Leacock (1978) it has been argued that the subordination of women relates to the growth of private property. I could therefore claim that with agriculture, domesticated animals, houses and other possessions in which the group had made long-term investments, the interests of the group came to be directed more carefully towards the control of the reproductive and productive output of the domestic context. Particularly as social ranking developed along with the adoption of agriculture (Bender 1978), it came to be in the interests of local groups to increase production and reproduction in order to increase output and increase abilities to give feasts and enter into exchanges. So women were possessed, controlled and restricted in the domestic context in order to reproduce and produce for competing social groups. The elaborate symbolism was involved in the domestication and ownership of women. The domestication of agriculture was dependent on the domestication and domination of women.

This state of affairs could be seen to last while kinship and domestic production and reproduction were the framework on which social and economic relations were built. But by the later Neolithic there is evidence of social power being based more on the control of other resources such as cattle, copper, warring and long-distance exchange. Writers such as Leacock (1978) and Gailey (1987) would argue that as these new sources of power became important, the status of women declined. As non-domestic and non-kinship sources of power became more dominant in the public economy, so the link provided by females between reproduction and production was broken or overtaken by other interests. As a result, reproduction and production became directed towards the public sphere (of exchange etc.), the public/domestic split was created or emphasised and the role of women in the domestic context devalued. Hence the symbolism associated with women and houses disappeared to be replaced by highly visible male symbolism linked to exchange, cattle and warring.

According to this second view, the period since Upper Palaeolithic hunter-gatherers saw a gradual decline in the power of women to control resources. They were first objectified and domesticated in domestic contexts and material symbols and were then further subordinated in the later Neolithic as they became less visible in the archaeological record.

This second view of increasing subordination of women certainly works well and has a nice evolutionary tone to it. There are a number of problems such as the assumption that the Upper Palaeolithic was a Garden of Eden in which women had equal status to men or at least a high degree of autonomy. And there is the problem that the model does not mention different types of women. Elder and younger women may have been treated very differently in such societies.

My difficulties with the two views (that women either were or were not powerful in the earlier Neolithic) were rather different and more personal. First, I realised that I was being highly partial and sexist in my interpretations. For example, I realised that I was treating male and female representation differently. Elaborate female symbolism in the earlier Neolithic was treated by me as a problem. It could either mean women were powerful or, as in the second theory which I preferred, they were powerless. Either way the evidence presented ambiguity and difficulty. When I reached the later Neolithic, on the other hand, the elaborate male symbolism was no problem at all. Here, according to either theory, the male symbolism represented male power. I was clearly using a double standard. I could accept real male power but found ways of rejecting real female power.

The second and main problem I had with my own interpretations was that I found I had no way of showing which theory was right. Were women more or less subordinated in the earlier Neolithic? I needed to be able to show who (males or females) really controlled resources, who was doing all the labour, who was making decisions, who was beating whom and so on. I had wanted to avoid or sidestep the problem that archaeologists can see representations of women and men better than they can get an idea of what men and women were actually doing, controlling or owning. But I kept being brought back to the question of whether the depicted men and women *really* had power.

At least in my data, however, there seemed to be no way of answering such a question. In fact I would hazard a guess that it is nearly always difficult to know what men and women (or any other social category) were *really* doing. The conventional procedures for answering the question include activity and burial associations. But even if spindle whorls are only found with women in graves and are found in 'female' parts of the house, we cannot assume that men did not do the weaving. We may be able to show from studies of human bones that women ate different or better food in a certain time period, but ultimately food too has its symbolic components and food associations do not provide a direct insight into who controlled food distribution.

I became disillusioned by these problems and ultimately wrote about the European Neolithic (Hodder 1990 and Chapter 16) without discussing gender issues at any length. It seemed so difficult to fill the representation–reality gap.

I now think that my decision was premature and derived from something which I seemed to have in abundance – male bias. I had assumed, despite being a proponent of the idea of 'symbols in action', that the Neolithic symbolism was ultimately unimportant. I had assumed that in order to understand the elaborate symbolism I had to get at the reality behind it. I had seen the signifiers, particularly the female signifiers, as passively manipulated in relation to some signified. I had assumed that power was really based on the control of resources (reproduction, production, copper, exchange, etc.) and that the symbols simply represented that real power. I was frustrated because I could not get beyond the light, insubstantial symbols to the deeper-voiced resources and powers which lay behind them.

This is a view of power which, for me at least, feminist critique has opened up. Moore (1988, 35) says that 'most feminist scholars would now agree, I think, that the cultural valuations given to women and men in society arise from something more than just their respective positions in the relations of production'. Cultural representations of gender rarely accurately reflect male–female relations, men's and women's activities, or men's and women's contributions in any given society.

So I realised that I had been trying to do the impossible because I had been underestimating the cultural construction of gender. I had been trying to equate representations with real powers without seeing that the two do not necessarily equate. While certain positions in the relations of production may be positively evaluated and represented in the cultural system, others may not. Perhaps more important, there are many types of power, some of which do not relate directly to the relations of production. Some groups may have to work within the interstices of dominant power relations, creating alternative dimensions of power through the negotiation of meaning. Representation, whether overt or muted, can itself be a form of power.

Of course I had known all this abstractly for some time, but in relation to gender in the Neolithic data I seemed to have become peculiarly blind to it. What I began to see as I started to criticise my own male bias, was that I had been wanting some positivist, universal relationships so that I could read off the relative roles of men and women from the relations of production. I wanted the relations of production to answer whether early Neolithic women were subordinate or not. As a result of my critique I came to see two problems with my male perspective on power.

First, there is no simple relationship between relations of production and gender domination because cultural values and representational systems intervene. Second, representational systems involving gender are constructed historically and specifically. Thus elaborate female symbolism in the domestic context might mean very different things in different societies. A good example of this is provided by Gailey (1987, 7), who shows how it used to be assumed that anthropologists could measure the powerlessness of women by measuring their deference behaviour to men. In fact, however, the meaning of deference varies and in some cultures it can mean not powerlessness but power.

Clearly I needed to return to the Neolithic example and start again by not assuming that there was one type of power. I needed to accept that there were different types of power in society, many cross-cutting and multivalent, and that the powers of men and women would have been defined both in relation to resources and in relation to symbolic systems which I would have to read in their own terms. The feminist critique gave an edge to that contextuality I had pretended to embrace. I needed to approach the question of the subordination of women in the Neolithic by realising, first, that the question was complex and multivalent and, second, by trying to understand the representation of men and women as contextually constructed and contextually meaningful.

I have now begun this more careful contextual reading of the historical complexity of the Neolithic data. I believe it is possible to construct detailed 'historical' accounts of the type developed by Le Goff (1985, 100) in his work on the medieval imagination. Le Goff argues that interdictions on flesh, sexuality, menstrual blood and women became stronger in the tenth to twelfth centuries AD because the Church was trying to separate itself from and to control the laity. The idea of the pure virginal priesthood (modelled on Christ the bachelor) was contrasted with the laity soiled in marriage. 'The church became a society of bachelors, which imprisoned lay society in marriage'. This account gives an insight into a complex situation in which the perspectives of women would need to be integrated, but it unambiguously situates gender roles and gender representation in a specific historical context.

Very briefly, I am attempting to show in the Neolithic in Europe that gender representation can be set within wider but specific historical circumstances. My reading of the burial tombs of the Neolithic in north and western Europe provides an example (Hodder 1990). The tombs of the SOM culture in the Paris Basin contain large numbers of human bones and the settlement data suggest that these represent kinship rather than residence units. The megalithic tombs of northwestern Europe generally provide independent evidence about the importance of kinship and communal labour (as seen in the construction of the monumental tombs). Some of the tombs contain evidence independent of gender data for a pervasive set of ideas about regeneration and renewal. In specific instances I can demonstrate that this general class of burial monument was surrounded in symbols of agricultural clearance and production, of continuity, duration and of life through death. By planting the dead in the ground, society was renewed and regenerated. Repetitive acts over the long term involving presentation of food and drink at the tombs, repetitive acts of rebuilding and renewal, of filling with earth and of burning, all suggest the centrality of ideas to do with regeneration, renewal and social reproduction.

Clearly this type of analysis needs to be extended to other Neolithic groups such as at Catal Huyuk or in southeast Europe, and it needs to be extended to the later time period. But I think that I am beginning to be able to argue that in the type of kinship/communal production/symbolic renewal system I have briefly described, the pervasive female symbolism can be contextually defined. In such a system the depiction of women at the entrances to SOM tombs comes to have a contextual meaning. In these tombs the necklaces and breasts of women are unambiguously shown and they occur towards the front of the tomb whereas axe depictions are found more to the interior of the tomb, including the inner recesses (Hodder 1990). From other contextual evidence it is reasonable to associate these axes with men. The female may not have been associated spatially and symbolically with the human bones in the tomb, nor with the esoteric knowledge involved in the sorting of the bones in its dark recesses. But it is the female one sees at the entrance to the tomb. Few people would have been able to get through the narrow passages into the SOM tombs at one time. Indeed it can be argued that the whole tomb was in some sense overtly female. It seems unreasonable to argue that, given the independent evidence for an overall social emphasis on reproduction and renewal, and given the multidimensional nature of power, women were powerless and totally subordinate in the social context of the SOM tombs. Rather, it seems more likely, given the historical context in which the tomb representations of women are found, that the representations helped constitute a real power for women. The female symbolism at the tombs occurred in relation to kinship and communal relations of production and in relation to specific ideological meanings which surrounded the economic relations and which were based on ideas of social reproduction, rebirth and renewal. In such a context I would argue that the female symbolism must have constituted a certain power for women, however much it might have been contested, contradicted and subordinated. After all, the female depictions are excluded from the interiors of the SOM tombs.

CONCLUSION

My general aim here has been to outline an approach to gender that is historical and hermeneutic while remaining reflexively critical – in other words an approach that I have dubbed contextual. It could be argued that a critical hermeneutic approach is necessary if we want to show how gender relations are experienced and given meaning, how they are used to define personhood and how they are involved in subtle ways in multidimensional relations of power. In so far as these issues are part of feminist archaeology, positivism is not an appropriate framework and I have heard others such as Alison Wylie make a similar point. Stacey and Thorne (1985) claim that feminist approaches have succeeded least in disciplines (like sociology, psychology, economics) more deeply anchored in positivism. It is in fields with a strong interpretive approach (history, literature, sociocultural anthropology) that feminism has most advanced. It may be archaeology's recent positivist history coupled with its increasing resource base in the sciences that has impeded the development of feminist archaeology for so long.

However inadequately and briefly I have presented my own contextual interpretation of the European Neolithic, I would argue that an overall theoretical shift is needed in the discipline before many of the most exciting aspects of feminism can take hold in archaeology. As Michelle Rosaldo said of this shift in anthropology, we must pursue not universal, general causality, but meaningful explanation. 'It now appears to me that woman's place in human social life is not in any direct sense a product of the things she *does*, but of the *meaning* her activities acquire through concrete social interaction' (Rosaldo 1980, 400). I hope the same can be said of man's place. But it is through writers such as Rosaldo and other feminist and gender studies that wider theoretical moves can be made in archaeology which incorporate critical and interpretive approaches to women, men and all areas of social life.

REFERENCES

Barstow, A. (1978) 'The uses of archaeology for women's history: James Mellaart's work on the Neolithic goddess at Catal Huyuk', *Feminist Studies* 4, 7–18.

Bender, B. (1978) 'Gatherer–hunter to farmer: a social perspective', *World Archaeology* 10, 204–22.

Draper, P. (1975) '!Kung women: contrasts in sexual egalitarianism in foraging and sedentary contexts', in R. R. Reiter (ed.) *Toward an Anthropology of Women*, New York: Monthly Review Press.

Gailey, C. W. (1987) *Kinship to Kingship*, Austin: University of Texas Press.

Hodder, I. (1987) 'Contextual archaeology: an interpretation of Catal Huyuk and a discussion of the origins of agriculture', *Bulletin of the Institute of Archaeology* 24, 43–56.

——— (1990) *The Domestication of Europe*, Oxford: Basil Blackwell.

Leacock, E. (1978) 'Women's status in egalitarian society: implications for social evolution', *Current Anthropology* 19, 247–75.

Le Goff, J. (1985) *The Medieval Imagination*, Chicago: University of Chicago Press.

Meeker, M., Barlow, K. and Lipset, D. (1986) 'Culture, exchange and gender: lessons from the Murik', *Cultural Anthropology* 1, 6–73.

Moore, H. (1988) *Feminism and Anthropology*, Cambridge: Polity Press.
Rosaldo, M. (1980) 'The uses and abuses of anthropology: reflections on feminism and cross–cultural understanding', *Signs* 5, 400.
Stacey, J. and Thorne, B. (1985) 'The missing feminist revolution in sociology', *Social Problems* 32, 301–16.
Weiner, A. B. (1978) 'The reproductive model in Trobriand society', *Mankind* 11, 175–86.

18

WRITING ARCHAEOLOGY: SITE REPORTS IN CONTEXT

I wish to begin by quoting from an 'Account of a Roman pavement, with wheat underneath it, found at Colchester' in *Archaeologia* 2 (Griffith 1773):

St Mary Hill, May 31, 1771

Dear Sir,

I take the first opportunity, after my return from Colchester, to send you some particulars relating to the wheat lately found there, under a Roman pavement, in the kitchen garden of Doctor Piggot, a physician, in Angel Lane in that town.

Between two and three years ago the Doctor having observed that some of his fruit trees, which stood in one continued line, did not thrive so well as the rest, he ordered a man to dig at a little distance from the outermost of them. . . . After digging to the depth of a yard and a half, there appeared a Roman pavement, consisting of rude and coarse tesellae or brick, without any material difference of colour, or any variety of figure arising from the disposition of them.

Having thus found what it was that checked the growth of his trees, he desisted from any further enquiry, till the beginning of this month, when he ordered a man to dig in the same place; who, having laid the ground open to the extent of five yards and a quarter in length, and two yards and an half in breadth, came to the extremity of the pavement on the east and south sides. . . .

An acquaintance having informed me of some wheat being found a few days before under a Roman pavement, I went immediately to the spot. . . .

I am, dear Sir,

Your faithful humble Servant
Guyon Griffith

I could have taken my second illustration from any recent excavation report. The 1978 CBA Research Report 28 on the *Excavations at Ashville*

Trading Estate, Abingdon (1974–1976) contains the following sentences (Parrington 1978, 6) in a section on Bronze Age ditches and cremation pits:

F1054 (Fig. 7) was 0.14 m deep and oval in plan being 0.7 m wide north–south and 1.3 m long east–west. In the fill of the feature were two complete pots (Fig. 27, No. 9 and 10, p. 28) and fragments of cremated bone (p. 92). Half a metre to the west of 1054 was another area of charcoal-flecked loam, F1033 (Fig. 7). F1033 was 0.36 m deep and circular in shape having a diameter of 0.25 m. The feature contained fragments of cremated bone (p. 92) and was cut into the fill of ditch 460.

Histories of archaeology need to notice the different ways in which archaeological texts are written through time. The differences between these two examples of archaeological writing do not simply reside in the recent account giving more references and measurements. Both reports do provide quantitative, objective data. Neither do the differences result simply from the explosion of archaeological data, even though the recent account is enormously longer than the two pages and one diagram of 1773. Rather, the whole way of writing has changed. The earlier account is imprecise but it is fixed in time and place. It tells a story of the excavation, with a sequence of events through time. And it involves named actors and their intentions. The more recent account reads to me as outside time and place, abstract and without an author, using a fixed descriptive code.

In examining this transformation, I have to select texts from the great variety and quantity of site reports from the eighteenth century to the present day. The way texts are written depends partly on who they are written for. An area specialist, concerned with detail, will only take note of the style of writing if it gets in the way of the detail. The wider audience of professional archaeologists, concerned with the story the text tells, will look at the way in which theory is brought to bear on data. Students will often want simplified texts, government departments will emphasize links to practical policies, and the popular readership will want readability without jargon. When comparing texts through time I need to compare like with like. A site report may differ considerably in style from a general or popular synthesis written by the same author. In my account I emphasise reports in the jourals of the established societies, with some consideration of book-length reports published by the main societies or government agencies.

I do not see the changes since the 1770s as the simple results of the application of 'science' in the nineteenth and twentieth centuries. Right from the beginning, the atmosphere of excavation reports in *Archaeologia* was scientific and rigorous. The very first sentence in the first volume of *Archaeologia*, published by the Society of Antiquaries in 1770, reads:

> The history and antiquities of nations and societies have been objects of inquiry to curious persons in all ages, either to separate falsehood from truth, and tradition from evidence, to establish what had probability for its basis, or to explode what rested only on the vanity of the inventors and propagators.

The growth of antiquarian research is linked to the general rise of the sciences (*Archaeologia* 1 (1770), 2):

> The arrangement and proper use of facts is history; – not a mere narrative taken up at random and embellished with poetic diction, but a regular and elaborate inquiry into every ancient record and proof.

Despite this early opposition – science and history on the one hand and narrative, the poetic and the personal on the other – the style of writing (trope) of site reports in the 1770s in *Archaeologia* was very different from our own. It allowed the narrator to be present in the text. Many of these early examples are 'letters from' or 'parts of a letter from' an individual to the Society of Antiquaries, often introduced by a Fellow of the Society. They frequently show deference to the nobles and churchmen who made up a large proportion of the Fellows. A relatively closed society received, controlled and published knowledge sent in from the outside world. The style of writing imposed by this power structure has two distinctive characteristics.

First, the report is fixed in time and place. The letters are always dated to a particular day (such as May 31, 1771), and the place of writing is also given. The events described also fix the report in a particular context. The first paragraph of Griffith's letter tells us that the report was written from memory and perhaps notes. The report is a letter, written at a particular time and place. If written the day after, presumably a different letter would have been written. The report appears to me, the reader, as located, particular, contingent, transient.

Second, the report frequently uses the first-person pronoun that is appropate to a letter. The author, the subject, the 'I', is undeniably present. In Griffith's letter the personal pronouns constantly remind the reader that the report is the opinion of an individual. And these early reports tie the descriptions of sites and excavations closely to individuals. In his letter of 1773 describing New Grange, Governor Pownall writes (1773, 258):

> examining very narrowly, with a candle in my hand, all the parts of this cemetery, I discovered on the flat stone . . . what I took to be

traces of letters. . . . These lines were of a breadth and depth in which I could lay the nail of my little finger. . . . As I had continued in this cave a much longer time than was prudent, by which I caught a violent illness . . . I gave over the task, referring it to be done at leisure by the surveyor, whom Dr. Norris was so good as to engage. Mr. Bovie accordingly traced this supposed inscription; and, as it appears to me, faithfully, and with due care . . .

Pownall further vouches for the accuracy of Mr Bovie's work, following the pattern in which individuals within the Society of Antiquaries give their stamp of personal approval to the published letters, by introducing them. The appearance of the site reports partly depends on a personal authority and privilege, themselves partly inherited within established structures. The individual and personal are emphasised in the texts, partly because power outside the text is also individual, personal and arbitrary.

Along with first-person pronouns go named individuals. Griffith refers to Dr Piggott the physician and to several workmen (significantly not identified by name). The reader of the letter, the 'you', is also taken into the context of the discoveries. Governor Pownall (1773, 250) writes of New Grange:

As most . . . the Barrows which we know of . . . are formed of earth, you will, upon your approach to this, be surprised to find it a pyramid of stone.

These early reports are full of the actions of individuals. They are to me not only more interesting to read, but also located in terms of the particular, the contingent.

The personalised eighteenth-century accounts include debate, controversy, and dialogue between different interpretations. When Governor Pownall (ibid., 252) tries to measure the height of New Grange,

This was done by Mr. Samuel Bovie, a land-surveyor in that part of the country. . . . I have some reason to doubt of his projection of the altitude. . . . Dr. Molineux . . . says, that the altitude is 150 feet, while Mr. Bovie makes it but 42. Neither of these accounts can be right. . . . I make the altitude in the whole about 70 feet . . . and as my eye . . . will judge of outlines and angles with an accuracy nearly approaching to measurement, I find myself . . . the rather more confirmed in my opinion. How Dr. Molineux could be led into the mistake that the altitude was 150 feet, I cannot conceive.

The contextualised and contingent nature of these early reports is also seen in their structuring by the narrative of discovery or by some other sequence of events. In reporting the Roman pavement at Colchester,

Griffith tells us: Dr Piggott had a problem with his fruit trees; he then found a pavement; two years later he dug again; an acquaintance told Guyon Griffith who went to visit; he saw the wheat under the pavement, but Dr Piggott was out so he could not verify how much wheat had been thrown away.

This emphasis on sequence is especially found in accounts of the opening of barrows. A report in *Archaeologia* 3 (Preston 1775, 273) begins:

> The labourers began by driving a level, and for some time found nothing worth notice. At length one of them, digging on the top of the barrow downwards, turned up . . . a piece of an urn, and soon after came to what he thought an urn, fixed in a large pot or vessel, and containing a small quantity of white ashes. . . . About a yard below these the workmen came to an orbicular pile of stones, resembling a vault. . . . On removing this pile, they came to a fine black mould . . .

Individual discoveries are placed in a sequence which organises the way the site and the finds are described. The reader knows that the site would have yielded a different story, if it had been dug differently in different circumstances.

As a result, I find a certain excitement in reading these eighteenth-century reports, and a tension as one follows the process of discovery. This excitement is enhanced by the use of personal pronouns and actor-oriented accounts. Interpretation, too, is linked into the description of the excavation. Imaginative and poetic terms are often used, but there is a keen identification of unwarranted interpretation as 'conjecture'. The understanding of the site is tied to the process of excavation itself. Hypotheses are rejected or adopted as the excavation continues. The meaning of the site is linked to the circumstances of recovery.

In the nineteenth century, the general scientific aims of excavation and archaeology remain, but the manner of writing seems gradually to shift. Letters are replaced by articles, although large parts of texts are sometimes presented as extended quotations. The first-person pronoun is still often used; even at the end of the century Pitt-Rivers (1894, 206) can begin an article on South Lodge, 'I was prevented by illness from excavating in the summer of 1892, but in April 1893, I returned to the work'; and the entire report uses the first person. Frequently the reader is still invited to situate herself within the text. For example, in the Reverend John Collingwood Bruce's report on the excavations ordered by the Duke of Northumberland on the Roman fort at Bremenium, 'on coming within the precincts of the station, the spectator will be struck with the mass of building which it contains. . . . A closer scrutiny will show . . . (1852, 137). Even descriptions and measurements can be seen as authored, personal and contingent. The Bremenium wall foundation does not have a maximum width of 16 or 17 feet, but 'Mr McLauchlan states the thickness of the foundations as measuring in several places 16 or 17 feet' (ibid., 136).

Although excavation reports become longer in the nineteenth century, they are often still organised according to the sequence of events of discovery and excavation. However, by the end of the century specialist reports become more common (e.g. Pitt-Rivers 1894), in which the aim is to place the artifacts into constructed archaeological typologies, including pottery typologies. There is more specialist jargon, such as 'central' and 'secondary' interments in barrows. A transformation occurs towards more distant, abstract, decontextualised accounts and towards archaeological terminologies within which finds are to be described. Of course, the old emphases on the 'I', the actor, dialogue, narrative sequence and interpretation tied to the contingent context of discovery, never wholly die out.

It is in reading reports of the late nineteenth and early twentieth centuries that we find a style which is familiar. In *Archaeologia* the reports are still papers 'read' to the society on a certain day so that some aura of the contingent, particular and privileged remains. But there is little evidence of personal pronouns, of authors or actors. In a report on Caerwent excavations the passive voice is used widely (Ashby 1906). A sandstone block 'was found', and 'it must be noted that'. The imperative seems to suggest there can only be one possible interpretation. Indeed, admitted interpretation has largely disappeared behind objective description. Thus, 'a comparison . . . will show that' (ibid., 118) – as if the observations as well as the artifacts had been found, and as if the description is self-evident, distanced from any onlooker or author. Reports are increasingly organised by feature (such as houses, gates, defences) rather than by the sequence of excavation.

In the first half of the twentieth century the same trends continue, so that by the time of Piggott's (1962) volume on the excavations of the West Kennet long barrow, limited personal information is placed in a brief preface. Although plans are signed and dated, the 'I', 'you', 'he' or 'she' are largely absent. Instead, 'the mound . . . was examined by a cutting', 'it was seen that' and 'it was quickly realised that'. In interpretive sections the use of 'we' (as in 'so far we have noted that') is more an imperious royal 'we' that emphasises the universal and the self-evident.

The writer and the excavator are absent, hidden within codes and institutions. Thus Piggott notes that 'the Ministry of Works made themselves responsible for preparing a plan of all visible stones . . . and for laying out a survey grid which would enable 10' squares to be excavated anywhere within its area'. This image of a public institution, the Ministry of Works, laying out a grid within which the excavation could take place, is a wonderful metaphor for the new style of writing. As legislation and public funding increased in archaeology and as the state became responsible for preserving the past for the nation, so standardised codes and procedures were introduced which depended less on personal authority and more on an abstract disciplinary code.

Piggott organises his 1962 report into the familiar sections of the modern order: introduction, description, the finds, discussion and appendices. The sequence of discovery, the contingent events of excavation, are reduced to one page of dry account. The main body of the report describes measurements and soils. Considerable space is devoted to defining archaeological terms which have little meaning except as categories – Ebbsfleet, Mortlake, Transepted Gallery-Graves of the Severn-Cotswold Series. The 'interpretation' largely consists of describing parallels.

In the reports of the 1970s and 1980s this new grid within which we all work has become increasingly formalised (as in the Frere and Cunliffe reports). The writing has become increasingly distant, objective, impersonal and universal. We have become blind to the fact that we are writing. It appears as if self-evident data are simply described in neutral terms. The description is undated, timeless and beyond history.

While a site report today still often has a main author, there are usually numerous other contributors and specialists. The site report has often become truly collective. But there is rarely any debate or uncertainty in the text, and dialogue among the collective rarely surfaces on the page. Most excavations involve differences of opinion about drawing sections, planning features, deciding on sequences and interpretation. Our decisions about what happened at a site change as we dig and analyse the finds. The supposed 'final' interpretation results from a series of contingent factors, and most excavators know that their 'final' account might well have been different if they could have excavated more or obtained more analytical results. But in the report, dialogue and contingency are written out. After the excavation is finished and a 'final' interpretation is reached, we work backwards and reorganise our data so that they are coherent. We publish this constructed account as if it simply describes what was there.

All the kinds of information that were central to the eighteenth-century account – the personal, the active, the sequential, the interpretive – are now marginalised to introductions or to discussions at the end. The introduction, describing the history of the excavation, usually has no bearing on the main body of the report, and the interpretation at the end is usually just a matter of chronology, typological parallels and functional arguments with little reference to the layers, pottery, flint, bones, seeds and snails that were so drily described in the previous pages. In some reports no discussion or interpretation at the end even exists. The coded descriptions of pots and layers are left hanging as self-evident.

AN INTERPRETATION

How can I explain the gradual shift from the contingent and contextualised in the eighteenth century to the modern, abstract, distanced and universal? Why do contingent conclusions appear today as unargued, dry descriptions of the self-evident? I have already linked the gradual shift in writing style to changing structures of power and of the production of knowledge. In the eighteenth century, scientific authority was identified with the personal authority of individuals including lords and bishops. In the twentieth century, power in the archaeological community has been dispersed. It resides in institutions and in the public space. The authority of the text is no longer personal, but lies in adherence to abstract codes. The self, history and uncertainty must be denied.

In *Discipline and Punish*, Foucault (1977) argues that, prior to the late eighteenth century in France, power was centred on the sovereign and nobility. It was personal and arbitrary; a king could suddenly, arbitrarily pardon an individual condemned to death. As this power came to be seen as excessive, another disciplinary power developed, not a great apparatus wielded *by* the state but dispersed *within* the system itself. The supervisors were themselves supervised within a humane, precise and democratic code. The code became increasingly impersonal; at the same time it involved surveillance and definition of individuals. Foucault argues that many of the human sciences developed in this period because of a need within society to survey and control individuals with precision, and because of a desire to identify objective, non-arbitrary codes to live by.

The growth of archaeology as a science in the nineteenth century in Britain fits with these developments. The past had been associated with tradition, established authority, superstition and the lack of science. In 1651 Bacon had written that 'too great a reverence for Antiquity is prejudicial to the advancement of science'. In the nineteenth century the scientific evidence for the antiquity of the human species confronted established views, including the views of the established church. To disperse knowledge about the past within an abstract, impersonal and objective code was to disperse the power and authority based on tradition. Power, no longer personal and arbitrary, was dispersed within the fabric of science and its institutions.

As the style of archaeological writing changed, legislation was gradually introduced which placed the archaeological past more completely into public hands. The first British act to be passed was the Ancient Monuments Protection Act in 1882 (Cleere 1984). 'Before 1882, the state undertook little or no responsibility within a sphere now generally recognized as the proper concern of any civilised state' (Clark 1934, 414).

270

Commissioners of Works would now be responsible for certain scheduled monuments. But it was not until the new act of 1913 that the Ancient Monuments Board was constituted with greater powers. The act of 1931 empowered the Commissioners of Works to carry out excavations. Indeed, Clark argued that the Commissioners were legally empowered to control all archaeological excavation in the country (ibid., 418).

Clark was in no doubt that the legislative programme was made possible by the establishment of archaeology as a non-arbitrary, objective science (ibid., 414): 'The study of British Archaeology has only within the last fifty years reached a degree of accuracy and discipline worthy of the expenditure of public funds.' Notice the clear link between the development of a disciplined discipline of archaeology and the transfer into the public domain of power over the past: 'It is of the utmost significance in this connection that the first scientific British archaeologist, General Pitt-Rivers, was appointed as first Inspector of Ancient Monuments under the Act of 1882' (ibid., 414). Clark noted that earlier archaeologists were acting in an arbitrary, privileged manner when they devastated monuments. The provision of a disciplinary code, dispersed and public, was part of a more general process of social transformation. The past, taken out of private hands, would no longer legitimate and constitute traditional privilege and personal authority (ibid., 414):

> The whole conception of the state exerting its power for the conservation of a national heritage at the expense of a narrowly conceived view of private property is of itself a product of recent constitutional changes, reflected in the successive extensions of the franchise between 1867 and 1918. The various Ancient Monuments Acts, etc. may be considered as manifestations of the same social conscience that successfully demanded such measures as the regulation of conditions of employment, insurance for work-people, provision for unemployed persons, compulsory education, suitable housing for the poor, and the nationalisation of certain resources such as petroleum.

CONTEMPORARY WRITING: SOME SUGGESTIONS

Other aspects of archaeological site reports follow the trend. Dated and signed illustrations with an individual's style have given way to anonymous, coded representations. But it is in the *writing* of site reports that there has been the plainest trend towards a more impersonal, abstract, timeless and objective style. The data that we excavate must be made available in code for others to use.

271

This impersonal style of writing, developed to deal with earlier problems, may in its turn now be losing its value. At best the reports are dull, excessively long, detailed and expensive and read by no one except the delirious specialist. It often seems to me as if the code has become everything, pursued for its own sake. The public value of the lists and dry descriptions is questionable. At worst, the scientific, objective and rigorous nature of the reports can be called into doubt. How can reports be adequately scientific in which it is difficult to see why a particular conclusion has been reached, by what process of argument, and with what uncertainties? We wish to make the data available to others. But how can they use the data critically if we tell them little about the context in which the data were collected? The published data can be evaluated only with knowledge of the contingent interpretive context in which they were identified as data. If archaeology is to develop as a rigorous science, we must acknowledge that the data are not self-evident.

Trends in the writing of history (e.g. White 1973) and ethnography (e.g. Clifford and Marcus 1986) may provide some clues for a new archaeological writing. These trends place a renewed emphasis on *rhetoric*, on writing from the point of view of the reader rather than the writer. Two important components of rhetoric are *narrative* and *dialogue*. I wish to discuss two aspects of narrative: the presence of the narrator and the emphasis on narrative sequence – the storyline. As regards the narrator, many archaeologists will have been told by teachers and editors to remove the 'I' from the text, to deny the self, the author. The authority of the text is to be placed outside the self in the faceless, objective discipline. Giving a place to the 'I', the narrator, in accounts of excavations, would help to situate the text, to disclose it as it really is, provisional and contingent, constructed by actors in the present.

An emphasis on narrative sequence or storyline would involve retaining some of the sequence of excavation and discovery within the text, and some of the sequence in which the ideas about the site developed. In the report – more honest, readable and exciting – the reader would see the ideas and interpretations as contingent. The site report could be written as a complex interweaving of sequences of events in the past (what happened on the site) and sequences of events in the present (what happened on the excavation). Most excavations have their dramas, their problems unsolved. The text would permit uncertainty and unresolved doubts and would narrate a truer picture of what had passed.

Dialogue would draw on the relationships between co-directors, between supervisors, between diggers, between specialists, so as to provide a flavour of debate and argument about the site. Few sites can be dug in total consensus. The disagreements should spill over into the text so that the reader can insert herself into a process of argument rather than having to consume pre-packaged, supposedly neutral fare.

Other attempts to deal with the current problems of archaeological writing might include the provision of funds to allow those writing site reports, or specialist reports, the opportunity to incorporate their information into interpretation. It cannot, in my view, be acceptable to use public funds to produce pages of dry detail unlinked (and often unlinkable) to any purpose, idea or theory. In preserving the heritage we have a duty to give it some meaning. We might also consider publishing much larger portions of site reports in microfiche form, leaving the text for narrative, dialogue and interpretation.

I do not argue that we should return to the eighteenth century in our writing, although rhetoric, narrative and dialogue were better provided in 1770 than they have been in the 1980s. But we now face the modern problems of overloaded, dull, unreadable reports, a separation of data and interpretation, concern about public funding of archaeology, the separation of field-professional, scientific specialist and academic interpreter, changes in our understanding of the nature of science, and so on. We may be able to learn from earlier experiences of writing archaeology, but we have to work the older ideas out in new ways.

REFERENCES

Ashby, T. (1906) 'Excavations at Caerwent, Monmouthshire, on the site of the Romano-British city of Venta Silurum, in the year 1905', *Archaeologia* 60, 111–30.

Clark, G. (1934) 'Archaeology and the state', *Antiquity* 8, 414–28.

Cleere, H. (1984) 'Great Britain', in H. Cleere (ed.) *Approaches to the Archaeological Heritage*, Cambridge: Cambridge University Press.

Clifford, J. and Marcus, G. (1986) *Writing Culture*, Berkeley (CA): University of California Press.

Collingwood Bruce, J. (1852) 'An account of the excavations at Bremenium', *Proceedings of the Archaeological Institute* 1, 135–56.

Foucault, M. (1977) *Discipline and Punish*, New York: Vantage.

Griffith, G. (1773) 'Account of a Roman pavement, with wheat underneath it, found at Colchester', *Archaeologia* 2, 286–90.

Parrington, M. (1978) *The Excavation of an Iron Age Settlement, Bronze Age Ring Ditches and Roman Features at Ashville Trading Estate, Abingdon (Oxfordshire) 1974–6*, London: Council for British Archaeology Research Report 28.

Piggott, S. (1962) *The West Kennet Long Barrow Excavations 1955–6*, London: HMSO.

Pitt-Rivers, A. H. L. F. (1894) 'Excavation of the South Lodge Camp, Rushmore Park: an entrenchment of the Bronze Age', *Wiltshire Archaeological and Natural History Magazine* 27, 206–22.

Pownall, T. (1773) 'A description of the sepulchral monument at New Grange, near Drogheda, in the county of Meath, in Ireland', *Archaeologia* 2, 236–75.

Preston, W. (1775) 'Account of opening one of the largest barrows on Sandford Moor, Westmoreland', *Archaeologia* 3, 273.

White, H. (1973) *Metahistory: the Historical Imagination in Nineteenth Century Europe*, Baltimore (MD): Johns Hopkins University Press.

19

ARCHAEOLOGY AND THE POST-MODERN

This contribution follows on from that of Merriman (1989) who showed the existence and social context of a 'heritage boom' in Britain over recent years (see also Hewison 1987). There has been a doubling of the number of museums in Britain since 1971 and they are currently opening at the rate of one every ten days. There has also been a sharp rise since the 1970s in the number of historic buildings open to the public. The four most visited tourist attractions in Britain are all museums. The Yorvik Centre receives about one million visitors a year.

I want to try and explain why this boom has occurred and discuss the roles archaeologists should play in relation to post-modern society. One immediate explanation for the heritage boom might be that it is linked to the rise in importance of green issues. After all, in the 1970s and 1980s the past was renamed a 'resource' (as in Cultural Resource Management) which needed protection. Perhaps also the increased awareness of the global scale of environmental issues and climatic change has produced a millennial perspective to which the long time-spans covered by archaeology seem relevant. But these answers do not explain the way in which people seem fascinated by the past in the current heritage boom. Why is it particularly centres such as Yorvik, with its time car visit to a moment frozen in Viking York, which do so well?

Rather, I want to relate the attraction of such experiences to post-modern society. The latter is not easy to define (Jameson 1984; Eagleton 1985; Harvey 1989), but I would emphasise pastiche, facade, commodification and depthlessness. This is a culture of 'sound bites', a 'Sony Walkman' society in which the individual subject is cut off, floating free, just another signifier itself fragmented into multiple levels of consciousness and into a conflicting assortment of 'beings'. In this decontextualised, ironic world the language of commerce and the commodity are embraced and played with. Everything is a 'trivial pursuit'.

Initially it seems odd that a post-modernism so defined should be linked to a heritage boom. Post-modernism is all about the present.

275

Lyotard (1984) argues for the collapse of 'metanarratives', overarching metaphysical philosophies or ultimate schemes. In this context Eagleton (1985) suggests that we are persuaded by post-modernism to recognise the ultimate utopia 'as nothing less than the present itself'. If meaning is always elsewhere in the chains of signification, and if social reality is always already commodified, then there can be no ultimate meaning. There is only the 'doing' in the present. Modernism believed in change, the present to be replaced by a better future. But post-modernism accepts that this idea of change or rupture is just repression. In doing so it effaces both history and future and celebrates the instant. Lowenthal, in his 1985 book *The Past is a Foreign Country*, argues that over the last two centuries the past has increasingly been made meaningless. Our ties with the past have been severed. It is now a different place with little relevance to the present.

So why in such a context should we be going through a heritage boom? In fact the past has found a new and central role in post-modernism. In this new relationship with the past we are not placed in history and we do not learn from it, but we are absorbed with the very foreignness and disconnected nature of the past. With the collapse of 'meaning' and 'cause', the producers of culture have nowhere to turn but the past (Jameson 1984). The past can be plundered to construct an incoherent present. The past can be 'versioned off' to produce, as in architecture or music, a meaningless 'mix' of images. This is a world in which one goes to a Moroccan restaurant in Las Vegas where the sound system plays Julio Iglesias and a man from Bombay does a belly dance to Greek music.

We have become image-addicted and the past has become our main source of relief. Post-modern architecture continually makes references to classical, Egyptian, art deco or childhood images. A Chippendale motif is referred to on Philip Johnson's AT and T building. It is trendy to be 'neo-'. Nostalgia is used heavily in marketing eveything from clothes to recipes. Films involving archaeology (such as *Indiana Jones*) or time travel (as in *Back to the Future*) abound. This post-modern past is one of images and of the vicarious thrill of time travel into other images. Re-enactment is thriving and in North America the Society for Creative Anachronism is expanding. This is not a past involving sequence, history or evolution. Traditional museums in which artifacts were arranged in long typological sequences covering centuries or millennia have been replaced by a visit to an instant frozen in time in Viking York with all the sounds and smells relived – a commodified, contrived depthlessness.

There are a number of characteristics of archaeology which make it suitable in the post-modern context of fragmented, decontextualised time. First, archaeologists dig up fragments, bits and pieces of pots and societies. The prehistoric past in particular is distant and we know little of the context in which prehistoric objects were produced. These material signals from the past are signifiers floating free from any signified, odd images without obvious meaning. And yet they require interpretation. They attract explanation. But the distance between past object and present interpretation creates an obviously constructed image. A present is created which is a world of transient images. Our image addiction seeks just another 'other', difference for its own sake.

Second, the paradox of the archaeological object is that it is real and tactile so that when we hold it, it seems to bring the past close and to allow us to experience another reality. But at the same time, that other reality is distant and unconnected to the present. To experience the past in this way is to experience the thrill of time travel, an archaeological 'tourism'. The closeness of the object which has itself travelled through time leads us to believe we can do the same. This 'I've seen Elvis' perspective is particularly evident in the process of excavation where archaeologists can physically dig through time and see what happened there from the physical remains.

Third, the materiality of the past means that it is ripe for commercialisation. People like collecting things and the archaeological past is already a commodity. The objects can be put on display, on mantelpieces or in expensive glass cases with focused lighting, to give them the appearance of value. The past is packaged and 'sold' as a commodity, both figuratively and literally. At least one can buy replicas as when at Yorvik the visit leads to a shop and to the minting and buying of your own Viking coin. We no longer talk of the past or of history but of the heritage industry. Local councils and commercial businesses are interested in starting museums because the past 'sells well'. It brings in tourists and creates wealth and jobs. The speed of the time cars at York is precisely calculated to maximise profit. In the Museum of the Iron Age at Andover the past is sensationalised by reference to the barbaric, weird habits of the Celts, in order to attract visitors.

Fourth, archaeologists often claim that in comparison with historical evidence their data allow access to popular, non-elite culture – to the everyday lives of past men and women. Certainly the materiality of archaeological data allows a popular, accessible approach to the past. Much post-modernism sees a synthesis of high and popular art and culture (as in the music of Philip Glass), or a mixing of classical with kitsch or Readers Digest culture. Whereas history is abstract and often intellectual, archaeological objects are immediately accessible and more open to commodification and consumerism.

In these various ways archaeology is well suited to the commodified fragmentation characteristic of post-modernism. What is the social context of this situation? To some degree this new view of the past could play a radical role in undermining claims about the past preferred by dominant groups. For example, the authoritarian view of an 'English' Heritage, increasingly problematic in a multicultural society, can be opened to other voices in the market-place. But on the whole, as Merriman has shown, the past represented in museums and heritage industries largely serves the interests of the better-educated middle classes. On the whole a fragmented past deconstructs historical connections and disempowers those groups who try to use the past to further their social strategies. It produces a universal culture in which our histories do not mean anything, except as nostalgia which is usually conservative in that it helps us to accept the present. More generally, although post-modernism may at times derive from a critique of established authority, it quickly becomes politically complacent and reinforces the consumer society of late capitalism as Jameson, Eagleton and Harvey have argued.

But the post-modern world is far from coherent. There are contradictory tendencies which involve conflicting uses of the past. The point is put well by Eagleton (1985). On the one hand, I am a consumer (of objects, taste, culture, style, heritage) who is supposed to be a decentred network of desire. I am supposed to close my eyes to the way in which my decentred consumerism affects the unemployed and the Third World. On the other hand, I am a father who faces problems of agency, duty, autonomy, authority and social responsibility. In this second, decidedly non post-modern world we cling to truths and ideologies. So alongside the post-modern collapse of metanarrative there emerges a counteracting desire for story, for meaning. It is particularly clear in archaeology and heritage that subordinate groups create connections with the past and try to situate themselves in relation to their heritage in order to form an alternative identity. They want the past to tell a story about themselves which confronts the dominant post-modern ethic.

There are various ways in which we can see this alternative use of a connected past by subordinate groups. First, in Merriman's survey it became clear that individuals who did not feel able to participate in the dominant post-modern heritage might be interested in local history or genealogy. In these ways personal or local ties with the past helped to situate people in the present and give them a sense of place. Second, around the world archaeology is increasingly being used by emerging nations and ethnic minorities to legitimate their claims to land or to further their contemporary political existence. Clear examples include the use of the site of Zimbabwe, the use of archaeology by Australian Aborigines or Canadian Inuit, and the claims by American Indians for the reburial of their ancestral remains (for other examples see Layton 1989). While the European experience has shown that nationalist uses of the past can also be repressive, links to the past can also be liberating.

278

Feminist rereadings of the past have also drawn attention to the import-ance of gender relations in long-term social change and challenged our assumptions about divisions of labour (Gero and Conkey 1991).

Third, the materiality of the archaeological past allows subordinate groups to ground their claims in a certain objectivity. Since archaeol-ogists deal not only with interpretations of interpretations but also with material data, it is possible to claim 'real' connections with the past, to show the 'real' complexity of Zimbabwe or to demonstrate 'real' Aborigine sites on the landscape. In this way it appears as if free-floating signifiers and uncoupled images can be countered with hard evidence by interested parties. Fourth, a past which is distant but which is nevertheless connected and 'real' has a great potential for the critique of established universals and taken-for-granteds. In an increasingly homo-genised world there is a danger that we eradicate all contemporary 'others'. As cultural diversity threatens to be reduced to a world same-ness, the notion that there might be other ways of thinking is less easy to maintain and the post-modern dispersal of meaning certainly contrib-utes to a lack of understanding of the 'other'. It is especially the dis-covery of new pasts by archaeologists which will leave open the possibility for recognising difference and for situating the present as a particular product of history. The material difference of the past, as long as it is contextually bound and connected to us, helps with anthropology to ensure against the presumed universality of western thought.

Fifth, in a very practical way archaeology gets in the way of mass commercial development which severs people from their histories and their landscapes. Developers literally trip up over the past as they find that some archaeological site stands in the way of their building or quarrying programme. Partly because of the rise in awareness of green issues, local planning departments in England increasingly withhold consent to developers until proper archaeological enquiry has been carried out. As a result most archaeology in the country is now carried out on a commercial basis rather than by public agencies. In many ways this change in the way archaeology is carried out in England has led to a post-modern commercialisation and trivialisation of the past as is seen also in the United States. But in England at least, popular interest in local pasts has often produced a counter-argument that development should cease or that it should fund heritage displays which in the midst of modern shopping malls, towns and building estates maintain links between people, their landscape and their heritage. Interpretive or heritage centres increasingly appear which make up the statistics of new museums but which are often not termed museums. They are more concerned with telling a story which gives local people a sense of place. I certainly found working as an archaeologist in the Fens in Cambridgeshire that in a fragmented post-modern world small local communities were willing to go to enormous lengths to retain access to a past which was materially connected to them.

The consumerised instant thrill of a post-modern heritage draws people in and threatens to alienate them from a past to which they might wish to be connected. It is certainly in the interests of devolopers and dominant groups in western society to commercialise the past and undermine the claims to legitimacy in the past made by subordinate groups. But really the two sides feed off each other. For example, in the public controversy about the building of a new town, planning consent may be negotiated against the construction of a heritage centre which for the first time gives people a local sense of place. And after all, the visitor to the frozen moment in Viking York is first taken back in a time car through the intervening centuries and the centre claims a historical integrity. The main reason for the heritage boom is that a new past, especially the material past, has become the site of struggle between two aspects of post-modernism. The material heritage is an appropriate location for the conflict between continuity and discontinuity, between the contextualised and the decontextualised. The past, renamed heritage, is an important arena for working out the opposed claims of our social responsibilities and our decentred consumer existence. Archaeology confronts a material reality with disconnected meanings and with the dominant view that 'anything goes'. Heritage is central to the issue of whether we are floating images or historical agents.

REFERENCES

Eagleton, T. (1985) 'Capitalism, modernism and post–modernism', *New Left Review* 152, 60–73.

Gero, J. and Conkey, M. (1991) *Engendering Archaeology: Women and Prehistory*, Oxford: Basil Blackwell.

Harvey, D. (1989) *The Condition of Post-modernity*, Oxford: Basil Blackwell.

Hewison, R. (1987) *The Heritage Industry*, London: Methuen.

Jameson, F. (1984) 'Post–modernism, or the cultural logic of late capitalism', *New Left Review* 146, 53–92.

Layton, R. (1989) *Conflict in the Archaeology of Living Traditions*, London: Unwin Hyman.

Lowenthal, D. (1985) *The Past is a Foreign Country*, Cambridge: Cambridge University Press.

Lyotard, J.-F. (1984) *The Post–modern Condition*, Manchester: Manchester University Press.

Merriman, N. (1989) 'Heritage from the other side of the glass case', *Anthropology Today* 5(2), 14–15.

INDEX